KT-498-988

MEMOIRS OF
A FOX-HUNTING MAN

Also by Siegfried Sassoon

THE COMPLETE MEMOIRS OF GEORGE SHERSTON
MEMOIRS OF AN INFANTRY OFFICER
SHERSTON'S PROGRESS
COLLECTED POEMS 1908–56
SELECTED POEMS

Edited by Rupert Hart-Davis
WAR POEMS OF SIEGFRIED SASSOON

MEMOIRS OF
A FOX-HUNTING MAN

BY

SIEGFRIED SASSOON

with decorations by
WILLIAM NICHOLSON

NORWICH CITY COLLEGE LIBRARY

Stock No.	192253		
Class	823·91 SAS		
Cat.		Proc.	

faber and faber

First published in Great Britain in 1928
by Faber and Faber Limited
3 Queen Square London WC1N 3AU
This edition first published in 1999

Printed and bound in Great Britain by
Mackays of Chatham PLC, Chatham, Kent

All rights reserved

© Siegfried Sassoon, 1928

Siegfried Sassoon is hereby identified as author of this work
in accordance with Section 77 of the Copyright,
Designs and Patents Act 1988.

*This book is sold subject to the condition that it shall not, by way of trade
or otherwise, be lent, resold, hired out or otherwise circulated without the
publisher's prior consent in any form of binding or cover other than that
in which it is published and without a similar condition including
this condition being imposed on the subsequent purchaser.*

A CIP record for this book is
available from the British Library
ISBN 0-571-20028-1

Cat.

2 4 6 8 10 9 7 5 3 1

CONTENTS

PART ONE: EARLY DAYS

I

My childhood was a queer and not altogether happy one. Circumstances conspired to make me shy and solitary. My father and mother died before I was capable of remembering them. I was an only child, entrusted to the care of an unmarried aunt who lived quietly in the country. My aunt was no longer young when I began to live in her comfortable, old-fashioned house with its large, untidy garden. She had settled down to her local interests, seldom had anyone to stay with her, and rarely left home. She was fond of her two Persian cats, busied herself sensibly with her garden, and was charitably interested in the old and rheumatic inhabitants of the village. Beyond this, the radius of her activities extended no further than the eight or ten miles which she could cover in a four-wheeled dog-cart driven by Tom Dixon, the groom. The rest of the world was what she described as "beyond calling distance".

Dixon was a smart young man who would have preferred a livelier situation. It was he who persuaded my aunt to buy me my first pony. I was then nine years old.

My aunt had an unexplained prejudice against sending me to school. So I remained at home until I was twelve—inefficiently tutored by a retired elementary schoolmaster, a gentle, semi-clerical old person who arrived every morning, taught me a limited supply of Latin, and bowled lobs to me on the lawn. His name (which I have not thought of for I don't know how many years) was Mr. Star.

Apart from my aunt's efforts to bring me up nicely, my early education was exclusively controlled by Mr. Star and Dixon, who supplemented Mr. Star's lobs with his more intimidating overarm bowling, and never lost sight of his intention to make a sportsman of me. For the vaguely apologetic old tutor in his black tail-coat I felt a tolerant affection. But it was Dixon who taught me to ride, and my admiration for him was unqualified. And since he was what I afterwards learnt to call "a perfect gentleman's servant", he never allowed me to forget my position as "a little gentleman": he always knew exactly when to become discreetly respectful. In fact, he "knew his place".

I have said that my childhood was not altogether a happy one. This must have been caused by the absence of companions of my own age. My Aunt Evelyn—who was full of common sense and liked people (children included) to be practical in their habits and behaviour—used to complain to Mr. Star that I was too fond of mooning aimlessly about by myself. On my eighth birthday she gave me a butterfly-net and a fretwork saw, but these suggestions were unfruitful. Now and again she took me to a children's party given by one of the local gentry: at such functions I was awkward and uncomfortable, and something usually happened which increased my sense of inferiority to the other children, who were better at everything than I was and made no attempt to assist me out of my shyness. I had no friends of my own age. I was strictly forbidden to "associate" with the village boys. And even the sons of the neighbouring farmers were considered "unsuitable"—though I was too shy and nervous to speak to them.

I do not blame my aunt for this. She was merely conform-

10

ing to her social code which divided the world into people whom one could "call on" and people who were "socially impossible". She was mistaken, perhaps, in applying this code to a small, solitary boy like myself. But the world was less democratic in those days, and it must not be thought that I received any active unkindness from Aunt Evelyn, who was tender-hearted and easy-going.

As a consequence of my loneliness I created in my childish day-dreams an ideal companion who became much more of a reality than such unfriendly boys as I encountered at Christmas parties. (I remember a party given by my aunt, in the course of which one of my "little friends" contrived to lock me in a cupboard during a game of hide-and-seek. And, to tell the truth, I was so glad to escape from the horrors of my own hospitality that I kept as quiet as a mouse for the best part of an hour, crouching on the floor of that camphor-smelling cupboard.) The "ideal companion" probably originated in my desire for an elder brother. When I began these reminiscences I did not anticipate that I should be describing such an apparently trivial episode—and I doubt whether such a thing can be called an episode at all—but among a multitude of blurred memories, my "dream friend" has cropped up with an odd effect of importance which makes me feel that he must be worth a passing mention. The fact is that, as soon as I began to picture in my mind the house and garden where I spent so much of my early life, I caught sight of my small, long-vanished self with this other non-existent boy standing beside him. And, though it sounds silly enough, I felt queerly touched by the recollection of that forgotten companionship. For some reason which I cannot explain, the presence of that "other boy" made my childhood unexpectedly clear, and brought me close to a number of things which, I should have thought, would have faded for ever. For instance, I have only just remembered the tarnished mirror which used to hang in the sunless passage which led to my schoolroom, and how, when I secretly stared at my small, white face in this mirror, I could hear the sparrows chirping in the ivy which grew thickly outside the windows. Somehow the sight of my own reflection increased my loneliness, till the voice of my aunt speaking to one of the servants on the stairs made me start guiltily away. . . .

And now, as I look up from my writing, these memories also seem like reflections in a glass, reflections which are becoming more and more easy to distinguish. Sitting here, alone with my slowly moving thoughts, I rediscover many little details, known only to myself, details otherwise dead and forgotten with all who shared that time; and I am inclined to loiter among them as long as possible.

II

Now that I come to think about it, it seems to me to be quite on the cards that, had my Aunt Evelyn employed an unpretentious groom-gardener (who would really have suited her original requirements far better than jaunty young Dixon) I should never have earned the right to call myself a fox-hunting man. Dixon's predecessor was a stolid old coachman who disliked riding. One of my earliest recollections is the advent of Dixon, who lost no time in persuading my aunt to pension off her pair of worn-out carriage horses, which he replaced by two comparatively juvenile animals "warranted quiet to ride or drive". Dixon dearly loved to do a deal, and my aunt was amenable to his influence. She even went so far as to sanction the purchase of a side-saddle, and although a timid and incompetent horsewoman, she came to the conclusion that riding was good for her health.

Two or three times a week, then, on fine days, shepherded

by the dignified and respectful groom, she was to be seen ambling along the lanes in a badly cut brown habit. She never attended a meet of the hounds however, for we lived in an unhunted part of the country, and the nearest meet was more than eight miles away.

So far as I was concerned, for several years "the hounds" remained a remote and mysteriously important rumour, continually talked about by Dixon, who never ceased to regret the remoteness of their activities. Foxes were few in our part of the country, and the farmers made no secret of shooting them. In fact ours was a thoroughly unsporting neighbourhood. There wasn't so much as a pack of beagles in the district. But Dixon was deeply imbued with sporting instincts. From the age of fourteen he had worked in stables, and had even shared, for a few months, the early rising rigours of a racing stable. He had been "odd man" to a sporting farmer in the Vale of Aylesbury, and had spent three years as undergroom to a hard-riding squire who subscribed handsomely to Lord Dumborough's Hounds. Dumborough Park was twelve miles from where my aunt lived, and in those days twelve miles meant a lot, from a social point of view. My aunt was fully two miles beyond the radius of Lady Dumborough's "round of calls". Those two miles made all the difference, and the aristocratic yellow-wheeled barouche never entered our unassuming white gate. I never heard my aunt express any regret for her topographical exclusion from the centre of county society. But for Dixon it was one of the lesser tragedies of life; he would have given anything to be able to drive "the mistress" over to Dumborough Park now and again, for the Kennels were there, and to him the Kennels were the centre of the local universe. As it was, he had to be content with a few garden-parties, where he could hob-nob with a crowd of garrulous grooms, and perhaps get a few words with that great man, Lord Dumborough's head coachman.

Nevertheless, as the slow seasons of my childhood succeeded one another, he rattled my aunt along the roads in her four-wheeled dogcart at an increasingly lively pace. He must have been very adroit in his management of my gentle relative and guardian, since he perpetually found some plausible excuse for getting rid of one of the horses. Invariably, and by gentle gradations toward his ideal "stamp of hunter", he replaced each criticizable quadruped with one that looked more like galloping and jumping. The scope of these manœuvrings was, of course, restricted by my aunt's refusal to pay more than a certain price for a horse, but Dixon always had his eyes open for a possible purchase from any sporting farmer or country gentleman within riding distance; he also assiduously studied the advertisements of the London horse sales, and when he had finally established his supremacy "the mistress" unprotestingly gave him permission to "go up to Tattersalls", whence he would return, sedately triumphant, accompanied by the kindly countenance of what he called "a perfect picture of an old-fashioned sort". (A "sort", as I afterwards learned, was a significant word in the vocabulary of hunting men.)

How vividly I remember Dixon's keen featured face, as he proudly paraded his latest purchase on the gravel in front of the house, or cantered it round the big paddock at the back of the stables, while my aunt and I watched, from a safe distance, the not infrequent symptoms of a sprightliness not altogether to her taste.

"Yess, 'm," he would say, in his respectful voice, as he pulled up and leant forward to clap the neck of the loudly snorting animal, "I think this mare'll suit you down to the ground."

"Fling you to the ground" would, in one or two cases, have been a more accurate prophecy, as Aunt Evelyn may have secretly surmised while she nervously patted the "new carriage-horse" which was waltzing around its owner and her small nephew! And there was, indeed, one regrettable occasion, when a good-looking but suspiciously cheap new-comer (bought at Tattersalls without a warrant) decided to do his best to demolish the dogcart; from this expedition my aunt returned somewhat shaken, and without having left any of the cards which she had set out to distribute on "old Mrs. Caploss, and those new people over at Amblehurst Priory". So far as I remember, though, the unblenching Dixon soon managed to reassure her, and the "funny tempered horse" was astutely exchanged for something with better manners.

"He looked a regular timber-topper, all the same," re-marked Dixon, shaking his head with affectionate regret for the departed transgressor. He had a warm heart for any horse in the world, and, like every good groom, would sit up all night with a hunter rather than risk leaving a thorn in one of its legs after a day's hunting.

So far as I know, Dixon never made any attempt to get a better place. Probably he was shrewd enough to realize that he was very well off where he was. And I am certain that my aunt would have been much upset if he had given notice. The great thing about Dixon was that he knew exactly where to draw the line. Beyond that line, I have no doubt, lay his secret longing to have an occasional day with the Dum-borough Hounds on one of his employer's horses. Obviously there was no hope that "the mistress" could ever be manipu-lated into a middle-aged enthusiasm for the hazards of the chase. Failing that, his only possible passport into the distant Dumborough Elysium existed in the mistress's nephew. He would make a sportsman of him, at any rate!

*   *   *

My first appearance in the hunting-field was preceded by more than three years of unobtrusive preparation. Strictly speaking, I suppose that my sporting career started even earlier than that. Beginning then with the moment when Dixon inwardly decided to increase my aunt's establishment by the acquisition of a confidential child's pony, I pass to his first recorded utterance on this, to me, important subject.

I must have been less than nine years old at the time, but I distinctly remember how, one bright spring morning when I was watching him assist my aunt into the saddle at her front door, he bent down to adjust a strap, and having done this to his final satisfaction made the following remark: "We'll soon have to be looking out for a pony for Master George, 'm."

His tone of voice was cheerful but conclusive. My aunt, who had, as usual, got her reins in a tangle, probably showed symptoms of demurring. She was at all times liable to be fussy about everything I did or wanted to do. As a child I was nervous and unenterprising, but in this case her opposition may have prejudiced me in favour of the pony. Had she insisted on my learning to ride I should most likely have felt scared and resentful.

As it was, I was full of tremulous elation when, one afternoon a few weeks later, Dixon appeared proudly parading a very small black pony with a flowing mane and tail. My aunt, realizing that it was about to become her property, admired the pony very much and wondered whether it went well in harness. But since it was already wearing a saddle, I soon found myself on its back, my aunt's agitated objections were rapidly overruled, and my equestrianism became an established fact. Grasping the pommel of the saddle with both hands, I was carried down the drive as far as the gate; the pony's movements were cautious and demure: on the return journey Dixon asked me whether I didn't think him a little beauty, but I was speechless with excitement and could only nod my assent. Even my aunt began to feel quite proud of me when I relinquished my apprehensive hold on the saddle and, for the first time in my life, gathered up the reins. Dixon greeted this gesture with a glance of approval, at the same time placing a supporting hand on my shoulder.

"Stick your knees in, sir," he said, adding, "I can see you'll make a rider all right."

He had never called me "sir" before, and my heart warmed toward him as I straightened my back and inwardly resolved to do him credit.

III

Although, in my mind's eye, that first pony is clearly visible to me, I am not going to delay my already slow progress toward fox-hunting by describing him in detail. It will be sufficient if I quote Dixon, who called him "a perfect picture of a miniature hunter". His name was Rob Roy, and I thought him the most wonderful pony in the world. Nimble and lightly built, his courageous character never caused him to behave with more than an attractive friskiness. My devotion to him was therefore well justified. But as I sit here reconstructing my life from those remote beginnings, which are so difficult to recover in their authentic aliveness, I cannot help suspecting that I was, by nature, only half a sportsman. Dixon did his best for me as he patiently coaxed me toward my first fence (the idea of "jumping" made me horribly nervous for fully twelve months after I became a proud owner of horseflesh), but there must have been moments when he had grave doubts about my future as a horseman.

When I began my rides on Rob Roy, Dixon used to walk beside me. Our longest expedition led to a place about three miles from home. Down in the Weald were some large hop-farms, and the hop-kilns were interesting objects. It was unusual to find more than two hop-kilns on a farm; but there was one which had twenty, and its company of white cowls was clearly visible from our house on the hill. As a special treat Dixon used to take me down there. Sitting on Rob Roy at the side of the road I would count them over and over again, and Dixon would agree that it was a wonderful sight. I felt that almost anything might happen in a world which could show me twenty hop-kilns neatly arranged in one field.

It is no use pretending that I was anything else than a dreaming and unpractical boy. Perhaps my environment made me sensitive, but there was an "unmanly" element in my nature which betrayed me into many blunders and secret humiliations. Somehow I could never acquire the knack of doing and saying the right thing: and my troubles were multiplied by an easily excited and emotional temperament. Was it this flaw in my character which led me to console my sense of unhappiness and failure by turning to that ideal companion whose existence I have already disclosed? The fantasies of childhood cannot be analysed or explained in the rational afterthoughts of experienced maturity. I am not attempting to explain that invisible but unforgotten playmate of mine. I can only say that he was a consolation which grew to spontaneous existence in my thoughts, and remained with me unfalteringly until gradually merged in the human presences which superseded him. When I say that he was superseded I mean that he faded out of my inward life when I went to school and came in crude contact with other boys. Among them he was obliterated but not replaced. In my memory I see him now as the only friend to whom I could confess my failures without a sense of shame. And what absurd little failures they were!

At this moment I can only recall a single instance, which happened about eighteen months after the arrival of Rob Roy. By that time I was going for rides of six or seven miles with Dixon, and the "leading-rein" was a thing of the past. I was also having jumping lessons, over a small brush-fence which he had put up in the paddock. One day, inflated with pride, I petitioned, rather shyly, to be allowed to go for a ride by myself. Without consulting my aunt, Dixon gave his permission; he seemed pleased, and entrusted me with the supreme responsibility of saddling and bridling the pony without his help. I managed to do this, in my bungling way, and I have no doubt that I felt extremely important when I tit-tupped down to the village in that sleepy afternoon sunshine of thirty years ago. Rob Roy probably shared my feeling of independence as he shook his little black head and whisked his long tail at the flies. I was far too big a man to look back as we turned out of my aunt's white gate into the dusty high road; but I can imagine now the keen sensitive face of Dixon, and his reticent air of amusement as he watched us go out into the world by ourselves. My legs were then long enough to give me a pleasant feeling of security and mastery over my mount.

"Here we are, Rob," I remarked aloud, "off for a jolly good day with the Dumborough."

And, in spite of the fact that it was a hot August afternoon, I allowed my imagination to carry me on into fox-hunting adventures, during which I distinguished myself supremely, and received the brush from the Master after a tremendous gallop over hill and vale. I must mention that my knowledge of the chase was derived from two sources: firstly, the things I had heard in my conversation with Dixon; and secondly, a vague but diligent perusal of the novels of Surtees, whose humorous touches were almost entirely lost on me, since I accepted every word he wrote as a literal and serious transcription from life.

Anyhow, I had returned home with the brush and received the congratulations of Dixon when my attention was attracted by an extra green patch of clover-grass by the roadside: I was now about a mile beyond the village and nearly double that distance from home. It seemed to me that Rob must be in need of refreshment. So I dismounted airily and intimated to him that he ought to eat some grass. This he began to do without a moment's delay. But there was mischief in Rob Roy that afternoon. With one knee bent he grabbed and munched at the grass with his diminutive muzzle as though he hadn't had a meal for a month. Nevertheless, he must have been watching my movements with one of his large and intelligent eyes. With characteristic idiocy I left the reins dangling on his neck and stepped back a little way to admire him. The next moment he had kicked up his heels and was cantering down the road in the direction of his stable. It seemed to me the worst thing that could possibly have happened. It would take me years to live down the disgrace. Panic seized me as I imagined the disasters which must have overtaken Rob Roy on his way home—if he *had* gone home, which I scarcely dared to hope. Probably his knees were broken and I should never be able to look Dixon in the face again. In the meantime I must hurry as fast as my dismounted legs could carry me. If only I could catch sight of that wretched Rob Roy eating some more grass by the roadside! If only I hadn't let him go! If only I could begin my ride all over again! How careful I would be!

Hot and flustered, I was running miserably towards the village when I turned a corner and saw, to my consternation, the narrow, stooping figure of Mr. Star. His eyes were on the ground, so I had time to slow down to a dignified walk. I advanced to meet him with all the nonchalance that I could muster at the moment. The silver-haired schoolmaster greeted me with his usual courtesy, as though he had forgotten that he had been attempting to teach me arithmetic and geography all the morning. But I was aware of the mild inquiry in his glance. If only I'd been carrying my green butterfly-net instead of the rather clumsy old hunting-crop of which I was usually so proud! I have never been a clever dissembler, so I have no doubt that my whole demeanour expressed the concealment of delinquency. Mr. Star removed his black wideawake hat, wiped his forehead with a red handkerchief, and genially ejaculated, "Well, well; what a gloriously fine afternoon we are having!"

As I was unable to say anything at all in reply, he continued, with gentle jocularity (running his eyes over the brown corduroy riding-suit which I was just beginning to grow out of), "And what have you done with your pony? You look almost as if you'd lost him."

At this appallingly intuitive comment I gazed guiltily down at my gaiters and muttered abruptly, "Oh, I'm going to take him out after tea; I was just out for a walk."

My voice died unhappily away into the dusty sunshine. . . . After tea! For all I knew, darling Rob Roy might be *dead* by then. . . . For two pins I could have burst into tears at that moment, but I managed to control my feelings: Mr. Star tactfully informed me that he must be getting on his way, and our constrained interview ended. Half an hour afterwards I slunk into the stable-yard with a sinking heart. Dixon's black retriever was dozing with his head out of his kennel under the walnut tree. No one seemed to be about. I could hear the usual intermittent snorts and stampings from inside the stable. There were two stalls and a loose-box. My pony occupied the stall in the middle. My heart thumped as I peeped over the door, the upper half of which was open. Rob Roy was facing me; he was attached to the "pillar-reins", still saddled and bridled. I am certain that his face wore a look of amusement. A sense of profound relief stole over me. . . . A moment later the stable-boy came whistling out of the barn with a bucket. On seeing me he grinned derisively and I retreated toward the house in dignified silence. As I passed the kitchen window Mrs. Sosburn, the fat, red-faced cook, dropped the cucumber which she was peeling and greeted me with a startled squeal.

"Lawks, Master Georgie, whatever 'ave you bin up to? The mistress 'as been in an awful state about you, and Dixon's gone down to the village to look for you. We thought you must 'ave broke your neck when the pony came trotting back without you."

And the well-meaning woman bustled officiously out to make sure I hadn't any bones broken, followed by the gaping kitchen-maid; a moment later the parlour-maid came helter-skelter out of the pantry, and I was inundated by exasperating female curiosity and concern.

"Gracious goodness! To think of him going off by himself like that, and no wonder he got thrown off, and the wonder was he wasn't killed, and the pony too," they chorused; whereupon my aunt's head popped out of an upper window, and they clucked like hens as they reassured her about my undamaged return.

Infuriated by all this feminine fussiness I pushed past them and scurried up the back stairs to the schoolroom, whither Aunt Evelyn immediately followed me with additional exclamations and expostulations. I was now not only humiliated but sulky, and had I been a few years younger my rudeness would have ended in my being smacked and sent to bed. As it was I was merely informed that unless I learnt to behave better I should never grow up into a nice man, and was left alone with my tragic thoughts. . . .

Next morning I paid my customary visit to the stable with a few lumps of sugar in my pocket. Dixon was polishing up a stirrup-iron at the door of the little harness room; he stopped in the middle of a jaunty snatch of song to give me his usual greeting. All my embarrassment faded out of me. His impas-

sive face made not the slightest reference to yesterday's cal-
amity and this tactful silence more than ever assured me of his
infinite superiority to those chattering females in the kitchen.

IV

Since the continuity of these memoirs is to depend solely
on my experiences as a sportsman, I need not waste many
words on the winter, spring, summer and autumn that
chronologically followed the last episode which I narrated.
Outwardly monotonous, my life was made up of that series
of small inward happenings which belong to the develop-
ment of any intelligent little boy who spends a fair amount of
time with no companion but himself. In this way I continued
to fabricate for myself an intensely local and limited world.
How faintly the vibrations of the outer world reached us on
that rural atmosphere it is not easy to imagine in this later and
louder age. When I was twelve years old I hadn't been to
London half a dozen times in my life, and the ten sleepy miles
to the county town, whither the village carrier's van went
three times a week, were a road to romance. Ten miles was a
long way when I was a child. Over the hills and far away, I
used to think to myself, as I stared across the orchards and
meadows of the Weald, along which ran the proverbially
slow railway line to London.

There were a few events which created in my mind an
impression out of proportion to the architecture of my earthly
ideas. Among them was Queen Victoria's Diamond Jubilee
(though I cannot pretend to remember exactly how it struck
me at the time, except that I counted fifty bonfires from the
hill near our house). This was balanced by Canterbury Cricket
Week. (I went there by train with Dixon and spent a long hot
day watching Prince Ranjitsinhjii make about 175 not out.

My aunt's black Persian cat was called Ranjii, which made the celebrated Indian cricketer quite a comfortable idea for me to digest.)

Almost my favourite books were *The Palace in the Garden* and *Four Winds Farm*, both by Mrs. Molesworth. Naturally there were other more impressive phenomena which cropped up in my mental existence, such as Scott's *Ivanhoe* and Longfellow's poem *Excelsior*, and Beethoven's piano sonatas. But all these things clothed themselves in local associations. Sir Walter Scott had no existence outside of my aunt's voice as she read him aloud in the evening, Longfellow was associated with Mr. Star in the schoolroom, Beethoven lived somewhere behind the faded silk on the back of the upright piano, and I never imagined any of them as in any other edition than those in which I knew them by sight. The large photograph of Watt's picture, "Love and Death", which hung in the drawing-room, gave me the same feeling as the "Moonlight" sonata (my aunt could only play the first two movements).

In this brightly visualized world of simplicities and misapprehensions and mispronounced names everything was accepted without question. I find it difficult to believe that young people see the world in that way nowadays, though it is probable that a good many of them do. Looking back across the years I listen to the summer afternoon cooing of my aunt's white pigeons, and the soft clatter of their wings as they flutter upward from the lawn at the approach of one of the well-nourished cats. I remember, too, the smell of strawberry jam being made; and Aunt Evelyn with a green bee-veil over her head. . . . The large rambling garden, with its Irish yews and sloping paths and wind-buffeted rose arches, remains to haunt my sleep. The quince tree which grew beside the little pond was the only quince tree in the world. With a sense of abiding strangeness I see myself looking down from an upper window on a confusion of green branches shaken by the summer breeze. In an endless variety of dream-distorted versions the garden persists as the background of my unconscious existence.

*   *   *

I had always been given to understand that I had a delicate constitution. This was one of the reasons which my aunt urged against my being sent to school when Mr. Pennett, the pink-faced solicitor who had charge of our affairs, paid us one of his periodic visits and the problem of my education was referred to in my presence. The solicitor used to come down from London for the day. In acknowledgment of his masculinity my aunt always conceded him the head of the table at lunch. I can remember him carving a duck with evident relish, and saying in somewhat unctuous tones, "Have you reconsidered, my dear Miss Evelyn, the well-worn subject of a school for our young friend on my left?"

And I can hear my aunt replying in a fluttering voice that she had always been nervous about me since I had pneumonia (though she knew quite well that it was only slight inflammation of the lungs, and more than two years ago at that). Fixing my gaze on his fat pearl tie-pin, I wondered whether I really should ever go to school, and what it would feel like when I got there. Nothing was said about Mr. Star, but Mr. Pennett usually had a private conversation with him on the subject of my progress.

"Your guardian seems an extremely well-informed gentleman," Mr. Star would say to me after one of these interviews. For Mr. Pennett had been to Harrow, and when Mr. Star spoke of him I was vaguely aware that he had made the modest old man feel even more humble than usual. My aunt was perfectly satisfied with Mr. Star, and so was I. But the solicitor knew that I was growing out of my tutor; and so, perhaps, did Mr. Star himself. . . . Indeed, I was getting to be quite a big boy for my age. People in the village were saying that I was "filling out a fair treat", and "shooting up no end". . . .

To one little incident I can give an exact date—not always an easy thing to do when one is looking back such a long way. It was in 1896, on the last Wednesday in May, and I had just returned from my afternoon ride. My aunt was out in the garden, wearing her leather gauntlets to cut some lilac, when I dashed excitedly across the lawn shouting, "Isn't it splendid, Auntie—the Prince of Wales has won the Derby!"

"Oh, how splendid—has he really?" she exclaimed, dropping the branch of white lilac which she had just snipped off the bush with her huge pair of scissors.

"Yes," I continued, bursting with the important news, "we stopped at the station on our way home, and the stationmaster showed Dixon the telegram."

"What was it called?" she queried.

"Persimmon, of course; I should have thought you'd have known that!"

"Really, Georgie dear, you shouldn't speak so rudely to your aunt."

I was silent for a moment, feeling crestfallen. Then I remarked, in a subdued voice: "Earwig was third."

"Earwig! What an odd name for a horse!" And then, as I bent down to pick up a spray of lilac, she added, "Good gracious, darling, how you've grown out of your riding-breeks! I really must get you another corduroy suit". . . .

But my increasing size had another and far more important effect. I was growing out of Rob Roy. My aunt showed her inevitable lack of initiative in the matter: she said that a small pony was safer for me. During the summer, however, Dixon persistently drew her attention to the obvious fact that my legs were getting nearer and nearer to the ground, although he had the highest respect for gallant little Rob Roy, who was beloved by all who knew him. The end of it was that a "perfect home" was found for him, and he trotted out of my life as gaily as he had trotted into it. After his departure I had a good cry by myself in the kitchen garden.

"I shall never be so fond of anyone again as I was of Rob Roy," I thought, mopping my eyes with a grubby handkerchief. Subsequent events proved my prophecy incorrect. And anyhow it was a fine day, early in September; a few minutes afterwards I was clambering up into a plum tree. The plums were particularly good that year.

*   *   *

As might be expected, Dixon lost no time in discovering an adequate substitute for my vanished favourite. For several weeks he remained reticent on the subject, except that once or twice he mentioned mysteriously that he thought he had heard of something. Conscientious enquiries among coachmen, innkeepers, and the local vet, and the insertion of an advertisement in the county paper, culminated in the arrival of a fourteen-hand, mouse-coloured Welsh cob called Sheila. The sight of Sheila struck awe into my heart. She looked as much too big for me as Rob Roy had looked too small. I also divined that she was enormously expensive.

"Do you really think Master George'll be able to manage her, Dixon?" asked my aunt, regarding Sheila with deprecatory approbation. Dixon reiterated his belief that the mare was thoroughly handy and as quiet as an old sheep: he added that we'd never get such a bargain again for thirty pounds.

"Jump on her back, Master George, and see if she doesn't give you a good feel," suggested that inexorably encouraging voice which was to make a sportsman of me. Whereupon he quickly circumvented the obvious fact that this was no jumping matter by giving me a leg-up into the saddle (a nearly full-sized one). There was no doubt at all that I was a long way from the ground. Rather timidly I surveyed the stable-yard from my new altitude. Then Dixon led the cob carefully through the gate into the paddock and she broke into a springy trot.

V

November, with its darkening afternoons and smell of burning weeds, found me gradually becoming acclimatized to "the new mare", as I importantly called her (using Dixonian phraseology). The groom was able to give me all his attention, since my aunt never rode in the winter. We now went longer distances; sometimes he would tell me that we were "on the edge of the Dumborough country", and he would pull up and point out to me, a few miles away, some looming covert where they often went to draw.

The Dumborough, as I afterwards discovered, was a scrambling sort of country to hunt in—heavily wooded and hilly. But as we turned away from its evening-lighted landscape I would listen eagerly to Dixon's anecdotes of the sport he had seen there. He spoke often of Mr. Macdoggart, Lord Dumborough's hard-riding agent, and how one year he had seen him win the Hunt Steeplechase by a short head from a famous "gentleman rider": and how, another year, Mr. Macdoggart had got concussion of the brain while riding in the same race.

Our afternoon expeditions usually took us in the Dumborough direction, and I suspect that Dixon always had a faint hope that we might "chip in with the hounds", though he knew too well that the foxes rarely ran our way. He also showed an increasing antipathy to the high road, and was continually taking short cuts across the country.

"It'll do them good to have a pipe-opener," he would say, turning in at a gate and setting his horse going up a long stretch of meadow, and my confidence in Sheila increased as I scuttled after him.

Sometimes we would pretend to be "riding a finish", and I would say, "Tom, show me how Mr. Macdoggart won the Hunt Cup on Nobleman."

I had never seen a race in my life; nor had I ever been to a meet of the hounds. But I assiduously studied the novels of Surtees, of which my aunt had a complete set. She dipped into them herself now and again, and we often used to talk about Mr. Jorrocks.

As Christmas approached Dixon drew her attention to my rapid improvement as a rider. Finally he took the bull by the horns and intimated that it would do me no harm to go and have a look at the hounds. She seemed taken aback by this, but he assured her that he would only take me as far as the meet. When she suggested that he could drive me there in the dogcart Dixon's face assumed such an air of disapproval that she gave way at once, and it became only a matter of waiting for the next "near meet".

"I think, 'm, you can rely on me to take proper care of Master George," he remarked rather stiffly; the next moment he looked at me with a grin of delight followed by a solemn wink with the eye furthest away from my aunt.

A few days later I found him studying the local paper in the leather-smelling little harness room. "They're meeting at Finchurst Green on Saturday," he announced with appropriate seriousness. It was an important moment in my life. Finchurst Green was not quite nine miles away.

*   *   *

It was a grey and chilly world that I went out into when I started for my first day's fox-hunting. The winter-smelling air met me as though with a hint that serious events were afoot. Silently I stood in the stable-yard while Dixon led

Sheila out of her stall. His demeanour was business-like and reticent. The horses and their accoutrements were polished up to perfection, and he himself, in his dark-grey clothes and hard black hat, looked a model of discretion and neatness. The only one who lacked confidence was myself.

Stuffing a packet of sandwiches into my pocket and pulling on my uncomfortably new gloves, I felt half aware of certain shortcomings in my outward appearance. Ought one really to go out hunting in a brown corduroy suit with a corduroy jockey-cap made to match the suit? Did other boys wear that sort of thing? . . . I was conscious, too, that Dixon was regarding me with an unusually critical eye. Mute and flustered, I mounted. Sheila seemed very fresh, and the saddle felt cold and slippery. As we trotted briskly through the village everything had an austerely unfamiliar look about it, and my replies to Dixon were clumsy and constrained.

Yet the village was its ordinary village self. The geese were going single file across the green, and Sibson, the lame shoeing-smith, was clinking his hammer on the forge as usual. He peered out at us as we passed, and I saluted him with a slightly forlorn wave of the hand. He grinned and ducked his head. Sheila had had her shoes looked to the day before, so he knew all about where we were going.

As we jogged out of the village, Dixon gazed sagaciously at the sky and said with a grim smile, "I'll bet they run like blazes to-day; there's just the right nip in the air," and he made the horses cock their ears by imitating the sound of a hunting-horn—a favourite little trick of his. Secretly I wondered what I should do if they "ran like blazes". It was all very well for *him*—he'd been out hunting dozens of times!

As we neared the meet I became more and more nervous. Not many of the hunting people came from our side of the country, and we saw no other horsemen to distract my attention until we rounded a bend of the road, and there at last was

Finchurst Green, with the hounds clustering in a corner and men in red coats and black coats moving to and fro to keep their horses from getting chilled. But this is not the last meet that I shall describe, so I will not invent details which I cannot remember, since I was too awed and excited and self-conscious to be capable of observing anything clearly.

Once we had arrived, Dixon seemed to become a different Dixon, so dignified and aloof that I scarcely dared to speak to him. Of course I knew what it meant: I was now his "young gentleman" and he was only the groom who had brought me to "have a look at the hounds". But there was no one at the meet who knew me, so I sat there, shy and silent —aware of being a newcomer in a strange world which I did not understand. Also I was quite sure that I should make a fool of myself. Other people have felt the same, but this fact would have been no consolation to me at the time, even if I could have realized it.

*   *   *

My first period of suspense ended when with much bobbing up and down of hats the cavalcade moved off along the road. I looked round for Dixon, but he allowed me to be carried on with the procession; he kept close behind me, however. He had been sensible enough to refrain from confusing me with advice before we started, and I can see now that his demeanour continued to be full of intuitive tactfulness. But he was talking to another groom, and I felt that I was being scrutinized and discussed. I was riding alongside of a large, lolloping lady in a blue habit; she did not speak to me; she confined herself to a series of expostulatory remarks to her horse which seemed too lively and went bouncing along sideways with its ears back, several times bumping into Sheila, whose behaviour was sedately alert.

Soon we turned in at some lodge gates, crossed the corner

of an undulating park, and then everyone pulled up outside a belt of brown woodland. The hounds had disappeared, but I could hear the huntsman's voice a little way off. He was making noises which I identified as not altogether unlike those I had read about in Surtees. After a time the chattering crowd of riders moved slowly into the wood which appeared to be a large one.

My first reaction to the "field" was one of mute astonishment. I had taken it for granted that there would be people "in pink", but these enormous confident strangers overwhelmed my mind with the visible authenticity of their brick-red coats. It all felt quite different to reading Surtees by the schoolroom fire.

But I was too shy to stare about me, and every moment I was expecting an outburst of mad excitement in which I should find myself galloping wildly out of the wood. When the outbreak of activity came I had no time to think about it. For no apparent reason the people around me (we were moving slowly along a narrow path in the wood) suddenly set off at a gallop and for several minutes I was aware of nothing but the breathless flurry of being carried along, plentifully spattered with mud by the sportsman in front of me. Suddenly, without any warning, he pulled up. Sheila automatically followed suit, shooting me well up her neck. The next moment everyone turned round and we all went tearing back by the way we had come. I found Dixon in front of me now, and he turned his head with a grin of encouragement.

Soon afterwards the hunt came to a standstill in an open space in the middle of the wood: the excitement seemed to be abating, and I felt that fox-hunting wasn't so difficult as I'd expected it to be. A little way below I could hear a confused baying of the hounds among the trees. Then, quite close to where I had halted, a tall man in a blue velvet cap and vermilion coat came riding out from among the undergrowth with one arm up to shield his face from the branches. His face was very red and he seemed upset about something. Turning in my direction he bawled out in an angry voice, "What the bloody hell do you think you're here for?"

For a moment I sat petrified with terror and amazement. He was riding straight at me, and I had no time to wonder what I had done to incur his displeasure. So I stared helplessly until I was aware that he had passed me and was addressing someone immediately behind my horse's heels. . . . Looking round I saw a surly-featured elderly man with side-whiskers: he was on foot and wore the weathered garments of a game-keeper.

"What the hell do you mean by leaving the main-earth unstopped?" the infuriated voice continued.

"Very sorry, m'lord," the man mumbled, "but I never heard you was coming till this morning, and——"

"Don't answer me back. I'll get you sacked for this when Major Gamble comes down from Scotland. I tell you I'm sick of you and your god-damned pheasants," and before the man could say any more the outraged nobleman was pushing his way into the undergrowth again and was bawling "Go on to Hoath Wood, Jack," to the invisible huntsman.

I looked at Dixon, whose horse was nibbling Sheila's neck. "That's the Master," he said in a low voice, adding, "his lord-ship's a rough one with his tongue when anyone gets the wrong side of him." Silently I decided that Lord Dumborough was the most terrifying man I had ever encountered. . . .

Dixon was explaining that our fox had gone to ground and I heard another man near me saying: "That blighter Gamble thinks of nothing but shooting. The place is crawling with birds, and the wonder is that we ever found a fox. Last time we were here we drew the whole place blank, and old D. cursed the keeper's head off and accused him of poisoning the foxes, so I suppose he did it to get a bit of his own back!"

Such was my introduction to the mysteries of "earth-stopping"....

The comparatively mild activities of the morning had occupied a couple of hours. We now trotted away from Major Gamble's preserves. It was about three miles to Hoath Wood; on the way several small spinneys were drawn blank, but Hoath Wood was a sure find, so Dixon said, and a rare place to get a gallop from. This caused a perceptible evaporation of the courage which I had been accumulating, and when there was a halt for the hunt-servants to change on to their second horses I made an attempt to dispel my qualms by pulling out my packet of sandwiches.

While I was munching away at these I noticed for the first time another boy of about my own age. Dixon was watching him approvingly. Evidently this was a boy to be imitated, and my own unsophisticated eyes already told me that. He was near enough to us for me to be able to observe him minutely. A little aloof from the large riders round him, he sat easily, but very upright, on a corky chestnut pony with a trimmed stump of a tail and a neatly "hogged" neck.

Reconstructing that far-off moment, my memory fixes him in a characteristic attitude. Leaning slightly forward from the waist, he straightens his left leg and scrutinizes it with an air of critical abstraction. He seems to be satisfied with his smart buff breeches and natty brown gaiters. Everything he has on is neat and compact. He carries a small crop with a dark leather thong, which he flicks at a tuft of dead grass in a masterly manner. An air of self-possessed efficiency begins with his black bowler hat, continues in his neatly-tied white stock, and gets its finishing touch in the short, blunt, shining spurs on his black walking boots. (I was greatly impressed by the fact that he wore spurs.) All his movements were controlled and modest, but there was a suggestion of arrogance in the steady, unrecognizing stare which he gave me when he

34

became conscious that I was looking at him so intently. Our eyes met, and his calm scrutiny reminded me of my own deficiencies in dress. I shifted uneasily in my saddle, and the clumsy unpresentable old hunting-crop fell out of my hand. Dismounting awkwardly to pick it up, I wished that it, also, had a thong (though this would make the double reins more difficult to manage) and I hated my silly jockey-cap and the badly-fitting gaiters which pinched my legs and always refused to remain in the correct position (indicated by Dixon). When I had scrambled up on to Sheila again—a feat which I could only just accomplish without assistance—I felt what a poor figure I must be cutting in Dixon's eyes while he compared me with that other boy, who had himself turned away with a slight smile and was now soberly following the dappled clustering pack and its attendant red-coats as they disappeared over the green, rising ground on their way to Hoath Wood.

*　　　*　　　*

By all the laws of aunthood we should by now have been well on our way home. But Dixon was making a real day of it. The afternoon hunt was going to be a serious affair. There never appeared to be any doubt about that. The field was reduced to about forty riders, and the chattersome contingent seemed to have gone home. We all went into the covert and remained close together at one end. Dixon got off and tightened my girths, which had got very loose (as I ought to have noticed). A resolute-looking lady in a tall hat drew her veil down after taking a good pull at the flask which she handed back to her groom. Hard-faced men rammed their hats on to their heads and sat silently in the saddle as though, for the first time in the day, they really meant business. My heart was in my mouth and it had good reason to be there. Lord Dumborough was keeping an intent eye on the ride which ran through the middle of the covert.

"Cut along up to the top end, Charlie," he remarked without turning his head; and a gaunt, ginger-haired man in a weather-stained scarlet coat went off up the covert in a squelchy canter.

"That's Mr. Macdoggart," said Dixon in a low voice, and my solemnity increased as the legendary figure vanished on its mysterious errand.

Meanwhile the huntsman was continuing his intermittent yaups as he moved along the other side of the wood. Suddenly his cheers of encouragement changed to a series of excited shoutings. "Hoick-holler, hoick-holler, hoick-holler!" he yelled, and then blew his horn loudly; this was followed by an outbreak of vociferation from the hounds, and soon they were in full cry across the covert. I sat there petrified by my private feelings; Sheila showed no symptoms of agitation; she merely cocked her ears well forward and listened.

And then, for the first time, I heard a sound which has thrilled generations of fox-hunters to their marrow. From the far side of the wood came the long shrill screech (for which it is impossible to find an adequate word) which signifies that one of the whips has viewed the fox quitting the covert. "Gone Away" it meant. But before I had formulated the haziest notion about it Lord Dumborough was galloping up the ride and the rest of them were pelting after him as though nothing could stop them. As I happened to be standing well inside the wood and Sheila took the affair into her own control, I was swept along with them, and we emerged on the other side among the leaders.

I cannot claim that I felt either excitement or resolution as we bundled down a long slope of meadowland and dashed helter-skelter through an open gate at the bottom. I knew nothing at all except that I was out of breath and that the air was rushing to meet me, but as I hung on to the reins I was aware that Mr. Macdoggart was immediately in front of me.

My attitude was an acquiescent one. I have always been inclined to accept life in the form in which it has imposed itself
upon me, and on that particular occasion, no doubt, I just felt
that I was "in for it". It did not so much as occur to me that
in following Mr. Macdoggart I was setting myself rather a
high standard, and when he disappeared over a hedge I took
it for granted that I must do the same. For a moment Sheila
hesitated in her stride. (Dixon told me afterwards that I actually hit her as we approached the fence, but I couldn't remember having done so.) Then she collected herself and jumped
the fence with a peculiar arching of her back. There was a
considerable drop on the other side. Sheila had made no mistake, but as she landed I left the saddle and flew over her head.
I had let go of the reins, but she stood stock-still while I sat
on the wet ground. A few moments later Dixon popped over
a gap lower down the fence and came to my assistance, and I
saw the boy on the chestnut pony come after him and gallop
on in a resolute but unhurrying way. I scrambled to my feet,
feeling utterly ashamed.

"Whatever made you go for it like that?" asked Dixon,
who was quite disconcerted.

"I saw Mr. Macdoggart going over it, and I didn't like to
stop," I stammered. By now the whole hunt had disappeared
and there wasn't a sound to be heard.

"Well, I suppose we may as well go on." He laughed as he
gave me a leg up. "Fancy you following Mr. Macdoggart
over the biggest place in the fence. Good thing Miss Sherston
couldn't see you."

The idea of my aunt seemed to amuse him, and he slapped
his knee and chuckled as he led me onward at a deliberate
pace. Secretly mortified by my failure I did my best to simu-
late cheerfulness. But I couldn't forget the other boy and how
ridiculous he must have thought me when he saw me rolling
about on the ground. I felt as if I must be covered with mud.

About half an hour later we found the hunt again, but I can remember nothing more except that it was beginning to get dark and the huntsman, a middle-aged, mulberry-faced man named Jack Pitt, was blowing his horn as he sat in the middle of his hounds. The other boy was actually talking to him—a privilege I couldn't imagine myself promoted to. At that moment I almost hated him for his cocksuredness.

Then, to my surprise, the Master himself actually came up and asked me how far I was from home. In my embarrassment I could only mutter that I didn't know, and Dixon interposed with "About twelve miles, m'lord," in his best manner.

"I hear he's quite a young thruster." . . . The great man glanced at me for a moment with curiosity before he turned away. Not knowing what he meant I went red in the face and thought he was making fun of me.

*   *   *

Now that I have come to the end of my first day's hunting I am tempted to moralize about it. But I have already described it at greater length than I had intended, so I will only remind myself of the tea I had at an inn on the way home. The inn was kept by a friend of Dixon's—an ex-butler who "had been with Lord Dumborough for years". I well remember the snug fire-lit parlour where I ate my two boiled eggs, and how the innkeeper and his wife made a fuss over me. Dixon, of course, transferred me to them in my full status of "one of the quality", and then disappeared to give the horses their gruel and get his own tea in the kitchen. I set off on the ten dark miles home in a glow of satisfied achievement, and we discussed every detail of the day except my disaster. Dixon had made enquiries about "the other young gentleman", and had learnt that his name was Milden and that he was staying at Dumborough Park for Christmas. He described him as a proper little sportsman; but I was reticent on the subject. Nor did I refer to the question of our going out with the hounds again. By the time we were home I was too tired to care what anybody in the world thought about me.

VI

It was nearly seven o'clock when we got home; as Aunt Evelyn had begun to expect me quite early in the afternoon, she was so intensely relieved to see me safe and sound that she almost forgot to make a fuss about my prolonged absence. Dixon, with his persuasive manner next morning, soon hoodwinked her into taking it all as a matter of course. He made our day sound so safe and confidential. Not a word was said about my having tumbled off (and he had carefully brushed every speck of mud off my back when we stopped at the inn for tea).

As for myself, I began to believe that I hadn't done so badly after all. I talked quite big about it when I was alone with my aunt at lunch on Sunday, and she was delighted to listen to everything I could tell her about my exploits. Probably it was the first time in my life that I was conscious of having got the upper hand of my grown-up relative. When she asked whether there were "any other little boys out on their ponies" I was nonplussed for a moment; I couldn't connect young Milden with such a disrespectful way of speaking. Little boys out on their ponies indeed! I had more than half a mind to tell her how I'd followed the great Mr. Macdoggart over that fence, but I managed to remind myself that the less said about that incident the better for my future as a fox-hunter.

"Yes," I replied, "there was a very nice boy on a splendid little chestnut. He's staying at Dumborough Park." When I told her his name she remembered having met some of his people years ago when she was staying in Northamptonshire.

They had a big place near Daventry, she said, and were a well-known sporting family. I packed these details away in my mind with avidity. Already I was weaving Master Milden into my day dreams, and soon he had become my inseparable companion in all my imagined adventures, although I was hampered by the fact that I only knew him by his surname. It was the first time that I experienced a feeling of wistfulness for someone I wanted to be with.

*   *   *

As a rule I was inclined to be stand-offish about children's parties, though there weren't many in our part of the world. There was to be a dance at Mrs. Shotney's the next Friday, and I wasn't looking forward to it much until my aunt told me that she had heard from Mrs. Cofferdam that Lady Dumborough was going to be there with a large party of jolly young people. "So perhaps you'll see your little hunting friend again," she added.

"He's not little; he looks about two years older than me," I retorted huffily, and at once regretted my stupidity. "My hunting friend!" I had been allowing her to assume that we had "made friends" out hunting. And when we were at the party she would be sure to find out that he didn't know me. But perhaps he wouldn't be there after all. Whereupon I realized that I should be bitterly disappointed if he wasn't.

At seven o'clock on Friday we set off in the village fly. While we jolted along in that musty-smelling vehicle with its incessantly rattling windows I was anxious and excited. These feelings were augmented by shyness and gawkiness by the time I had entered the ballroom, which was full of antlers and old armour. Standing by myself in a corner I fidgeted with my gloves. Now and again I glanced nervously round the room. Sleek-haired little boys in Eton jackets were engaging themselves for future dances with pert little girls in short frocks. Shyness was being artificially dispelled by solicitous ladies, one of whom now swooped down on me and led me away to be introduced to equally unenterprising partners. The room was filling up, and I was soon jostling and bumping round with a demure little girl in a pink dress, while the local schoolmaster, a solemn man with a walrus moustache, thrummed out "The Blue Danube" on an elderly upright piano, reinforced by a squeaky violinist who could also play the cornet; he often did it at village concerts, so my partner informed me, biting her lips as someone trod on her foot. Steering my clumsy course round the room, I wondered whether Lady Dumborough had arrived yet.

There was Aunt Evelyn, talking to Mrs. Shotney. She certainly didn't look half bad when you compared her with other people. And old Squire Maundle, nodding and smiling by the door, as he watched his little granddaughter twirling round and round with a yellow ribbon in her hair. And General FitzAlan with his eyeglass—he looked a jolly decent old chap. . . . He'd been in the Indian Mutiny. . . . The music stopped and the dancers disappeared in quest of claret-cup and lemonade. "I wonder what sort of ices there are," speculated my partner. There was a note of intensity in her voice which was new to me.

*   *   *

"Oh, *do* come on, Denis, the music's begun," cried a dark attractive girl with a scarlet sash—tugging at the arm of a boy who was occupied with an ice. When he turned to follow her I recognized the rider of the chestnut pony. From time to time as the evening went on I watched him enjoying himself with the conspicuous Dumborough Park contingent, which was dominating the proceedings with a mixture of rowdiness and hauteur. Those outside their circle regarded them with envious and admiring antagonism. By a miracle I found myself sitting opposite Denis Milden at supper, which was at one long table. He looked across at me with a reserved air of recognition.

"Weren't you out last Saturday?" he asked. I said yes.

"Rotten day, wasn't it?" I said yes it was rather.

"That's a nice cob you were on. Jumped a bit too big for you at that fence outside Hoath Wood, didn't she?" He grinned good-humouredly. I went red in the face, but managed to blurt out a confused inquiry after the health of his chestnut pony. But before he could reply the Dumborough boy had shouted something at him and I was obliged to pay attention to the little girl alongside of me.

"Do you hunt much?" she inquired, evidently impressed by what she had overheard. Rather loftily I replied that I hunted whenever I got the chance, inwardly excusing myself with the thought that it wasn't my own fault that I'd only had one chance so far. . . .

I was now positively enjoying the party, but shortly afterwards Aunt Evelyn came gliding across the dark polished floor at the end of a polka and adroitly extricated me from the festivities. . . . "Really, darling, don't you think it's almost time we went home?"

I wished she wouldn't call me darling in public, but I fetched my overcoat and followed obediently down to the draughty entrance hall. Denis happened to be sitting on the stairs with his partner. He jumped up politely to allow my aunt to pass. I shot a shy glance at his face.

"Coming to Heron's Gate on Tuesday?" he asked. Deeply gratified, I said I was afraid it was too far for me.

"You ought to try and get there. They say it's one of the best meets." He sat down again with a nod and a smile.

"Wasn't that young Milden—the nice-mannered boy you spoke to as we went out?" asked Aunt Evelyn when our rattle-trap conveyance was grinding briskly down the gravel road to the lodge gates.

"Yes," I replied; and the monosyllable meant much.

VII

Next morning I was a rather inattentive pupil, but Mr. Star rightly attributed this to the previous night's gaieties and was lenient with me, though my eyes often wandered through the window when they ought to have been occupied with sums, and I made a bad mess of my dictation. Mr. Star was still great on dictation, though I ought to have been beyond such elementary exercises at the age of twelve. "Parsing" was another favourite performance of his.

The word parse always struck me as sounding slightly ridiculous: even now it makes me smile when I look at it; but it conjures up for me a very clear picture of that quiet schoolroom: myself in a brown woollen jersey with my elbows on the table, and my tutor in his shabby tail-coat, chalking up on the blackboard, for my exclusive benefit, the first proposition of Euclid. Above the bookcase (which contained an odd assortment of primers, poetry, and volumes of adventure) hung a map of the world—a shiny one, which rolled up. But the map of the world was too large for me that morning, and I was longing to look at the local one and find out how far it was to Heron's Gate (and where it was).

As soon as Mr. Star had gone home to his little house in the village I slyly abstracted the ordnance map from the shelf where my aunt kept it (she was rather fond of consulting the map), and carried it back to the schoolroom with a sensation of gloating uncertainty. Heron's Gate was hard to find, but I arrived at it in the end, marked in very small print with *Wind-*

mill right up against it and a big green patch called *Park Wood* quite near. I wondered what it would look like, and at once visualized a large, dim bird sitting on a white gate. . . . I had never seen a heron, but it sounded nice. . . . But when I began measuring the distance with a bit of string both bird and gate were obliterated by the melancholy number of miles which meandered across the map. The string told its tale too plainly. Heron's Gate was a good twelve miles to go. . . .

The situation now seemed desperate, but Dixon might be able to do something about it. Without saying a word to Aunt Evelyn I waited until we were well away on our afternoon ride, and then asked, quite casually, "Have you ever been to Heron's Gate, Tom?" (I had been telling him about the dance, but had not mentioned Denis Milden.) Dixon gravely admitted that he knew Heron's Gate quite well. There was a short silence, during which he pulled his horse back into a walk. "Is it far from us?" I remarked innocently. He pondered for a moment. "Let's see—it's some way the other side of Hugget's Hill. . . . About twelve miles from us, I should think." I fingered Sheila's mane and tried another tack. "How far were we from home when we finished up the other night?"

"About twelve miles."

Unable to restrain myself any longer, I blurted out my eagerness to go to the meet next Tuesday. I never suspected that Dixon had known this all the time, though I might have guessed that he had looked up the list of meets in the local paper. But he was evidently pleased that my sporting instinct was developing so rapidly, and he refrained from asking why I specially wanted to go to Heron's Gate. It was enough for him that I wanted to go out at all. We duped Aunt Evelyn by a system of mutual falsification of distances (I couldn't find the map anywhere when she wanted to look it up), and at half-past eight on the Tuesday morning, in glittering sunshine, with a melting hoar-frost on the hedgerows, we left home for Heron's Gate.

*   *   *

Emboldened by the fact that I was going out hunting with an inward purpose of my own, I clip-clopped alongside of Dixon with my head well in the air. The cold morning had made my fingers numb, but my thoughts moved freely in a warmer climate of their own. I was being magnetized to a distant meet of the hounds, not so much through my sporting instinct as by the appeal which Denis Milden had made to my imagination. That he would be there was the idea uppermost in my mind. My fears lest I should again make a fool of myself were, for the moment, as far below me as my feet. Humdrum home life was behind me; in the freshness of the morning I was setting out for an undiscovered country. . . .

My reverie ended when Sheila slithered on a frozen puddle and Dixon told me to pay attention to what I was doing and not slouch about in the saddle. Having brought me back to reality he inspected his watch and said we were well up to time. A mile or two before we got to the meet he stopped at an inn, where he put our horses into the stable for twenty minutes, "to give them a chance to stale". Then, seeing that I was looking rather pinched with the cold, he took me indoors and ordered a large glass of hot milk, which I should be jolly glad of, he said, before the day was out. The inn-parlour smelt of stale liquor, but I enjoyed my glass of milk.

The meet itself was an intensified rendering of my initiatory one. I was awed by my consciousness of having come twelve miles from home. And the scene was made significant by the phrase "one of their best meets". In the light of that phrase everything appeared a little larger than life: voices seemed louder, coats a more raucous red, and the entire atmosphere more acute with imminent jeopardy than at Finchurst Green.

Hard-bitten hunting men rattled up in gigs; peeled off their outer coverings, and came straddling along the crowded lane to look for their nags. Having found them, they spoke in low tones to the groom and swung themselves importantly into the saddle as though there were indeed some desperate business on hand. . . .

Heron's Gate was a featureless wayside inn at the foot of a green knoll. I had not yet caught a glimpse of Denis when the procession moved away toward Park Wood, but I looked upward and identified the bulky black Windmill, which seemed to greet me with a friendly wave of its sails, as much as to say, "Here I am, you see—a lot bigger than they marked me on the map!" The Windmill consoled me; it seemed less inhuman, in its own way, than the brusque and bristling riders around me. When we turned off the road and got on to a sodden tussocked field, they all began to be in a hurry; their horses bucked and snorted and shook their heads as they shot past me—the riders calling out to one another with uncouth matutinal jocularities.

I was frightened, and I might have wondered why I was there at all if I had been old enough to analyse my emotions. As it was I felt less forlorn and insecure when we pulled up outside Park Wood and I caught sight of Denis on his chestnut pony. For the time being, however, he was unapproachable. With a gesture of characteristic independence he had turned his back on the jostling riders, who were going one by one into the wood through a narrow hunting-gate. I envied the unhesitating self-reliance with which he cantered along the field, turned his pony to put it at the low fence, and landed unobtrusively in the wood. It was all accomplished with what I should to-day describe as an unbroken rhythm. Thirty years ago I simply thought "Why can't I ride like that?" as I tugged nervously at Sheila's sensitive mouth and only just avoided bumping my knee against the gate-post as I went blundering

46

into the covert. Dixon conducted me along one of the by-paths which branched from the main ride down the middle.

"We'll have to keep our ears open or they'll slip away without us," he remarked sagely. "It's an awkward old place to get a fox away from, though, and we may be here most of the morning." Secretly I hoped we should be.

Where we rode the winter sunshine was falling warmly into the wood, though the long grass in the shadows was still flaked with frost. A blackbird went scolding away among the undergrowth, and a jay was setting up a clatter in an ivied oak. Some distance off Jack Pitt was shouting "Yoi-over" and tooting his horn in a leisurely sort of style. Then we turned a corner and came upon Denis. He had pulled his pony across the path, and his face wore a glum look which, as I afterwards learnt to know, merely signified that, for the moment, he had found nothing worth thinking about. The heavy look lifted as I approached him with a faltering smile, but he nodded at me with blunt solemnity, as if what thoughts he had were elsewhere.

"Morning. So you managed to get here." That was all I got by way of greeting. Somewhat discouraged, I could think of no conversational continuance. But Dixon gave him the respectful touch of the hat due to a "proper little sportsman" and, more enterprising than I, supplemented the salute with "Bit slow in finding this morning, sir?"

"Won't be much smell to him when they do. Sun's too bright for that." He had the voice of a boy, but his manner was severely grown up.

There was a brief silence, and then his whole body seemed to stiffen as he stared fixedly at the undergrowth. Something rustled the dead leaves; not more than ten yards from where we stood, a small russet animal stole out on to the path and stopped for a photographic instant to take a look at us. It was the first time I had ever seen a fox, though I have seen a great many since—both alive and dead. By the time he had slipped out of sight again I had just begun to realize what it was that had looked at me with such human alertness. Why I should have behaved as I did I will not attempt to explain, but when Denis stood up in his stirrups and emitted a shrill "Huick-holler", I felt spontaneously alarmed for the future of the fox.

"Don't do that; they'll catch him!" I exclaimed.

The words were no sooner out of my mouth than I knew I had made another fool of myself. Denis gave me one blank look and galloped off to meet the huntsman, who could already be heard horn-blowing in our direction in a maximum outburst of energy.

"Where'd ye see 'im cross, sir?" he exclaimed, grinning at Denis with his great purple face, as he came hustling along with a few of his hounds at his horse's heels.

Denis indicated the exact spot; a moment later the hounds had hit off the line, and for the next ten or fifteen minutes I was so actively preoccupied with my exertions in following Dixon up and down Park Wood that my indiscretion was temporarily obliterated. I was, in fact, so busy and flurried that I knew nothing of what was happening except that "our fox" was still running about inside the wood. When he did take to the open he must have slipped away unnoticed, for after we had emerged the hounds feathered dubiously over a few fields and very soon I found myself at a standstill.

Dixon was beside me, and he watched intently the mysterious operations of Jack Pitt, who was trotting across a ploughed field with the pack behind him. Dixon explained that he was "making a cast". "He must be a long way ahead of us; they could scarcely speak to him after they took the line out of covert," he commented.

All this was incomprehensible to me, but I was warned by my previous blunder and confined myself to a discreet nod. Dixon then advised me not to wear my cap on the back of my head: I pulled the wretched thing well down over my eyes and made a supreme effort to look like a "hard man to hounds". . . . I watched the riders who were chatting to one another in sunlit groups: they seemed to be regarding the proceedings of Jack Pitt with leisurely indifference.

Denis, as usual, had detached himself from his immediate surroundings, and was keeping an alert eye on the huntsman's head as it bobbed up and down along the far side of the fence. Dixon then made his only reference to my recent misconception of the relationship between foxes and hounds. "Young Mr. Milden won't think much of you if you talk like that. He must have thought you a regular booby!" Flushed and mortified, I promised to be more careful in future. But I knew only too well what a mollycoddle I had made myself in the estimation of the proper little sportsman on whom I had hoped to model myself. . . . *"Don't do that; they'll catch him!"* . . . It was too awful to dwell on. Lord Dumborough would be certain to hear about it, and would think worse of me than ever he did of a keeper who left the earths unstopped. . . . And even now some very sporting-looking people were glancing at me and laughing to one another about something. What else could they be laughing about except my mollycoddle remark? Denis must have told them, of course. My heart was full of misery. . . . Soon afterwards I said, in a very small voice, "I think I want to go home now, Tom." . . . On the way home I remembered that Denis didn't even know my name.

PART TWO:
THE FLOWER SHOW MATCH

I

Ten minutes late, in the hot evening sunshine, my train bustled contentedly along between orchards and hop gardens, jolted past the signal-box, puffed importantly under the bridge, and slowed up at Baldock Wood. The station was exactly the same as usual and I was very pleased to see it again. I was back from Ballboro' for the summer holidays. As I was going forward to the guard's van to identify my trunk and my wooden play-box, the station-master (who, in those days, wore a top-hat and a baggy black frock-coat) saluted me respectfully. Aunt Evelyn always sent him a turkey at Christmas.

Having claimed my luggage I crossed the bridge, surrendered my ticket to a red-nosed and bearded collector, who greeted me good-naturedly, and emerged from the station with my cricket bat (which was wrapped in my cricket pads) under my arm. Dixon was waiting outside with a smart pony and trap. Grinning at me with restrained delight, he instructed my luggage-trundling porter to put it on the village omnibus and I gave the man the last sixpence of my journey-money. As we rattled up the road the unpunctual train with a series of snorts and a streamer of smoke sauntered sedately away into the calm agricultural valley of its vocation.

How jolly to be home for the holidays, I thought to myself. So far neither of us had said a word; but as soon as we were out of the village street (it wasn't our own village) he gave the pony a playful flick of the whip and made the following remark: "I've got a place for you in to-morrow's team." Subdued triumph was in his voice and his face.

"What, for the Flower Show Match!" I exclaimed, scarcely able to believe my ears. He nodded.

Now the Flower Show Match was the match of the year, and to play in it for the first time in my life was an outstanding event: words were inadequate. We mutually decided not to gush about it.

"Of course, you're playing too?" I inquired. He nodded again. Dixon was one of the mainstays of the village team—a dashing left-hand bat and a steady right-arm bowler. I drew a deep breath of our local air. I was indeed home for the holidays! Expert discussion of to-morrow's prospects occupied the remaining mile and a half to the house.

"Miss Sherston won't half be pleased to see you," he said as we turned briskly in at the white gate. "She misses you no end, sir."

Aunt Evelyn had heard us coming up the drive, and she hurried across the lawn in her white dress. Her exuberant welcome ended with: "But you're looking rather thin in the face, dear. . . . Don't *you* think Master George is looking rather thin, Dixon? . . . We must feed him up well before he goes back." Dixon smiled and led the pony and cart round to the stable yard.

"And now, dear, whatever do you think has happened? I've been asked to help judge the vegetables at the Flower Show to-morrow. Really, I feel quite nervous! I've never judged anything except the sweet peas before. Of course, I'm doing them as well." With great restraint I said that I was sure the vegetables would be very interesting and difficult.

"I'm playing in the match," I added, with casual intensity. Aunt Evelyn was overjoyed at the news, and she pretended to be astonished. No doubt she had known about it all the time. The roast chicken at dinner tasted delicious and my bed felt ever so much more comfortable than the one at school.

*   *   *

My window was wide open when I went to bed, and I had left the curtains half-drawn. I woke out of my deep and dreamless sleep to a gradual recognition that I was at home and not in the cubicled dormitory at Ballboro'. Drowsily grateful for this, I lay and listened. A cock was crowing from a neighbouring farm; his shrill challenge was faintly echoed by another cock a long way off.

I loved the early morning; it was luxurious to lie there, half-awake, and half-aware that there was a pleasantly eventful day in front of me. . . . Presently I would get up and lean on the window-ledge to see what was happening in the world outside. . . . There was a starling's nest under the window where the jasmine grew thickest, and all of a sudden I heard one of the birds dart away with a soft flurry of wings. Hearing it go, I imagined how it would fly boldly across the garden: soon I was up and staring at the tree-tops which loomed motionless against a flushed and brightening sky. Slipping into some clothes I opened my door very quietly and tiptoed along the passage and down the stairs. There was no sound except the first chirping of the sparrows in the ivy. I felt as if I had changed since the Easter holidays. The drawing-room door creaked as I went softly in and crept across the beeswaxed parquet floor. Last night's half-consumed candles and the cat's half-empty bowl of milk under the gate-legged table seemed to belong neither here nor there, and my own silent face looked queerly at me out of the mirror. And there was the familiar photograph of "Love and Death", by Watts, with its secret meaning which I could never quite formulate in a thought, though it often touched me with a vague emotion of pathos. When I unlocked the door into the garden the early morning air met me with its cold purity; on the stone step were the bowls of roses and delphiniums and sweet peas which Aunt Evelyn had carried out there before she went to bed; the scarlet disc of the sun had climbed an inch above the hills. Thrushes and blackbirds hopped and pecked busily on the dew-soaked lawn, and a pigeon was cooing monotonously from the belt of woodland which sloped from the garden toward the Weald. Down there in the belt of river-mist a goods train whistled as it puffed steadily away from the station with a distinctly heard clanking of buffers. How little I knew of the enormous world beyond that valley and those low green hills.

*   *   *

From over the fields and orchards Butley Church struck five in mellow tones. Then the clock indoors whizzed and confirmed it with a less resonant tongue. The Flower Show Match was hours away yet—more than six hours in fact. Suppose I'd better go back to bed again, I thought, or I'll be feeling tired out before the match begins. Soon the maids would be stirring overhead, padding about the floor and talking in muffled voices. Meanwhile I stole down to the pantry to cut myself a piece of cake. What a stuffy smelling place it was, with the taps dripping into the sink and a bluebottle fly buzzing sleepily on the ceiling. I inspected the village grocer's calendar which was hanging from a nail. On it there was a picture of "The Relief of Ladysmith". . . . Old Kruger and the Boers. I never could make up my mind what it was all about, that Boer War, and it seemed such a long way off. . . . Yawning and munching I went creaking up to my room. It was broad daylight out of doors, but I was soon asleep again.

After breakfast there was no time to be wasted. First of all I had to rummage about for the tin of "Blanco", which was nowhere to be found. Probably the parlour-maid had bagged it; why on earth couldn't they leave things alone? I knew exactly where I'd left the tin at the end of last holidays —on the shelf in the schoolroom, standing on an old case of beetles (of which, for a short time, I had been a collector). And now, unless I could find the tin quickly, there'd never be time for me to "Blanco" my pads, for they took ever so long to dry in the sun, even on a blazing hot day like this one. . . .

"Really; it's a bit thick, Aunt Evelyn; someone's taken my tin of 'Blanco'," I grumbled. But she was already rather fussed, and was at that moment preoccupied in a serious discussion with Mabb, the gardener, about the transportation of the crockery which she was lending for the Cricket Tea.

In a hasty parenthesis she confessed that she had given the tin to Dixon only a week or two ago, so I transferred myself and my grimy pads to the harness room, where I discovered Dixon putting the finishing touches to his white cricket boots; he had already cleaned mine, and he apologized for not having done my pads, as he had been unable to find them. While I busied myself with dabbing and smearing the pads we had a nice chat about county cricket; he also told me how he had taken a "highly commended" at the Crystal Palace Dog Show with one of the smooth-haired collies which he had recently begun breeding. There had been a lull in his horse-buying activities after I went to school; since then I had given up my riding, as my aunt could not afford to keep a cob specially for me to ride in the holidays. So Dixon had consoled himself with his collies and village cricket: and the saddles were only used when he was exercising the sedate horse which now shared the carriage work with the smart little pony Rocket.

Leaving my pads to dry in the sun, I sauntered contentedly back to the house to have a squint at the morning paper, which never arrived until after breakfast. I had a private reason for wanting to look at the *Morning Post*. I was a firm believer in predestination, and I used to improvise superstitions of my own in connection with the cricket matches I played in. Aunt Evelyn was rustling the newspaper in the drawing-room, where she was having a short spell of inactivity before setting forth to judge the vegetables and sweet peas. Evidently she was reading about politics (she was a staunch Tory).

"I can't understand what that miserable Campbell-Bannerman is up to: but thank heaven the Radicals will never get in again," she exclaimed, handing me the sheet with the cricket news on it.

Carrying this into the garden I set about consulting the omens for my success in the match. I searched assiduously through the first-class scores, picking out the amateurs whose names, like my own, began with S, and whose initial was G. There were only two that day: the result was most unsatisfactory. *G. Shaw run out, 1: G. Smith, c. Lilley, b. Field, 0.* According to that I should score half a run. So I called in professional assistance, and was rewarded with: *Shrewsbury, not out, 127.* This left me in a very awkward position. The average now worked out at 64. The highest score I had ever made was 51, and that was only in a practice game at Ballboro'. Besides, 51 from 64 left 13, an unlucky number. It was absurd even to dally with the idea of my making sixty-four in the Butley Flower Show Match. Anything between twenty and thirty would have been encouraging. But Aunt Evelyn's voice from the drawing-room window informed me that she would be starting in less than ten minutes, so I ran upstairs to change into my flannels. And, anyhow, the weather couldn't have been better. . . . While we were walking across the fields Aunt Evelyn paused on the top of a stile to remark that she felt sure Mr. Balfour would be a splendid Prime Minister. But I was meditating about Shrewsbury's innings. How I wished I could bat like him, if only for one day!

*   *   *

The village of Butley contained, as one of its chief characters, a portly and prosperous saddler named William Dodd. It was Dodd who now greeted us at the field-gate and ushered Aunt Evelyn into the large, tropical-temperatured tent where the judges had already begun their expert scrutiny of the competing vegetables.

In the minds of most of the inhabitants of Butley William Dodd was an immemorial institution, and no village affairs could properly be transacted without his sanction and assistance. As a churchwarden on Sundays his impressive demeanour led us to suppose that, if he was not yet on hat-raising terms with the Almighty, he at any moment expected to be. During a Parliamentary Election he was equally indispensable, as he supervised the balloting in the village schoolroom; and the sanguine solemnity with which he welcomed the Conservative candidate left no doubt at all as to his own political opinions. He was a man much respected by the local gentry, and was on free and easy terms with the farmers of the neighbourhood. In fact, he was a sort of unofficial mayor of the village, and would have worn his robes, had they existed, with dignity and decorum. Though nearer fifty than forty, he was still one of the most vigorous run-getters in the Butley eleven, and his crafty underarm bowling worked havoc with the tail-end of many an opposing team. On Flower Show day he was in all his glory as captain of the cricket team and secretary and treasurer of the Horticultural Society, and his manner of receiving my aunt and myself was an epitome of his urbane and appreciative attitude toward the universe with which the parish of Butley was discreetly associated. Waggish persons in the village had given him the nickname "Did-I-say-Myself". Anyone who wanted to discover the origin of this witticism could do so by stopping outside the saddler's shop on a summer morning for a few minutes of gentle gossip. Laying aside whatever implement of his craft he happened to be using, he would get up and come to the door in his protuberant apron, and when interrogated about "the team for to-morrow", "Let me see," he would reply in a gravely complacent voice, "Let me see, there's Mr. Richard Puttridge; and Myself; my brother Alfred; Tom Dixon; Mr. Jack Barchard; young Bob Ellis—and did I say Myself?"—and so on, counting the names on his stubby fingers, and sometimes inserting "and I think I said Myself" again toward the end of the recital. But his sense of his own importance was justified when he had a bat in his hand. No one could gainsay that.

Having, so to speak, received the freedom of the Flower Show from this worthy man, there was nothing more for me to do until the rest of the players had arrived. At present there wasn't a cricketer to be seen on the small but well-kept ground, and it seemed unlikely that the match would start before noon. It was now a little after eleven and a cloudless day. Sitting in the shadow of a chestnut tree I watched the exertions of a muscular man with a mallet. He was putting up a "coconut shy" in the adjoining meadow, where a steam roundabout, some boat-swings, a shooting gallery, and other recreative facilities were in readiness for the afternoon. On the opposite side of the cricket field had been erected a Tea Tent, which would contain such spectators as were prevented, by their social status, from shying at coconuts or turning almost upside-down in a boat-swing. The ground sloped from the Tea Tent to the side where I was sitting (twenty-five summers ago), so that the genteel onlookers were enabled to feel themselves perceptibly above the rest of the proceedings.

Behind the Tent was a thick thorn hedge; beyond the hedge ran the dusty high road to the village. In the later afternoon of a cricket match there would be several dilatory vehicles drawn up on the other side of the hedge, and the drivers would watch the game in Olympian detachment. There would be the carrier's van, and the brewer's dray, and the baker's cart, and the doctor's gig, and sometimes even a wagon-load of hay. None of them ever seemed to be pressed for time, and once they were there they were likely to stay till the end of the innings. Rooks would be cawing in the vicarage elms, and Butley, with its huddle of red roofs and square church tower, was a contented-looking place.

In my retrospect the players are now beginning to appear in ones and twos. Some skim easily across the greensward on bicycles; others arrive philosophically on foot, pausing to inspect the wicket, which has a nasty habit of causing fast bowling to "bump" after a spell of dry weather.

Dixon and I were having a little practice up against the fence when Aunt Evelyn emerged from the Flower Show Tent with a bevy of head-gardeners. She signalled to me, so I clambered over the palings and went up to her. She only wanted to tell me that she would be back again after lunch and did so hope she wouldn't miss my innings.

"I'm feeling quite proud that Master George is playing in the match," she exclaimed, turning to a short, clean-shaven, small-eyed man in a square bowler hat and his dark Sunday suit, who was standing near her. And then, to me, she added, "I was just congratulating Mr. Bathwick on his wonderful vegetables. We've given him the first prize, and he thoroughly deserves it. You never *saw* such tomatoes and cucumbers! I've been telling Mr. Bathwick that he's a positive *example* to us all!" . . .

Sam Bathwick, who had a very large mouth, grinned bashfully, though his heavy, sallow face had an irrepressibly artful look about it. He farmed a little bit of land in an out-of-the-way corner of the parish, and was reputed to have put by more money than he admitted to.

Climbing over the fence again I became aware of the arrival of the Rotherden eleven in a two-horse brake. It was close on twelve o'clock, but they'd had a fourteen-mile drive and the road was up and down hill all the way. How enormous they looked as they sauntered across the ground—several of them carrying cricket bags. I should be lucky if I made any runs at all against such men as they were!

*　　*　　*

Butley Church clock was tolling twelve while our opponents were bearing down on us from the other side of the field, with William Dodd already half-way across to meet them. But the Rotherden men appeared to be in no great hurry to begin the game as they stopped to have a look at the wicket. Meanwhile Butley bells chimed sedately to the close of the mellow extra celebration which Providence allowed them every three hours without fail. . . .

"I suppose they've got their best team?" I faltered to Dixon, whose keen gaze was identifying the still distant stalwarts.

"You bet they have!" he replied with a grim smile.

Two of the tallest men had detached themselves from the others and were now pacing importantly down the pitch with Dodd between them. Dixon indicated this group. "They've got Crump and Bishop, anyhow," he remarked. . . . Crump and Bishop! The names had a profound significance for me. For many years I had heard Dixon speak of them, and I had even watched them playing in a few Flower Show Matches. Heavily built men in dark blue caps, with large drooping moustaches, one of them bowling vindictively at each end and Butley

59

wickets falling fast; or else one of them batting at each end and Butley bowling being scored off with masterful severity.

But they had also produced a less localized effect on me. Rotherden was on the "unhunted" side of our district; it was in a part of the country which I somehow associated with cherry-blossom and black-and-white timbered cottages. Also it had the charm of remoteness, and whenever I thought of Crump and Bishop, I comprehensively visualized the whole fourteen miles of more or less unfamiliar landscape which lay between Butley and Rotherden. For me the names meant certain lovely glimpses of the Weald, and the smell of mown hayfields, and the noise of a shallow river flowing under a bridge. Yet Crump was an ordinary auctioneer who sold sheep and cattle on market days, and Bishop kept the "Rose and Crown" at Rotherden.

III

Butley had lost the toss. As we went on to the field I tightened the black and yellow scarf which I wore round my waist; the scarf proved that I had won a place in my House Eleven at school, and it was my sole credential as a cricketer. But to-day was more exciting and important than any House Match, and my sense of my own inferiority did not prevent me from observing every detail of the proceedings which I am now able to visualize so clearly across the intervening years.

The umpires in their long white coats have placed the bails on the stumps, each at his own end, and they are still satisfying themselves that the stumps are in the requisite state of exact uprightness. Tom Seamark, the Rotherden umpire, is a red-faced sporting publican who bulks as large as a lighthouse. As an umpire he has certain emphatic mannerisms. When appealed to he expresses a negative decision with a severe and stentorian "Not Oout": but when adjudicating that the batsman is out, he silently shoots his right arm toward the sky—an impressive and irrevocable gesture which effectively quells all adverse criticism. He is, of course, a tremendous judge of the game, and when not absorbed by his grave responsibilities he is one of the most jovial men you could meet with.

Bill Sutler, our umpire, is totally different. To begin with, he has a wooden leg. Nobody knows how he lost his leg; he does not deny the local tradition that he was once a soldier, but even in his cups he has never been heard to claim that he gave the limb for Queen and Country. It is, however, quite certain that he is now a cobbler (with a heavily waxed moustache) and Butley has ceased to deny that he is a grossly partisan umpire. In direct contrast to Tom Seamark he invariably signifies "not out" by a sour shake of the head: when the answer is an affirmative one he bawls "Hout" as if he'd been stung by a wasp. It is reputed that (after giving the enemy's last man out leg-before in a closely-fought finish) he was once heard to add, in an exultant undertone: "and I've won my five bob." He has also been accused of making holes in the pitch with his wooden leg in order to facilitate the efforts of the Butley bowlers.

The umpires are in their places. But it is in the sunshine of my own clarified retrospection that they are wearing their white coats. While I was describing them I had forgotten that they have both of them been dead for many years. Nevertheless, their voices are distinctly audible to me. "Same boundaries as usual, Bill?" shouts Seamark, as loudly as if he were talking to a deaf customer in his tap-room. "Same *as* usual, Muster Seamark; three all round and four over the fence. Draw at six-thirty, and seven if there's anything in it," says Sutler. And so, with an intensified detachment, I look around me at the Butley players, who are now safely distributed in the positions which an omniscient Dodd has decreed for them.

I see myself, an awkward overgrown boy, fielding anxiously at mid-on. And there's Ned Noakes, the whiskered and one-eyed wicketkeeper, alert and active, though he's forty-five if he's a day. With his one eye (and a glass one) he sees more than most of us do, and his enthusiasm for the game is apparent in every attitude. Alongside of him lounges big Will Picksett, a taciturn good-natured young yokel; though over-deliberate in his movements. Will is a tower of strength in the team, and he sweeps half-volleys to the boundary with his enormous brown arms as though he were scything a hayfield. But there is no more time to describe the fielders, for Dodd has thrown a bright red ball to Frank Peckham, who is to begin the bowling from the top end. While Crump and Bishop are still on their way to the wickets I cannot help wondering whether, to modern eyes, the Butley team would not seem just a little unorthodox. William Dodd, for example, comfortably dressed in a pale pink shirt and grey trousers; and Peter Baitup, the ground-man (whose face is framed in a "Newgate fringe") wearing dingy white trousers with thin green stripes, and carrying his cap in his belt while he bowls his tempting left-hand slows. But things were different in those days.

In the meantime Bill Crump has taken his guard and is waiting with watchful ease to subjugate the first ball of the match, while Peckham, a stalwart fierce-browed farmer, takes a final look round the field. Peckham is a fast bowler with an eccentric style. Like most fast bowlers, he starts about fifteen paces from the wicket, but instead of *running* he *walks* the whole way to the crease, very much on his heels, breaking his aggressive stride with a couple of systematic hops when about half-way to his destination. Now he is ready. Seamark pronounces the word "Play!" And off he goes, walking for all he is worth, gripping the ball ferociously, and eyeing the batsman as if he intended to murder him if he can't bowl him neck and crop. On the ultimate stride his arm swings over, and a short-pitched ball pops up and whizzes alarmingly near Crump's magnificent moustache. Ned Noakes receives it rapturously with an adroit snap of his gauntlets. Unperturbed, and with immense deliberation, Crump strolls up the pitch and prods with his bat the spot where he has made up his mind that the ball hit the ground on its way toward his head. The ground-man scratches his nose apologetically. "Don't drop 'em too short, Frank," says Dodd mildly, with an expostulatory shake of his bristly grey cranium. Thus the match proceeds, until, twenty-five years ago, it is lunch time, and Rotherden has made seventy runs with three wickets down. And since both Crump and Bishop have been got rid of, Butley thinks it hasn't done badly.

*   *   *

The Luncheon Tent stood on that part of the field where the Flower Show ended and the swings and roundabouts began. Although the meal was an informal affair, there was shy solemnity in the faces of most of the players as they filtered out of the bright sunshine into the sultry, half-lit interior, where the perspiring landlord of the "Chequers" and his buxom wife were bustling about at the climax of their preparations. While the cricketers were shuffling themselves awkwardly into their places, the brawny barman (who seemed to take catering less seriously than his employers) sharpened the carving-knife on a steel prong with a rasping sound that set one's teeth on edge while predicting satisfactory slices or lamb and beef, to say nothing of veal and ham pie and a nice bit of gammon of bacon.

As soon as all were seated Dodd created silence by rapping the table; he then put on his churchwarden face and looked toward Parson Yalden, who was in readiness to take his cue. He enunciated the grace in slightly unparsonic tones, which implied that he was not only Rector of Rotherden, but also a full member of the M.C.C. and first cousin once removed to Lord Chatwynd. Parson Yalden's parishioners occasionally complained that he paid more attention to cricket and pheasant shooting than was fit and proper. But as long as he could afford to keep a hard-working curate he rightly considered it his own affair if he chose to spend three days a week playing in club and country-house matches all over the county. His demeanour when keeping wicket for his own parish was both jaunty and magisterial, and he was renowned for the strident and obstreperous bellow to which he gave vent when he was trying to bluff a village umpire into giving a batsman out "caught behind". He was also known for his habit of genially engaging the batsman in conversation while the bowler was intent on getting him out, and I have heard of at least one occasion when he tried this little trick on the wrong man. The pestered batsman rounded on the rather foxy-faced clergyman with, "I bin playing cricket nigh on thirty years, and parson or no parson, I take the liberty of telling you to hold your blasted gab."

But I hurriedly dismissed this almost unthinkable anecdote when he turned his greenish eyes in my direction and hoped, in hearty and ingratiating tones, that I was "going to show them a little crisp Ballboro' batting".

The brisk clatter of knives and forks is now well started, and the barman is busy at his barrel. Conversation, however, is scanty, until Tom Seamark, who is always glad of a chance to favour the company with a sentiment, clears his throat impressively, elevates his tankard, fixes Jack Barchard with his gregarious regard, and remarks, "I should like to say, sir, how very pleased and proud we all are to see you safe 'ome again in our midst." Jack Barchard has recently returned from the

Boer War where he served with the Yeomanry. The "sentiment" is echoed from all parts of the table, and glasses are raised to him with a gruff "Good 'ealth, sir," or "Right glad to see you back, Mr. Barchard." The returned warrior receives their congratulations with the utmost embarrassment. Taking a shy sip at my ginger-beer, I think how extraordinary it is to be sitting next to a man who has really been "out in South Africa". Barchard is a fair-haired young gentleman farmer. When the parson suggests that "it must have been pretty tough work out there", he replies that he is thundering glad to be back among his fruit trees again, and this, apparently, is about all he has to say about the Boer War.

But when the meal was drawing to an end and I had finished my helping of cold cherry-tart, and the barman began to circulate with a wooden platter for collecting the half-crowns, I became agonizingly aware that I had come to the match without any money. I was getting into a panic while the plate came clinking along the table, but quiet Jack Barchard unconsciously saved the situation by putting down five shillings and saying, "All right, old chap, I'll stump up for both." Mumbling, "Oh, that's jolly decent of you," I wished I could have followed him up a hill in a "forlorn hope". . . . He told me, later on, that he never set eyes on a Boer the whole time he was in South Africa.

*   *   *

The clock struck three, and the Reverend Yalden's leg-stump had just been knocked out of the ground by a vicious yorker from Frank Peckham. "Hundred and seventeen. Five. Nought," shouted the Butley scorer, popping his head out of the little flat-roofed shanty which was known as "the pavilion". The battered tin number-plates were rattled on to their nails on the scoring-board by a zealous young hobbledehoy who had undertaken the job for the day.

"*Wodger* say last man made?" he bawled, though the scorer was only a few feet away from him.

"Last man, *Blob*."

The parson was unbuckling his pads on a bench near by, and I was close enough to observe the unevangelical expression on his face as he looked up from under the brim of his panama hat with the M.C.C. ribbon round it. Mr. Yalden was not a popular character on the Butley ground, and the hobbledehoy had made the most of a heaven-sent opportunity.

From an undersized platform in front of the Horticultural Tent the Butley brass band now struck up "The Soldiers of the Queen". It's quite like playing in a county match, I thought, as I scanned the spectators, who were lining the fence on two sides of the field. Several easily recognizable figures from among the local gentry were already sauntering toward the Tea Tent, after a gossiping inspection of the Flower Show. I could see slow-moving Major Carmine, the best dressed man in Butley, with his white spats and a carnation in his buttonhole; and the enthusiastic curate, known as "Hard Luck" on account of his habit of exclaiming, "Oh, hard luck!" when watching or taking part in games of cricket, lawn tennis, or hockey. He was escorting the Miss Pattons, two elderly sisters who always dressed alike. And there was Aunt Evelyn, with her red sunshade up, walking between rosy-faced old Captain Huxtable and his clucking, oddly dressed wife. It was quite a brilliant scene which the Butley Band was doing its utmost to sustain with experimental and unconvincing tootles and drum-beatings.

Soon afterwards, however, the Soldiers of the Queen were overwhelmed by the steam-organ which, after a warning hoot, began to accompany the revolving wooden horses of the gilded roundabout with a strident and blaring fanfaronade. For a minute or two the contest of cacophonies continued.

But in spite of a tempestuous effort the band was completely outplayed by its automatic and unexhaustible adversary. The discord becoming intolerable, it seemed possible that the batsmen would "appeal against the music" in the same way that they sometimes "appeal against the light" when they consider it inadequate. But William Dodd was equal to the emergency; with an ample gesture he conveyed himself across the ground and prohibited the activity of the steam-organ until the match was finished. The flitting steeds now revolved and undulated noiselessly beneath their gilded canopy, while the Butley Band palavered peacefully onward into the unclouded jollity of the afternoon.

* * *

The clock struck four. Rotherden were all out for 183 and Tom Dixon had finished the innings with a confident catch on the boundary off one of Dodd's artfully innocent lobs. No catches had come my way, so my part in the game had been an unobtrusive one. When Dodd and Picksett went out to open our innings it was a matter of general opinion in the Beer Tent that the home team had a sporting chance to make the runs by seven o'clock, although there were some misgivings about the wicket and it was anticipated that Crump and Bishop would make the ball fly about a bit when they got to work.

Having ascertained that I was last but one on the list in the score-book, I made my way slowly round the field to have a look at the Flower Show. As I went along the boundary in front of the spectators who were leaning their elbows on the fence I felt quite an important public character. And as I shouldn't have to go in for a long while yet, there was no need to feel nervous. The batsmen, too, were shaping confidently, and there was a shout of "Good ole Bill! That's the way to keep 'em on the carpet!" when Dodd brought off one of his celebrated square-cuts to the hedge off Bishop's easy-actioned fast bowling. Picksett followed this up with an audacious pull which sent a straight one from Crump skimming first bounce into the Tea Tent, where it missed the short-sighted doctor's new straw hat by half an inch and caused quite a flutter among the tea-sipping ladies.

"Twenty up," announced the scorer, and the attendant hobbledehoy nearly fell over himself in his eagerness to get the numbers up on the board. A stupendous appeal for a catch at the wicket by the Reverend Yalden was countered by Sutler with his surliest shake of the head, and the peg-supported umpire was the most popular man on the field as he ferried himself to his square-leg location at the end of the over. Forty went up; then Dodd was clean bowled by Crump.

" 'Ow's *that*?" bawled a ribald Rotherden partisan from a cart in the road, as the rotund batsman retreated; warm but majestic, he acknowledged the applause of the onlookers by a slight lifting of his close-fitting little cap. Everybody was delighted that he had done so well, and it was agreed that he was (in the Beer Tent) "a regular chronic old sport" and (in the Tea Tent) "a wonderful man for his age". Modest Jack Barchard then made his appearance and received a Boer War ovation.

Leaving the game in this prosperous condition, I plunged into the odoriferous twilight of the Horticultural Tent. I had no intention of staying there long, but I felt that I owed it to Aunt Evelyn to have a look at the sweet peas and vegetables at any rate. In the warm muffled air the delicate aroma of the elegant sweet peas was getting much the worst of it in an encounter with the more aggressive smell of highly polished onions. Except for a couple of bearded gardeners who were conferring in professional undertones, I had the tent to myself. Once I was inside I felt glad to be loitering in there, alone and away from the optical delirium of the cricket. The brass band had paused to take breath: now and again the brittle thud of a batsman's stroke seemed to intensify the quiescence of the floralized interior.

As I sniffed my way round I paid little attention to the card-inscribed names of the competitors (though I observed that the Miss Pattons had got second prize for a tasteful table decoration): I found many of the flowers tedious and un-pleasing—more especially the bulbous and freckled varieties with the unpronounceable names—the kind of flowers which my aunt always referred to as "gardeners' greenhouseries". On the whole the fruit and vegetables gave me most enjoy-ment. The black cherries looked delicious and some of the green gooseberries were as large as small hen's eggs. The two gardeners were concentrating on Sam Bathwick's first-prize vegetables and as they seemed to grudge making way for me I contented myself with a glimpse of an immense marrow and some very pretty pink potatoes. As I passed, one of the gardeners was saying something about "copped 'im a fair treat this time", and I absent-mindedly wondered who had been copped. When I emerged the home team had lost two more wickets and the condition of the game was causing grave anxiety. Reluctantly I drifted toward the Tea Tent for a period of social victimization.

*   *   *

The Tea Tent was overcrowded and I found Aunt Evelyn sitting a little way outside it in comparative seclusion. She was in earnest communication with Miss Clara Maskall, a remarkable old lady who had been born in the year of the Battle of Waterloo and had been stone-deaf for more than sixty years.

My aunt was one of the few people in the neighbourhood who enjoyed meeting Miss Maskall. For the old lady had a way of forgetting that the rest of the world could hear better than she could, and her quavering comments on some of the local gentlefolk, made in their presence, were often too caustic to be easily forgotten. She was reputed to have been kissed by King George the Fourth. She was wearing a bunched-up black silk dress, and her delicately withered face was framed in a black poke-bonnet, tied under the chin with a white lace scarf. With her piercingly alert eyes and beaky nose she looked like some ancient and intelligent bird. Altogether she was an old person of great distinction, and I approached her with an awful timidity. She had old-fashioned ideas about education, and she usually inquired of me, in creaking tones, whether I had recently been flogged by my schoolmaster.

But the menace of Roman Catholicism was her most substantial and engrossing theme; and up to the age of ninety she continued to paste on the walls of her bedroom every article on the subject which she could find in *The Times* and the *Morning Post*. Aunt Evelyn told me that the walls were almost entirely papered with printed matter, and that she had more than once found Miss Maskall sitting on the top step of a library ladder reading some altitudinous article on this momentous question of "the Scarlet Woman". To the day of her death she never so much as trifled with a pair of spectacles. But she was still very much alive when I saw her at the Flower Show Match. Sitting bolt upright in a wicker-chair, she scrutinized me keenly and then favoured me with a friendly little nod without losing touch with what my aunt was engaged in telling her by "finger-talk".

"*What* is it the man has been doing, Evelyn?" she asked, her queer, uncontrolled voice quavering up to a bird-like shrillness. There was something rather frightening about her defective intonation.

"Write it down; write it down," she screeched, clawing a tablet and pencil out of her lap and consigning them to Aunt Evelyn, who hurriedly scribbled two or three lines and returned the tablet for her to read aloud; "such a dreadful thing, the judges have found out that Bathwick has been cheating with his prize vegetables". She passed it back with a tremulous cackle.

"How did he do it?" More scribbling, and then she read out, "He bought all the vegetables at Ashbridge. The judges suspected him, so they went to his garden in a pony trap and found that he has *no glass*—not even a cucumber frame." Miss Maskall chuckled delightedly at this, and said that he ought to be given a special prize.

"I call it downright dishonest. Almost as bad as embezzlement," wrote Aunt Evelyn who, as one of the judges, could scarcely be expected to treat the offence in a spirit of levity.

Miss Clara now insisted that she must herself inspect the fraudulent vegetables. Rising energetically from her chair, she grasped her ebony stick with an ivory knuckled hand and shaped an uncompromising course for the Horticultural Tent with Aunt Evelyn and myself in tow. The villagers at the gate made way for her with alacrity, as though it had dawned on them that she was not only the most ancient, but by far the most interesting object to be seen at the Flower Show Match.

*   *   *

Miss Maskall had made the game seem rather remote. She cared nothing for cricket, and had only come there for an afternoon sprec. But she was taciturn during her tour of the Flower Show: when we tucked her into her shabby old victoria she leant back and closed her eyes. Years ago she must have had a lovely face. While we watched her carriage turn the corner I wondered what it felt like to be eighty-seven; but I did not connect such antiquity with my own future. Long before I was born she had seen gentlemen playing cricket in queer whiskers and tall hats.

71

Next moment I was safely back in the present, and craning my neck for a glimpse of the score-board as I hustled Aunt Evelyn along to the Tea Tent. There had been a Tea Interval during our absence, so we hadn't missed so very much. Five wickets were down for ninety and the shadows of the cricketers were growing longer in the warm glare which slanted down the field. A sense of my own share in the game invaded me and it was uncomfortable to imagine that I might soon be walking out into the middle to be bowled at by Crump and Bishop, who now seemed gigantic and forbidding. And then impetuous Ned Noakes must needs call Frank Peckham for an impossibly short run, and his partner retreated with a wrathful shake of his head. Everything now depended on Dixon who was always as cool as a cucumber in a crisis.

"Give 'em a bit of the long handle, Tom!" bawled someone in the Beer Tent, while he marched serenely toward the wicket, pausing for a confidential word with Noakes who was still looking a bit crestfallen after the recent catastrophe. Dixon was a stylish left-hander and never worried much about playing himself in. Bishop was well aware of this, and he at once arranged an extra man in the outfield for him. Sure enough, the second ball he received was lifted straight into the long-off's hands. But the sun was in the fielder's eyes and he misjudged the flight of the catch. The Beer Tent exulted vociferously. Dixon then set about the bowling and the score mounted merrily. He was energetically supported by Ned Noakes. But when their partnership had added over fifty, and they looked like knocking off the runs, Noakes was caught in the slips off a bumping ball and the situation instantly became serious again.

Realizing that I was next in but one, I went off in a fluster to put my pads on, disregarding Aunt Evelyn's tremulous "I do hope you'll do well, dear". By the time I had arrived on the other side of the ground, Amos Hickmott, the wheelwright's son, had already caused acute anxiety. After surviving a tigerish appeal for "leg-before", he had as near as a toucher run Dixon out in a half-witted endeavour to escape from the bowling. My palsied fingers were still busy with straps and buckles when what sounded to me like a deafening crash warned me that it was all over with Hickmott. We still wanted seven runs to win when I wandered weakly in the direction of the wicket. But it was the end of an over, and Dixon had the bowling. When I arrived the Reverend Yalden was dawdling up the pitch in his usual duck-footed progress when crossing from one wicket to the other.

"Well, young man, you've got to look lively this time," he observed with intimidating jocosity. But there seemed to be a twinkle of encouragement in Seamark's light blue eye as I established myself in his shadow.

Dixon played the first three balls carefully. The fourth he smote clean out of the ground. The hit was worth six, but "three all round and four over" was an immemorial rule at Butley. Unfortunately, he tried to repeat the stroke, and the fifth ball shattered his stumps. In those days there were only five balls to an over.

Peter Baitup now rolled up with a wide grin on his fringed face, but it was no grinning moment for me at the bottom end when Sutler gave me "middle-and-leg" and I confronted impending disaster from Crump with the sun in my eyes. The first ball (which I lost sight of) missed my wicket by "a coat of varnish" and travelled swiftly to the boundary for two byes, leaving Mr. Yalden with his huge gauntlets above his head in an attitude of aggrieved astonishment. The game was now a tie. Through some obscure psychological process my whole being now became clarified. I remembered Shrewsbury's century and became as bold as brass. There was the enormous auctioneer with the ball in his hand. And there I, calmly resolved to look lively and defeat his destructive aim.

The ball hit my bat and trickled slowly up the pitch. "Come on!" I shouted, and Peter came gallantly on. Crump was so taken by surprise that we were safe home before he'd picked up the ball. And that was the end of the Flower Show Match.

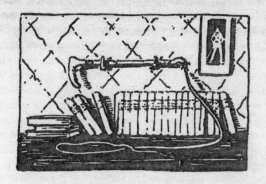

PART THREE: A FRESH START

I

Except for the letters written to me by Mr. Pennett I have no documentary evidence concerning the young man who was existing under my name in the summer after I left Cambridge. The fact that I have preserved them is a proof that I was aware of their significance, although it is now nearly twenty years since I last read them through. In these days they would be typewritten; but in those days they were fair-copied by a clerk, and the slanting calligraphy helps me to recapture my faded self as I was when I apprehensively extracted them from their envelopes. Even now they make rather uncomfortable reading, and I find myself wondering how their simple-minded recipient managed to repel such an onslaught of worldly wisdom.

But Tom Dixon was still about the place to pitchfork me

75

into the village cricket team; and it happened that it was on a showery June morning, when I was setting out for one of the Butley matches, that I received the first really uncomfortable letter from Mr. Pennett. We were playing over at Rotherden, which meant an early start, as it was fourteen miles away. So I slipped the letter into my pocket unopened and perused it at intervals later on in the day. My Aunt Evelyn, I may say, never made any attempt to influence me in my choice of a career. Like me, she preferred to procrastinate, and her intuition probably warned her that my mind was unlikely to habituate itself to the quibbling technicalities of the legal profession. But whatever she thought she kept to herself. She was still addicted to saying that I was "none too strong", and this delicacy of constitution which she ascribed to me was in itself a more than adequate argument against my overtaxing my health with tedious textbooks in the unwholesome air of a London office.

"George is a boy who ought not to be interfered with too much," she would say. And I agreed with her opinion unreservedly.

Mr. Pennett, however, had conscientiously dictated to his clerk a couple of pages of expostulation and advice with the unmistakable object of interfering with me as much as possible. But the letter remained in my pocket until after we had arrived at Rotherden.

The air was Elysian with early summer and the shadows of steep white clouds were chasing over the orchards and meadows; sunlight sparkled on green hedgerows that had been drenched by early morning showers. As I was carried past it all I was lazily aware through my dreaming and unobservant eyes that this was the sort of world I wanted. For it was my own countryside, and I loved it with an intimate feeling, though all its associations were crude and incoherent. I cannot think of it now without a sense of heartache, as if it contained something which I have never quite been able to discover.

Thus we jogged and jingled along in the rumbling two-horse brake with the Butley team talking their parish talk, and every house and hamlet animating William Dodd to some local-flavoured anecdote. Dodd was in a holiday humour, and there wasn't much that he didn't know about the living-memoried local history which lay between Butley and Rotherden. The doings of the county cricket team were also discussed; Dodd had watched them at Dumbridge last week and had spoken to Blythe, who was, in his opinion, the best slow left-hand bowler in England. The road went up and down hill by orchards and hop-gardens and parks crowded with ancient oaks. Nearly all the way we were looking, on our left-hand side, across the hop-kiln-dotted Weald. And along the Weald went the railway line from London to the coast, and this gave me a soberly romantic sense of distances and the outside world of unfamiliar and momentous happenings. I knew very little about London, and I had never been across the Channel, but as I watched a train hurrying between the level orchards with its consequential streamer of smoke, I meditated on the coast-line of France and all the unvisualized singularity of that foreign land. And then Rotherden Church hove in sight with its square battlemented tower, and we turned into the stableyard of the "Rose and Crown", where Bert Bishop, the landlord, was waiting to welcome us—a stouter man than he used to be, but still as likely as not to hit up a hundred.

*　　　*　　　*

Butley batted first. I was in eighth. Mr. Pennett's letter was still in my pocket. Sitting on a gate in a remote corner of ground I opened the envelope with a sinking heart. Mr. Pennett wrote as follows:

77

"My dear George, I have learned from your College Tutor, much to my regret, that you have gone down from Cambridge, at any rate for this term. I think that you have made a mistake in so doing and that this arises from perhaps a lack of appreciation on your part of the value of an University education. One of the objects of an University career is to equip the student for the battle of life, and as you grow older you will find that people are estimated in the world by the results which they have obtained at the Varsity. It is a kind of stamp upon a man and is supposed to indicate the stuff of which he is made. With a degree you start with so much capital to the good, but if on the other hand having once commenced an University career you abandon it, the fact will militate against you in almost everything you undertake hereafter. Although you are nearly twenty-two you cannot be expected yet to look at things in precisely the same light as those who have had more experience, but knowing as I do the great importance of the whole matter I do most earnestly beg you to reconsider the decision at which you have arrived. G. Sherston, M.A., will rank higher than plain G. Sherston, and the mere fact of your being able to attach the magic letters to your name will show that whatever may be your capabilities you have at any rate grit and perseverance. I hope, therefore, that you will see that the step you have taken is one of unwisdom and that before it is too late you will carefully reconsider it. Forgive this homily, but I am sure that whether it is to your taste or not you will at least acknowledge that it proceeds from a strong desire to be of use to you from— your sincere friend, Percival G. Pennett."

It amuses me now when I think of the well-meaning lawyer dictating that letter in his Lincoln's Inn office, and of myself with my gaze recoiling from the wiseacre phraseology to follow a rook which was travelling overhead with querulous cawings. Everything the letter said was so true; and yet, I wondered, was it really possible for P.G.P. to tell me what was best for my future? His letter had one effect which would have astonished him. Worried and put out of temper by it, I slouched to the wicket after lunch without caring a hoot whether I stayed there or not. The result was that, favoured by a fair amount of luck, I "carted" the bowling all over the field; at the end of our innings I was not out forty-three. This was the highest score I had ever made for the village; and, although we lost the match by five wickets, I finished the day in a glow of self-satisfaction which was undamped by a tremendous thunderstorm which overtook us on our way home.

*   *   *

Mr. Pennett's procedure for bringing me to my senses about "an University degree" was an excellent example of preaching to the winds. Good advice seldom sinks into the wayward mind of a young man, and in this case the carefully composed phrases meant nothing to me. The utmost I could do was to transmute his prudent precepts into some such sentiment as this: "The silly old blighter is trying to make me stay up at Cambridge when I'm absolutely fed up with the whole concern." Not that I made any serious attempt to "carefully reconsider" my decision. I had not yet begun to train myself to think rationally about anything. No one was ever less capable of putting two and two together than I was. And he made a strategic mistake when he adjured me to "look ahead".

I very much doubt whether anybody wants to look ahead unless he is anxious to escape from one condition into another more desirable one. Children hanker to be grown-up because they want liberty. But why should a young man who has inherited a net income of about six hundred a year find it easy or necessary to imagine himself as ten or twenty years older? If I ever thought of myself as a man of thirty-five it was a visualization of dreary decrepitude. The word maturity had no meaning for me. I did not anticipate that I should become *different*; I should only become *older*. I cannot pretend that I aspired to growing wiser. I merely *lived*, and in that condition I drifted from day to day. Ignorantly unqualified to regulate the human mechanism which I was in charge of, my self-protective instincts were continually being contradicted by my spontaneously capricious behaviour. When Mr. Pennett referred me to what he called "after-life", he was unaware that for me the future was a matter of the four seasons of the year. There was next autumn, and next winter, and after that next spring. But this summer was the only thing that I cared about. The phrase "after-life" was also vaguely confused with going to church and not wanting to be dead—a perplexity which can be omitted from a narrative in which I am doing my best to confine myself to actual happenings. At the age of twenty-two I believed myself to be unextinguishable.

II

It was a wet and windy afternoon toward the end of September. We were on our way home from a seaside place in Devonshire, where we had been staying for a change of air. Aunt Evelyn was going through a period of bad health, and her headaches were probably much worse than she admitted. Anyhow, she had been content to do very little, and I caused her no anxiety, for I had "taken up golf" and most of my time and energy had evaporated on the links. The people I played with at Bidmouth were equally engrossed by the game, and if they had any ideas about things other than golf they showed no inclination to share them with me. Aunt Evelyn wasn't sorry to be going home again; there was plenty to be done in the garden, and how the cats had got on without her she couldn't imagine.

Of my own sensations about our return I have no recollection: I may have felt vaguely dissatisfied, but I did not consciously allow myself to criticize the purposeless existence I was leading. At Waterloo Station we changed from one train to another for the final stage of our "through" journey. On account of her feeling unwell, Aunt Evelyn had taken first-class tickets, and this made me conscious that we had a social position to keep up. Gratified by the obsequious attentions of the green-flagged guard, I couldn't help wishing that my aunt had tipped him more than a shilling. As she remarked, he was such a very nice-mannered man, and I assumed that he was expecting half a crown.

At any rate, it was a relief to settle down in a corner of the dark blue cushioned compartment after my aunt's unnecessary fussification about the luggage. Raindrops trickled down the windows as we steamed out of the station, and I was glad to avert my gaze from the dingy and dilapidated tenements and warehouses which we were passing. Poverty was a thing I hated to look in the face; it was like the thought of illness and bad smells, and I resented the notion of all those squalid slums spreading out into the uninfected green country. While I perused a magazine called *Golf Illustrated* I stole an occasional glance at the two very first-class looking passengers who occupied the other corners of the compartment. One of them was a grey-haired lady with a crocodile-skin dressing-case and a fur cloak. She was reading a book with an air of refined hauteur. The other was a middle-aged man with a neatly trimmed grey beard and a glossy top-hat which he had ceremoniously arranged on the rack above him. He was glancing at *Blackwood's Magazine*, and he had a bunch of violets in the buttonhole of his opulent dark blue overcoat. From the tone of voice in which he inquired whether she would prefer the window down a little I inferred that the lady was a stranger to him. Compared with these influential-looking people,

Aunt Evelyn in her countrified tweed coat and skirt and her dowdy little hat seemed only just presentable. I had yet to make the significant discovery that the most distinguished personages are sometimes the most untidy.

Fortunately for her peace of mind, my aunt was much too tired to worry about the impression which her exterior might be creating on two complete strangers who were surveying her for the first and probably the last time on earth. What she really cared about was a cup of hot tea. But we should be in the train another hour, and we couldn't possibly get home before six o'clock. Aunt Evelyn, however, though she seldom travelled, was not without resourcefulness in the matter of railway journeys, and what she didn't know about picnics wasn't worth knowing. Now among the numerous light articles which she had brought into the carriage there was a certain plebeian-looking basket which contained every facility for making tea. Most essential among the facilities was a patent spirit-lamp for boiling the water; and this lamp was apt to misbehave itself and produce an unpleasing smell. Had we been alone I should have been willing enough to set it alight, and the whole business would have been quite companionable and cosy. But now, with those impeccably dressed people in their corners, I felt nothing except discomfort and disapproval when my aunt became busy with her basket. I totally dissociated myself from her preparations, while she muddled about with the lamp, which for some time refused to function and then flared up with sudden explosive ardour.

"I was quite afraid it was going to be tiresome," she remarked, screening it with the *Pall Mall Gazette* and looking across at me with a smile. But the expected response was absent. I glowered contemptuously at the apparatus which she had placed on the floor. She then began measuring out the tea. In the meantime I was conscious that our fellow-travellers

82

were exchanging scandalized glances, and their haughtiness intensified itself with every phase of the capricious conduct of the lamp.

"There now! It's gone out again!" exclaimed Aunt Evelyn, who had become slightly flustered, since she had observed that she was getting herself into bad odour with the other passengers.

By dint of striking several more matches and much twiddling of the wick she got the conflagration well under way again, although she had some difficulty in shielding it against a dangerous draught caused by the gentleman, who had let down his window with expostulating asperity.

As for me, I considered that Aunt Evelyn was making a regular exhibition of herself, and when her persistence had been rewarded by a cloud of steam and she held out a cup of moderately hot China tea, I felt so annoyed that I could almost have chucked it out of the window. However, I expressed my feelings adequately by muttering, "No, I don't want any," and putting my paper up as a barrier between myself and the objectionable sight of Aunt Evelyn sipping her tea with mechanical enjoyment. As there was a spare cup in the basket she politely said to the lorgnette-raising lady, "May I offer you a cup of tea, madam?" But the amenity was declined with an air of social remoteness.

For the remainder of the journey I couldn't bring myself to say another word, and Aunt Evelyn endured my sulky silence—wearily apologetic. By the time we were home I knew quite clearly that my attitude toward the tea-making had been odious; and the more I realized it the more impossible it seemed for me to make amends by behaving gently to her. It was one of those outwardly trivial episodes which one does not forget.

It was now an accepted fact that I had quitted Cambridge University. During that autumn I was limply incorporating myself with Aunt Evelyn's localized existence. Nothing was being said on the subject of what I was going to do, and I cannot remember that the problem was perplexing my thoughts, or that I felt any hankerings for more eventful departments of human experience. I was content to take it easy until something happened. But since I had no responsibilities and no near relatives except my aunt whose connection with the world beyond her own "round of calls" was confined to a few old friends who seldom wrote to her, the things which could happen were humdrum and few.

"What are you doing to-day, George?" asks Aunt Evelyn, as she gets up from the breakfast table to go down to the kitchen to interview the cook.

"Oh, I shall probably bike over to Amblehurst after lunch for a round of golf," I reply.

Over at Amblehurst, about four miles away, there is a hazardless nine-hole course round Squire Maundle's sheep-nibbled park. The park faces south-west, sloping to a friendly little river—the Neaze—which at that point, so I have been told, though I never troubled to verify it—divides the counties of Kent and Sussex. On the other side of the river is the village. Squire Maundle's clanging stable clock shares with the belfry of the village school the privilege of indicating the Amblehurst hours. My progress up and down the park from one undersized green to another is accompanied by the temperate clamour of sheep-bells (and in springtime by the loud litanies of baa-ing lambs and anxious ewes). The windows of Squire Maundle's eighteenth-century mansion overlook my zigzag saunterings with the air of a county family dowager who has not yet made up her mind to leave cards on those new people at the Priory. As a rule I have the links to myself, but once in a while "young" Squire Maundle (so-called because his eighty-seven-year-old father is still above ground) appears on the skyline in his deer-stalker hat, with a surly black retriever at his heels and we play an amicable round.

Without wishing to ridicule him, for he was always kind and courteous, I may say that both his features and his tone of voice have something in common with the sheep who lift their mild munching faces to regard him while he plays an approach shot in his cautious, angular, and automatic style. He is one of those shrewdly timorous men who are usually made a butt of by their more confident associates. Falstaff would have borrowed fifty pounds off him, though he has the reputation of being close with his money. His vocabulary is as limited as his habit of mind, and he speaks with an old-fashioned word-clipping conciseness. His lips are pursed up as if in a perpetual whistle. The links—on which he knows every tussock and ant-hill intimately—are always "in awful good condition"; and "That's a hot'un!" he exclaims when I make a long drive, or "That's for Sussex!" (a reference to the remote possibility that my ball may have gone over the river). But the best instance I can give of his characteristic mode of expressing himself is one which occurred when I once questioned him about a group of little grey stones among the laurel bushes outside his stable-yard. After whistling to his retriever he replied, "House-dogs bury in the shrubbery: shooting-dogs bury in the park". . . .

Aunt Evelyn always enjoyed a game of croquet with him at a garden party.

But in my spontaneous memories of Amblehurst I am always playing by myself. The sun is in my eyes as I drive off at the "long hole" down to the river, and I usually slice my ball into a clump of may trees. I am "trying to do a good score"—a purpose which seldom survives the first nine holes —but only half my attention is concentrated on the game. I am wondering, perhaps, whether that parcel from the second-hand bookshop at Reading will have arrived by the afternoon post; or I am vaguely musing about my money affairs; or thinking what a relief it is to have escaped from the tyranny of my Tripos at Cambridge. Outside the park the village children are making a shrill hubbub as they come out of school. But the sun is reddening beyond the straight-rising smoke of the village chimneys, and I must sling my clubs across my shoulder and mount my bicycle to pedal my way along the narrow autumn-smelling lanes. And when I get home Aunt Evelyn will be there to pour out my tea and tell me all about the Jumble Sale this afternoon; it was such a success, they made more than six pounds for the Mission to Deep-Sea Fishermen.

*　　　*　　　*

The days were drawing in, though it was only the second week in October.

"There's a nice fire up in the schoolroom, Mr. George; and a parcel of books come by the carrier's van," said Miriam, when she was taking away the tea things.

Miriam (and I might well have mentioned her before, since she had already been with Aunt Evelyn for nearly seven years) was a gaunt woman who had looked more than middle-aged ever since I first saw her. Miriam's hair had perhaps begun by being golden, but it was now a faded yellow remnant, drawn tightly back from her broad forehead and crowned by a skimpy lace cap. Her wide-set eyes had a strained and patient expression, as though expecting to be rather sharply ordered to lug a heavy scuttle of coals up four flights of steep stairs. She was unobtrusively humpbacked and round shouldered, which suggested that when not carrying scuttles upstairs she had been burdened with heavy trays or had been stooping over a scullery sink to wash and wipe a lifetime of crockery. Her voice, too, had a long-suffering note in it—most noticeable when she was doing her best to be gay. These outward characteristics were the only legacy which she had received from her late mistress who had for a long period of years exploited Miriam's abnormal willingness for work. In such drudgery she had used up her youth and maturity, thereby acquiring an habitual capacity for taking on her own shoulders a load of domestic duties which never seemed to have struck her as being excessive. She was what is known as "a treasure". The difficulty, as Aunt Evelyn often said, was to persuade her to sit down and shut her eyes for a few minutes and allow the other maids to do their fair share of the housework. But Aunt Evelyn's kindness only stimulated Miriam to renewed activity, and her response to ordinary civility and consideration reflected no credit at all on her former employer. In those days I used to look upon her as a bit of a joke, and I took for granted the innumerable little jobs she did for me. She was no more than an odd-looking factotum, whose homely methods and manners occasionally incurred my disapproval, for I had a well-developed bump of snobbishness as regards flunkeydom and carriage-and-pair ostentation as a whole. Now and again, however, I was remotely affected by the smile which used to light up her sallow humble face when I said something which pleased her. It is the memory of that smile which has helped me to describe her. For there was a loveliness of spirit in her which I did not recognize until it was too late for her to know it.

*　　　*　　　*

On my way up to the schoolroom, which had formerly been known as "the day-nursery", I decided that the name needed further promotion. "Study" was inappropriate and sounded elderly. "Smoking-room" wouldn't do either, because I hadn't begun smoking yet, although puffing my pipe by the fireside on winter evenings was a comfortable idea. "Library", I thought (pausing in the dark passage with a hand on the brass door-knob) was too big a jump from "schoolroom". Besides, there wasn't any library. "Library" meant glass-fronted bookcases with yellow busts of Julius Caesar and Cicero on the top. Entering the fire-lit room, I pounced on the bulky package which Miriam had deposited on the table. "Book-room", I thought, as I tugged impetuously at the thick string. And "book-room" it rather tentatively became.

There was no doubt that I had a fondness for books—especially old ones. But my reading was desultory and unassimilative. Words made a muddled effect on my mind while I was busy among them, and they seldom caused any afterthoughts. I esteemed my books mostly for their outsides. I admired old leather bindings, and my fancy was tickled by the thought of firelight flickering on dim gilt, autumn-coloured backs—rows and rows of them, and myself in an armchair musing on the pleasant names of Addison and Steele, Gibbon and Goldsmith. And what wonderful bargains were to be discovered in the catalogues of second-hand booksellers at Birmingham! Only last week I had acquired (for seven and sixpence) *Dr. Burnet's Rights of Princes in the Disposing of Ecclesiastical Benefices*, 1685. FIRST EDITION. *Original sheep*, scarce. And there were Tillotson's Sermons, ten imposing volumes in sage green morocco. I had bought them along with a twelve-volume edition of Doctor Johnson's Works (in contemporary sprinkled calf), and had even read a few of the shorter *Lives of the Poets* (such as Garth, Broome, Mallet, and Sprat). I had also made a short-winded effort to read *Rasselas*. . . .

And now (disentangling the cord and rending the brown paper wrappings) Pope's *Homer* had actually arrived. Six folio volumes, first edition, and they had only cost fifteen bob plus the postage. When I wrote for them (to a philanthropist named Cowler, at Reading) I made sure that someone else would have snapped them up. But no; here they were; in quite good condition, too. And how splendid, to be able to read both Pope and Homer at once! Homer had been impossible to enjoy in the fifth form at Ballboro', but he would seem ever so much easier now. I resolved to read exactly a hundred lines every day until I waded through the whole six volumes. And when I'd marshalled them on the top shelf —for they were too tall to fit into any other—between the quarto sets of Smollett's *History of England* and Tickell's *Addison*, I solemnly abstracted the first volume of the Iliad and made a start.

> *The wrath of Peleus' son and that dire spring*
> *Of woes unnumbered, heavenly goddess, sing. . . .*

IV

To those who are expecting to see me in the saddle again it may seem that I have delayed over-long in acquiring my first hunter. But I take this opportunity of reminding my invisible audience that there was no imperative reason why I should ever have bought a horse at all; in fact candour compels me to confess that if I had been left to my own devices I should probably have spent the forty-five guineas on something else. For though I was living so quietly and paying Aunt Evelyn nothing for my keep, I never seemed to have much of a balance at the bank. And Mr. Pennett, who appeared to consider me utterly irresponsible in matters of money, had so far refused to disgorge more than £450 a year out of my estimated income of £600. So, what with buying books and a new bicycle, and various other apparently indispensable odds and ends, I found myself "going in for economy" when early in January Dixon began his campaign to revive my interest in the stable.

During the winter I had been taking a walk every afternoon. I usually went five or six miles, but they soon became apathetic ones, and I was conscious of having no genuine connection with the countryside. Other people owned estates, or rented farms, or did something countrified; but I only walked along the roads or took furtive short cuts across the fields of persons who might easily have bawled at me if they had caught sight of me. And I felt shy and "out of it" among the local landowners—most of whose conversation was about shooting. So I went mooning, more and more moodily, about the looming landscape, with its creaking-cowled hop-kilns and whirring flocks of starlings and hop-poles piled in pyramids like soldiers' tents. Often when I came home for five o'clock tea I felt a vague desire to be living somewhere else—in 1850, for instance, when everything must have been so comfortable and old-fashioned, like the Cathedral Close in Trollope's novels. The weather was too bad for golf, and even "young" Squire Maundle was obliged to admit that the Amblehurst course was in far from first-rate condition. And there never seemed to be any reason for going to London, although, of course, there were interesting things to see there. (Aunt Evelyn was always intending to run up for the day and go to a matinee of Beerbohm Tree's new Shakespearean production.)

I seldom spoke to anyone while I was out for my walks, but now and again I would meet John Homeward, the carrier, on his way back from the county town where he went three days a week. Homeward was a friendly man: I always "passed the time of day" with him. He was a keen cricketer and one of Dixon's chief cronies. The weather and next year's cricket were the staple topics of our conversation. Homeward had been making his foot-pace journeys with his hooded van and nodding horse ever since I could remember, and he seemed an essential feature of the ten miles across the Weald to Ashbridge (a somnolent town which I associated with the smell of a brewery and the grim fact of people being hung in the gaol there). All the year round, whether there was snow on the ground or blossom on the fruit trees, the carrier's van crawled across the valley with its cargo of utilities, but Homeward was always alone with his horse, for he never took passengers. In my mind's eye he is invariably walking beside his van, for he always got out at the steep hill which winds down to the Weald. His burly figure and kindly bearded face must have gone up and down that hill about five thousand times before he retired to prosper with a small public-house. I used to wonder what he thought about while on the road, for he had the look of a man who was cogitant rather than vegetative. Dixon told me that he spent his whole time weighing the pros and cons of the half-crown bets which he made on races. In matters connected with the Turf he was a compendium of exact knowledge, and his profession allowed him ample leisure to make up his mind about likely outsiders and nicely handicapped horses at short odds.

Another feature of the local landscape was Joey, who worked on the roads, mostly at flint-breaking. I never knew his real name, though I'd known him by sight ever since I could remember. He was a lizard-faced man and the skin of his throat hung loose and shrivelled. I had named him Joey— in my mind—after a tortoise which I had owned when I was a child. Sitting on a heap of stones on the main road, alone with the humming telegraph poles and the clack of his hammer, he always saluted me as I passed, but I never conversed with him and he never seemed to get any older. He might have been any age between forty and seventy. . . .

But I must hurry along a bit, for it is high time that I was on the back of my new hunter.

*   *   *

On New Year's Day I was half-pedestrian and half-bicyclist, with no idea of being anything else. Within a week I found myself a full-blown horse-owner, and was watching Dixon exerting himself with a hammer and chisel as he opened the neat wooden case which contained a new saddle from that old-established West End firm, Campion & Webble. The responsibility for these stimulating occurrences rested with Dixon.

One morning after breakfast Miriam announced that Dixon had something he particularly wished to speak to me about and was waiting in the servants' hall. Wondering what on earth it would be, I asked her to send him up to the book-room. I was there before him; a minute or two later the sound of his deliberate tread was audible in the passage; he knocked portentously and entered respectfully, introducing a faint odour of the stables. He had an air of discreetly subdued excitement and there was a slight flush about the cheekbones of his keen face. Without delay he produced a copy of *Horse and Hound* from his pocket, unfolded it carefully, and handed it to me, merely saying, "I want you to have a look at *that*, sir." *That*, as indicated by his thumb, was the following item in Tattersall's weekly sale list.

"The Property of Cosmo Gaffikin, Esq., Harkaway III. Chestnut gelding; aged; sixteen hands; a good hunter; an exceptionally brilliant performer; well known with the Dumborough Hounds, with whom he has been regularly hunted to date. Can be seen and ridden by appointment with Stud Groom, Mistley House, Wellbrook."

I read the advertisement in a stupefied way, but Dixon allowed me no time for hesitation or demur.

"It struck me, sir, that you might do worse than go over and have a look at him," he remarked, adding, "I saw him run in the Hunt Cup two years ago; he's a very fine stamp of hunter."

"Did he win?" I asked.

"No, sir. But he ran well, and I think Mr. Gaffikin made too much use of him in the first mile or two." For lack of anything to say I re-read the advertisement.

"Well, sir, if you'll excuse me saying so, you don't get a chance like that every day."

An hour later Dixon had got me into the dogcart and was driving me over to Wellbrook—a distance of ten miles. It was a mild, grey morning, and as I felt that I had lost control over what was happening, there was no need to feel nervous about the impending interview. In response to my tentative inquiries Dixon displayed a surprisingly intimate knowledge of everything connected with Harkaway and his present owner, and when I suggested that the price expected would be too high for me he went so far as to say that he had very good reason to believe that he could be bought for fifty pounds.

When we arrived at Mistley House it soon became clear even to my unsuspicious mind that the stud groom had been expecting us. When Harkaway was led out of his stable my first impression was of a noticeably narrow animal with a white blaze on his well-bred and intelligent face. But I felt more impelled to admire than to criticize, and a few minutes later Mr. Gaffikin himself came clattering into the stable-yard on a jaunty black mare with a plaited mane. The stud groom explained me as "Mr. Sherston, sir; come over from Butley to have a look at Harkaway, sir." Mr. Gaffikin was about thirty-five and had a rather puffy face and full-sized brown moustache. He was good-humoured and voluble and slangy and easy going, and very much the sportsman. He had nothing but praise for Harkaway, and seemed to feel the keenest regret at parting with him.

"But the fact is," he explained confidentially, "the old horse isn't quite up to my weight and I want to make room for a young 'chaser. But you're a stone lighter than I am, and he'd carry you like a bird—like a bird, wouldn't you, old chap?"—and he pulled Harkaway's neat little ears affectionately. "Yes," he went on, "I don't mind telling you he's the boldest performer I've ever been on. Nailing good hunter. I've never known him to turn his head. Absolute patent-safety; I can guarantee you that much, Mr. Sherston."

Whereupon he urged me to jump on the old horse's back and see how I liked the feel of him. (He used the adjective "old" as if in the case of Harkaway age was an immensely valuable quality.) Conscious of the disparity between my untidy grey flannel trousers and Mr. Gaffikin's miraculously condensed white gaiters and perfectly cut brown breeches, I clambered uncouthly into the saddle. As I jogged out of the yard I felt myself unworthy of my illustrious conveyance. Conscious of the scrutiny of the experts whose eyes were upon me, I also felt that Mr. Gaffikin was conferring a privilege on me in affording me this facility for making up my mind about "the old horse". When I had been down to the gate and back again everyone agreed that Harkaway and myself were admirably suited to one another.

"I'm asking fifty for him—and he'd probably make a bit more than that at Tatts. But I'm awful keen to find the old chap a really good home, and I'd be glad to let you have him for forty-five," Mr. Gaffikin assured me, adding, "Forty-five *guineas*: it's very little for a horse of his class, and he's got many a hard season in him yet." I agreed that the price was extremely moderate. "Well, you must come in and have a bit of lunch, and then we can talk it over." But it was obvious that the transaction was as good as concluded, and Dixon had already made up his mind to put a bit more flesh on the old horse before he was much older.

That evening I composed a mildly defiant letter to Mr. Pennett, explaining that I had found it necessary to buy a horse, and asking him to provide me with an extra fifty pounds.

*　　　*　　　*

The arrival of Harkaway was a red-letter day for our uneventful household. Dixon and I had agreed to say nothing about it to Aunt Evelyn, so there was a genuine surprise when we were finishing our lunch two days later and Miriam almost fell through the dining-room door with a startled expression on her face and exclaimed, "Oh, sir, your horse has come, and he don't half look a beauty!"

"Good gracious, George, you don't mean to tell me you've bought a horse?" said Aunt Evelyn, fluttering up out of her chair and hastening to the window.

Sure enough, there was Harkaway with Dixon on his back, and we all three went outside to admire him. Aunt Evelyn accepted his advent with unqualified approval, and remarked that he had "such a benevolent eye". Dixon, of course, was beaming with satisfaction. Miriam hovered on the doorstep in a state of agitated enthusiasm. And altogether it seemed as if I had accomplished something creditable. Self-satisfied and proprietary, I stroked the old horse's neck, and felt as though in him, at least, I had an ally against the arrogance of the world which so often oppressed me with a sense of my inferiority. But the red-letter day was also a lawyer's letter day. My complacency was modified by Mr. Pennett's reply, which arrived in the evening. When I had carried it upstairs and digested it I had an uncomfortable feeling that the schoolroom was still the schoolroom in spite of its new and more impressive name. In fairness to the writer I must again quote his letter *in toto*, as he would have phrased it.

"Dear George, I confess I am disappointed with your letter. £450 a year is a big sum and should be more than ample for *all* your requirements. I do not propose to comment on the fact that you have found it necessary to buy a horse, although I am not surprised that you find that time hangs heavy on your hands. When I last saw you I told you that in my view the best thing you could do would be to qualify to be called to the Bar, that you should go into a barrister's chambers and work there steadily until you were called. The training is excellent, it gives you an insight into business matters, and enables you to acquire the power of steady concentration. I have also intimated to you as strongly as I could that you are wasting your time and energies in pursuing a course of desultory reading. I consider it a shame that a young fellow with your health and strength and more than average amount of brains should be content to potter around and not take up some serious calling and occupation. I venture to prophesy that this will one day be brought home to you and perhaps too late. My view is, 'Don't ride the high horse.' He won't carry you across country and the chances are you will come a cropper at your fences. Yours sincerely, Percival G. Pennett, P.S.—£50 is a large sum to spend for the object you propose. I am therefore paying into your account £35, which sum will be deducted from the next instalment of your income."

Dismissing the idea of working steadily in a barrister's chambers, which was too unpalatable to be dwelt on, however briefly, I wondered whether the truth of Mr. Pennett's prophecy would ever be "brought home to me". It was a nuisance about the money, though; but Harkaway had been brought home to me, anyhow. So I consolidated my position by writing out a cheque to Cosmo Gaffikin, Esq., there and then. After that I erected an additional barrier against the lawyer's attack on my liberties by settling down to a steady perusal of *Mr. Sponge's Sporting Tour*, which I had brought up from the drawing-room. And while I relished Mr. Sponge's desultory adventures I made up my mind to go out with the Dumborough Hounds as soon as I felt myself qualified to appear in public on my exceptionally brilliant performer.

*   *   *

If Mr. Pennett could have prevented me from purchasing Harkaway (or any other quadruped) he would have done so. It was his mundane duty as my ex-guardian and acting trustee. Nor can it be denied that Dixon's loyalty to his profession required him to involve me as inextricably as possible in all that concerned the equine race. Dixon had emerged victorious. A raw youth who refuses to read for the Bar is persuaded by the family groom to buy a horse. How tame it sounds! But there was a lot more in it than that—a statement which can be applied to many outwardly trivial events in life when one takes the trouble to investigate them. And while I am still at the outset of my career as a fox-hunting man, I may as well explain Dixon's method of collaborating with me in my progress toward proficiency. When I made my fresh start and began to ride the gallant old chestnut about the wintry lanes I was inwardly awake to the fact that I knew next to nothing about horses and hunting and was an indifferent rider. And Dixon knew it as well as I did. But his policy was to watch me learn to find my way about the fox-hunting world, supplementing my ignorance from his own experience in an unobtrusive manner. He invariably allowed me to pretend that I knew much more than I really did. It was a delicately adjusted, mutual understanding. I seldom asked him a straight question or admitted any ignorance, and he taught me by referring to things as though I already knew them. I can remember no instance when he failed in this tactful behaviour and his silences were beyond praise.

Meanwhile I am still reading *Mr. Sponge* in the schoolroom. But it must not be supposed that I launched myself in the hunting-field with unpremeditative temerity. Far from it. It was all very well to be reading about how Mr. Sponge bought a new pair of top-boots in Oxford Street sixty years ago. But the notion of my inexpert self acquiring such unfamiliar accoutrements seemed problematic and audacious. My trepidation blinded me to the obvious fact that bootmakers were willing, and even eager, to do their best for me. Nevertheless, I enjoyed dressing up as a sportsman, and the box-cloth gaiters which I had bought in Ashbridge were a source of considerable satisfaction when they encased my calves, and Miriam's long-suffering face looked in at the book-room door with "Your horse, sir"—for Dixon liked to bring the horse round to the front door when I was going out for a ride.

I always went out alone, for the driving horse was a nonentity and seldom appeared without the dogcart. Also, as I have already explained, I was making my equestrian experiment without active interference or supervision. When I got home again Dixon would ask, "Did he go all right?" and I would hang about the loose-box while Harkaway was being rubbed down. I always had a few things to tell Dixon about my two hours' exercise—how I'd been through the Hookham woods and had given him a nice gallop, and how I'd jumped the hedge by Dunk's Windmill on the way home (it was a very small hedge, and I lost a stirrup and very nearly fell off, but there was no need to mention that). And then we would agree that the old horse was looking grand and improving every day. It was also agreed that Mr. Gaffikin must have given him a pretty thick time out hunting and that a spell of easy work would do him all the good in the world.

Until the middle of February his reappearance with the hounds was not referred to. But one afternoon (when I had modestly admitted that we had jumped a small stile when taking the short cut between Clay Hill and Marl Place) Dixon interrupted his hissing to look up at me, and said in his most non-committal tone, "I see they're meeting at Finchurst Green on Tuesday." The significance of this remark was unmistakable. The next day I bicycled to Ashbridge and bought a pair of ready-made "butcher-boots".

*   *   *

Of all the pairs of hunting boots which I have ever owned, the Ashbridge pair remain vividly in my mind as a long way the worst. Judged by the critical standard which I have since acquired, their appearance was despicable. This was equalled by the difficulty of struggling into them, and the discomfort they caused while I wore them. Any long-legged "thruster" will tell you that a smart pair of boots is bound to cause trouble for the first few days. It is the penalty of smartness. (And I have heard of a young man with a broken ankle who, though almost fainting with the pain of his boot being pulled off, was able to gasp out: "Don't cut it; they're the best pair Craxwell's ever made for me.") But the Ashbridge boots, when I started for Finchurst Green, hung spurless on each side of Harkaway, stiff, ill-shaped, and palpably provincial in origin. And for some reason known only to their anonymous maker, they persistently refused to "take a polish". Their complexion was lustreless and clammy, although Aunt Evelyn's odd man had given them all the energy of his elbow. But it wasn't until I had surreptitiously compared them with other boots that I realized their shortcomings (one of the worst of which was their lack of length in the leg). A boot can look just as silly as a human being.

However, I had other anxieties as I rode to the meet, for I

was no less shy and apprehensive than I had been on my way to the same place ten years earlier. At the meet I knew no one except Mr. Gaffikin, who came oscillating up to me, resplendent in his pink coat and wearing a low-crowned "coachy" hat cocked jauntily over his right ear. After greeting me with the utmost geniality and good-fellowship, he fell into a portentous silence; bunching up his moustache under his fleshy nose with an air of profound cogitation and knowingness, he cast his eye over Harkaway. When he had concluded this scrutiny he looked up and unforeseeably ejaculated, "Is that a Sowter?" This incomprehensible question left me mute. He leant forward and lifted the flap of my saddle which enabled me to blurt out, "I got it from Campion and Webble." (Sowter, as I afterwards discovered, is a saddle-maker long established and highly esteemed.) Mr. Gaffikin then gratified me greatly by his approval of Harkaway's appearance. In fact, he'd "never seen the old horse looking fitter". During the day I found that the old horse was acting as my passport into the Dumborough Hunt, and quite a number of people eyed him with pleased recognition, and reiterated his late owner's encomiums about his condition.

But as it was a poor day's sport and we were in the woods nearly all the time, my abilities were not severely tested, and I returned home satisfied with the first experiment. Harkaway was not a difficult horse to manage, but I did wish he would walk properly. He was a most jogglesome animal to ride on the roads, especially when his head was toward his stable.

*　　　*　　　*

Three nondescript days with the Dumborough were all the hunting I did on Harkaway during the remainder of that season. But the importance which I attached to the proceedings made me feel quite an accredited fox-hunter by the time Dixon had blistered Harkaway's legs and roughed him off in readiness for turning him out in the orchard for the summer. The back tendon of his near foreleg was causing a certain anxiety. February ended with some sharp frosts, sharp enough to make hunting impossible; and then there was a deluge of rain which caused the country to be almost unrideable. The floods were out along the Weald, and the pollard willows by the river were up to their waists in water.

On one of my expeditions, after a stormy night, at the end of March, the hounds drew all day without finding a fox. This was my first experience of a "blank day". But I wasn't as much upset about it as I ought to have been, for the sun was shining and the primrose bunches were brightening in the woods. Not many people spoke to me, so I was able to enjoy hacking from one covert to another and acquiring an appetite for my tea at the "Blue Anchor". And after that it was pleasant to be riding home in the latening twilight; to hear the "chink-chink" of blackbirds against the looming leafless woods and the afterglow of sunset; and to know that winter was at an end. Perhaps the old horse felt it, too, for he had settled into the rhythm of an easy striding walk instead of his customary joggle.

I can see the pair of us clearly enough; myself, with my brow-pinching bowler hat tilted on to the back of my head, staring, with the ignorant face of a callow young man, at the dusky landscape and its glimmering wet fields. And Harka-way with his three white socks caked with mud, his "goose-rump", and his little ears cocked well forward. I can hear the creak of the saddle and the clop and clink of hoofs as we cross the bridge over the brook by Dundell Farm; there is a light burning in the farmhouse window, and the evening star glitters above a broken drift of half-luminous cloud. "Only three miles more, old man," I say, slipping to the ground to walk alongside him for a while.

It is with a sigh that I remember simple moments such as

those, when I understood so little of the deepening sadness of life, and only the strangeness of the spring was knocking at my heart.

V

I was now eager to find out all I could about riding and hunting, and it was with this object in view that I made up my mind to go to the Ringwell Hunt Point-to-Point Races. I had already been to the Dumborough Hunt Steeplechases on Easter Monday and had seen Mr. Gaffikin ride a whirlwind finish on his black mare. He was beaten by half a length, and I lost ten shillings. Even to my inexperienced eyes it seemed as if he was far too busy with his arms and legs as he came up the straight. He appeared to be trying to go much faster than his mount, and the general effect differed from what I had seen described in sporting novels, where the hero never moved in his saddle until a few strides from the post, when he hit his thoroughbred once and shot home a winner.

What with the crowds jostling in front of the bellowing bookmakers, the riders in their coloured jackets thrashing their horses over the fences and the dress and demeanour of the sporting gentlefolk, there was a ferocity in the atmosphere of Dumborough Races which made me unable to imagine myself taking an active part in such proceedings, although it was obviously the thing to do, and to win such a race as the Hunt Cup would be a triumph to which I could not even aspire.

So I went home feeling more warned than edified, and it was a relief to be reading Tennyson in my room while the birds warbled outside in the clear April evening, and the voice of Aunt Evelyn called to one of her cats across the lawn. But I still wanted to go to the Ringwell Point-to-Points, for Dixon had said that it was "a real old-fashioned affair", and from the little I had seen and heard of the Ringwell country I had got an idea that it was a jolly, Surtees-like sort of Hunt, and preferable to the Dumborough.

The Ringwell Hunt was on the other side of the Dumborough; its territory was almost double as large, and it was a four-day-a-week country, whereas the Dumborough only went out on Tuesdays and Saturdays. The races were being held about three miles from Downfield, the county town, which was in the middle of the Ringwell country. So in order to get there I had to bicycle nearly seven miles and then make the twenty-five mile train journey from Dumbridge to Downfield. It was a journey which subsequently became tediously familiar, but it felt almost adventurous on the fine mid-April day which I am describing.

In deference to the horsey events which I was intent on witnessing, I was wearing my box-cloth gaiters, and as I bicycled out of the unhunted Butley district I felt that I was indeed on my way to a region where things really happened. In fact, I might have been off to Melton Mowbray, so intense were my expectations. As the train puffed slowly into Sussex I eyed the densely wooded Dumborough country disparagingly. At the point where, so far as I could judge, there should have been a noticeable improvement, the landscape failed to adapt itself to my anticipations. The train had entered Ringwell territory, but there was still a great deal of woodland and little open country.

As we got nearer Downfield the country became more attractive-looking, and I estimated every fence we passed as if it had been put there for no other purpose than to be jumped by Harkaway. I had yet to become aware of the farmer's point of view. A large crowd of people riding over someone else's land and making holes in the hedges is likely to create all sorts of trouble for the Master of Hounds, but I had not thought of it in that way. The country was there to be ridden over. That was all. I knew that I ought to shut the gates behind me (and some of them were an awful nuisance to open, when Harkaway was excited), but it had not occurred to me that a hole in a fence through which fifty horses have blundered is much the same as an open gate, so far as the exodus of a farmer's cattle is concerned. However, this problem of trespassing by courtesy has existed as long as fox-hunting, and it is not likely to be solved until both the red-coated fraternity and the red-furred carnivorous mammal which they pursue have disappeared from England's green and pleasant land. But I was occupied with my speculations about the point-to-point course, and at Harcombe Mill, the last little station before Downfield, I got out of the train, lonely but light-hearted.

The direction of the course was indicated by a few gigs and other vehicles on the road, and by a thin stream of pedestrians who were crossing some upland fields by a footpath. When I came to the crest of the hill I caught sight of some tents on a tree-clustered knoll about a mile away, and the course evidently made a big ring round this central point. A red flag stuck on the top of an oak tree was the only indication of a racecourse, though here and there a hairy-looking hedge had been trimmed for a space of a few yards.

An elderly labourer was sitting in a ditch eating his bread and cheese and I asked him which way they went.

"Ay, it's a tricky old course, and no mistake," he remarked, "and the ground be terrible heavy down along the brook, as some of 'em'll find afore they're much older."

Following his directions I made my way from one obstacle to another, inspecting each one carefully. Most of them looked alarming, and though the brook was not quite so wide as I had expected, it had boggy banks. As there was still plenty of time before the first race I was able to go about half-way round the course before I joined the throng of people and carriages on the hillside.

The course, though I was not aware of it at the time, was one of the old-fashioned "sporting" type, and these races had a strong similarity to the original point-to-point which was run over a "natural" line of country, where the riders were told to make their way to some conspicuous point and back again as best they could. The Harcombe course was "natural" in so far as there were no flags stuck in the fences, a fair proportion of which had been left in that state which the farmer had allowed them to assume. This type of course has now been almost universally superseded by a much tamer arrangement where the riders usually go twice round a few fields, jumping about a dozen carefully made-up fences which can be galloped over like hurdles.

On the cramped Harcombe course there were nearly fifty obstacles to be surmounted, and most of them were more suited to a clever hunter than to an impetuous and "sketchy" jumper. Consequently these races were slower and more eventful than the scurrying performances which in most provincial hunts are still called point-to-point races. A course of the Harcombe type, though almost too interesting for many of the riders, had grave disadvantages for the spectators, who saw little except the start and the finish. But the meeting had a distinctive character of its own—the genuinely countrified flavour of a gathering of local people.

When I arrived at the centre of operations the farmers and puppy-walkers were emerging from the marquee where they had been entertained by the Hunt, and their flushed, convivial faces contributed to the appropriate atmosphere of the day. They had drunk the Master's health and were on the best of terms with the world in general. Had I been inside the tent as representative of the *Southern Daily News*, I should probably have reported the conclusion of his speech in something very like the following paragraph:

"He was glad to say that they had had a highly successful

season. A plentiful supply of foxes had been forthcoming and they had accounted for fifty-eight and a half brace. They had also killed three badgers. He would like to repeat what he had said at the commencement of his speech, namely, that it must never be forgotten that the best friend of the fox-hunter was the farmer. (Loud applause.) And he took the liberty of saying that no hunt was more fortunate in its farmers than the Ringwell Hunt. Their staunch support of the hunt was something for which he had found it impossible to express his appreciation in adequate terms. An almost equal debt of gratitude was due to the Puppy Walkers, without whose invaluable aid the huntsman's task would be impossible. Finally he asked them to do everything in their power to eliminate the most dangerous enemy of the hunting-man—he meant barbed wire. But he must not detain them any longer from what promised to be a most interesting afternoon's sport; and amidst general satisfaction he resumed his seat."

*   *   *

I bought a race-card and went in the direction of "the paddock", which was a hurdled enclosure outside some farm buildings. Several people nodded to me in a friendly manner, which made me feel more confident, although it puzzled me, for I couldn't remember that I had seen any of them before. The first race was almost due to start, and the bookmakers were creating a background of excitement with their crescendo shoutings of "Even money the Field" and "Two to one bar one".

"I'll lay five to one Monkey Tricks; five to one Monkey Tricks," announced a villainous-looking man under a vast red umbrella—his hoarse and strident voice taking advantage of a momentary lull in the lung-bursting efforts of the ornaments of his profession on either side of him. "Don't forget the Old Firm!" he added.

Looking down from above the heads and shoulders of their

indecisive clients, the Old Firms appeared to be urging the public to witness some spectacle which was hidden by the boards on which their names were gaudily displayed. The public, however, seemed vaguely mistrustful and the amount of business being done was not equivalent to the hullaballoo which was inciting them to bet their money.

There was a press of people outside the paddock; a bell jangled, and already the upper halves of two or three red- or black-coated riders could be seen settling themselves in their saddles; soon there was a cleavage in the crowd and the eight or ten competitors filed out; their faces, as they swayed past me, varied in expression, from lofty and elaborate unconcern to acute and unconcealed anxiety. But even the least impressive among the cavalcade had an Olympian significance for my gaze, and my heart beat faster in concurrence with their mettlesome emergency, as they disappeared through a gate in the wake of the starter, a burly, jovial-faced man on a stumpy grey cob.

"Having a ride to-day, sir?" asked a cadaverous blue-chinned individual, who might have been either a groom or a horse-dealer. Rather taken aback by this complimentary inquiry, I replied with a modest negation.

"I see your brother's riding Colonel Hesmon's old 'oss in the 'Eavy Weights. He might run well in this deep going," he continued.

I did not disclaim the enigmatic relationship, and he lowered his voice secretively. "I'm putting a bit on Captain Reynard's roan for this race! I've heard that he's very hot stuff." And with a cunning and confidential nod he elbowed his way toward the line of bookmakers, who were now doing a last brisk little turn of business before the destination of the Light Weight Cup was decided over "Three and a half miles of fair hunting country".

The card informed me that Lieut-Col. C. M. F. Hesmon's

Jerry was to be ridden by Mr. S. Colwood. "It can't be Stephen Colwood, can it?" I thought, visualizing a quiet, slender boy with very large hands and feet, who had come to my House at Ballboro' about two years after I went there. Now I came to think of it his father had been a parson somewhere in Sussex, but this did not seem to make it any likelier that he should be riding in a race.

At any rate, I wanted to see this Colwood, for whose brother I had been mistaken, and after the next race I walked boldly into the paddock to see the horses being saddled for the Heavy Weights. There were only five of them, and none of the five looked like going very fast, though all were obviously capable of carrying fourteen stone on their backs. But since one of them had got to come in first, their appearance was creating an amount of interest quite disproportionate to their credentials as racehorses, and their grooms and owners were fussing around them as if they were running in the Grand National.

"I've told the boy that if he wins I'll *give him the horse,*" exclaimed an active little old gentleman with a straggling grey moustache and a fawn-coloured covert coat with large pearl buttons: his hands were full of flat lead weights, which he kept doling out to an elderly groom, who was inserting them in the leather pouches of a cloth which was to go under the saddle.

"Yes, the old fellow's looking well, isn't he?" he went on, dropping another lump of lead into the groom's outstretched hand. "I don't think I've ever seen him look fitter than he does to-day." He gazed affectionately at the horse, a dark bay with unclipped legs and a short, untidily trimmed tail.

People kept on coming up and greeting the affable and excited owner with cordial civility and he made the same remarks to each of them in turn. "Yes, I've told the boy that if he wins I'll *give him the horse*—are you quite sure those girths are all right, Dumbrell?" (to the groom, who was continuing his preparations with stoical deliberation) "and 'pon my word I'm not at all sure he won't win—the old fellow's fit to run for his life—never saw him look better—and I know the boy'll ride him nicely—most promising boy—capital eye for a country already—one of the keenest young chaps I've ever known."

"Well, Colonel, and how's the old horse?" ejaculated an exuberant person in a staring check suit and a protuberant canary-coloured waistcoat, extending an immense red hand toward the little man—who dropped the lead weights in a fluster with "Ah, my dear chap, how are you—how are you —delighted to see you"—followed by a reiteration of his repertoire about "the boy" and "the old horse".

The fact that this was Lieut-Col. C. M. F. Hesmon was conveyed to me by the arrival of my former schoolfellow, Stephen Colwood. "Ah, there you are, my boy—that's capital," said the Colonel, moderating his agitation in order to adopt the important demeanour of an owner giving his final admonitions to a gallant young gentleman rider.

Stephen, who was wearing a pink silk cap and a long-skirted black hunting-coat, silently received from the groom the saddle and weight-cloth and disappeared into the weighing tent, accompanied by the Colonel, who was carrying a cargo of surplus lead. When they reappeared Stephen looked even more pale and serious than before. At the best of times he had a somewhat meditative countenance, but his face usually had a touch of whimsicality about it, and this had been banished by the tremendous events in which he was at present involved.

The combined efforts of Colonel and groom were now solemnly adjusting the saddle and weight-cloth (though it is possible that the assistance of the Colonel might have been dispensed with). Meanwhile the old hunter was standing as quiet as a carriage horse.

Stephen was holding the bridle, and in the picture which my memory retains of him at that moment he is looking downward at the horse's lowered head with that sensitive and gentle expression which was characteristic of him. It was nearly three years since I had last set eyes on him, but I had known him fairly well at school. As I watched him now I felt almost as nervous as if I were about to ride the Colonel's horse myself. I assumed that it was the first race he had ever ridden in, and knew that he was feeling that if anything went wrong it would be entirely his own fault and that he would never be able to look the Colonel in the face again if he were to make a fool of himself. And he had probably been suffering from such apprehensions for several days beforehand. It was not surprising that he patted Jerry's philosophic profile with a visibly shaking hand. Then he looked up, and encountering my sympathetic gaze his face lit up with recognition. It was a time when he badly needed some such distraction, and he at once made me feel that I was an opportune intruder.

"Why, it's old Sherston!" he exclaimed. "Fancy you turning up like this!" And he gave me a wry grin which privately conveyed his qualms.

He told me afterwards that there were two things which he wished at that moment: either that the race was all over, or that something would happen to prevent it taking place at all. It is sometimes forgotten that without such feelings heroism could not exist.

He then made me known to the Colonel, who greeted me with a mixture of formality and heartiness and insisted that I must come round to his brake and have a glass of port and a sandwich after the race.

It seemed as though my diffident arrival on the scene had somehow relieved their anxieties, but a moment later the stentorian voice of the starter was heard saying, "Now, gentlemen, I'm going down to the post," and I stood back while Stephen was given a leg up by the groom. Then he bent his head to hear the Colonel's final injunctions about "not making too much of the running" and "letting him go at his own pace at the fences", ending with a heartfelt valediction. Stephen was then turned adrift with all his troubles in front of him. No one could help him any more.

Colonel Hesmon looked almost forlorn when the horse and his long-legged rider had vanished through the crowd. He had the appearance of a man who has been left behind. And as I see it now, in the light of my knowledge of after-events, there was a premonition in his momentarily forsaken air. Elderly people used to look like that during the War, when they had said good-bye to someone and the train had left them alone on the station platform. But the Colonel at once regained his spryness: he turned to me to say what a pity it was that the course was such a bad one for the spectators. Then he got out his field-glasses and lost consciousness of everything but the race.

✳   ✳   ✳

The horses appeared to be galloping very slowly when they came in sight for the last time. I was standing up on the hill and couldn't see them distinctly. They had undoubtedly taken a long time to get round the course. Three of them jumped the last fence in a bunch, and Jerry was one of the three. For years afterwards that last fence was a recurrent subject of conversation in the Colwood family, but there was always a good deal of uncertainty about what actually happened. Stephen admitted that it was "a bit of a mix-up". Anyhow, one of them fell, another one pecked badly, and Jerry disengaged himself from the group to scuttle up the short strip of meadow to win by a length.

The Colonel, of course, was the proudest man in Sussex, and I myself could scarcely believe that Stephen had really won. The only regrettable element was provided by the dismal face of the man who was second. This was a Mr. Green, a lean and lanky gentleman farmer in a swallow-tailed scarlet coat—not a cheerful-looking man at the best of times. He made no secret of the fact that, in his opinion, Stephen had crossed him at the last fence, but as he never got beyond looking aggrieved about it no one really minded whether Mr. Green had been interfered with or not, and Jerry's victory appeared to be an extremely popular one. The Colonel was bombarded with cordialities from all and sundry, and kept on exclaiming, "I said I'd give the boy the horse if he won and I'm dashed glad to do it!"

Stephen, who now emerged after weighing in, wore an expression of dreamy enthusiasm and restricted himself to a repetition of one remark, which was, "By Gosh, the old horse jumped like a stag"; now and again he supplemented this with an assertion that he'd never had such a ride in his life. He gazed at the old horse as if he never wanted to look at anything else again, but the Colonel very soon piloted him away to the port and sandwiches. As they were going Stephen pulled me by the arm with, "Come on, you queer old cuss; you aren't looking half as bright as you ought to be." As a matter of fact I was thinking what a stagnant locality I lived in compared with this sporting Elysium where everything seemed a heyday of happiness and good fortune.

When we had regaled ourselves with the Colonel's provisions, Stephen led me off into the fields to watch the Farmers' Race, which was usually a very amusing show, he said. As we strolled along by ourselves I told him how I'd been mistaken for one of his brothers, and I asked what had happened to his family that day. He told me that both his brothers were abroad. Jack, the elder one, had gone to India with his regiment a month ago. The younger one was in the navy, and was with the Mediterranean Fleet.

"They're both of them as keen as mustard on the chase.

It'll be pretty mouldy at the Rectory without them when hunting starts again," he remarked.

I asked why his father wasn't there to see him ride. His face clouded. "The Guv'nor'll be as sick as muck at missing it. Poor old devil, he had to take a ruddy funeral. Fancy choosing the day of the point-to-points to be buried on!". . .

*   *   *

It was after eight o'clock when I got home and Aunt Evelyn was beginning to wonder what had happened to me. I had enjoyed my day far more than I could possibly have anticipated, but my gentle and single-minded relative came in for nothing but my moody and reticent afterthoughts and I was rather ungracious to poor Miriam when she urged me to have a second helping of asparagus. Her face expressed mild consternation.

"What, no more asparagus, sir? Why it's the first we've had this year!" she exclaimed.

But I scowled at the asparagus as if it had done me an injury. What was asparagus to me when my head was full of the Colonel and his Cup, and the exhilarating atmosphere of the Ringwell Hunt? Why on earth had Aunt Evelyn chosen such a rotten hole as Butley to live in? Anyhow, Stephen had asked me to go and stay at Hoadley Rectory for the Polesham Races next week, so there was that to look forward to. And Aunt Evelyn, who had relapsed into a tactful silence (after trying me with the latest news from her bee-hives) was probably fully aware that I was suffering from the effects of an over-successful outing.

PART FOUR:
A DAY WITH THE POTFORD

I

The summer was over and the green months were discarded like garments for which I had no further use. Twiddling a pink second-class return ticket to London in my yellow-gloved fingers (old Miriam certainly had washed them jolly well) I stared through the carriage window at the early October landscape and ruminated on the opening meet in November. My excursions to London were infrequent, but I had an important reason for this one. I was going to try on my new hunting clothes and my new hunting boots. I had also got a seat for Kreisler's concert in the afternoon, but classical violin music was at present crowded out of my mind by the more urgent business of the day.

I felt as though I had an awful lot to do before lunch. Which had I better go to first, I wondered (jerking the window up as the train screeched into a tunnel), Craxwell or Kipward? To tell the truth I was a bit nervous about both of them; for when I had made my inaugural visits the individuals who patrolled the interiors of those eminent establishments had received me with such lofty condescension that I had begun by feeling an intruder. My clothes, I feared, had not quite the cut and style that was expected of them by firms which had the names of reigning sovereigns on their books, and I was abashed by my ignorance of the specialized articles which I was ordering. Equilibrium of behaviour had perhaps been more difficult at the bootmaker's; so I decided to go to Kipward's first.

Emerging from Charing Cross I felt my personality somehow diluted. At Baldock Wood Station there had been no doubt that I was going up to town in my best dark blue suit, and London had been respectfully arranged at the other end of the line. But in Trafalgar Square my gentlemanly uniqueness had diminished to something almost nonentitive.

Had I been able to analyse my psychological condition I could have traced this sensation to the fact that my only obvious connections with the metropolis were as follows: Mr. Pennett in Lincoln's Inn Fields (he was beginning to give me up as a bad job) and the few shops where I owed money for books and clothes. No one else in London was aware of my existence. I felt half-inclined to go into the National Gallery, but there wasn't enough time for that. I had been to the British Museum once and the mere thought of it now made me feel bored and exhausted. Yet I vaguely knew that I ought to go to such places, in the same way that I knew I ought to read *Paradise Lost* and *The Pilgrim's Progress*. But there never seemed to be time for such edifications, and the Kreisler concert was quite enough for one day.

So I asserted my independence by taking a hansom to the tailor's, which was some distance along Oxford Street. I wasn't very keen on taxicabs, though the streets were full of them now.

The lower half of Kipward & Son's shop window was fitted with a fine wire screening, on which the crows and vultures of several still undethroned European Majesties were painted. In spite of this hauteur the exterior now seemed quite companionable, and I felt less of a nobody as I entered. A person who might well have been Mr. Kipward himself advanced to receive me; in his eyes there was the bland half-disdainful interrogation of a ducal butler; for the moment he still seemed uncertain as to my credentials. On the walls were some ant-lered heads and the whole place seemed to know much more about sport than I did. His suavely enunciated "what name?" made the butler resemblance more apparent, but with his, "Ah, yes, Mr. Sherston of course; your coat and breeches are quite ready for you to try, sir", and the way he wafted me up a spacious flight of stairs, he became an old-fashioned inn-keeper who had been in first-rate service, and there seemed nothing in the world with which he was not prepared to accommodate me. To have asked the price of so much as a waistcoat would have been an indecency. But I couldn't help wondering, as I was being ushered into one of the fitting compartments, just how many guineas my black hunting-coat was going to cost.

A few minutes later I was sitting on a hard, shiny saddle and being ciphered all over with a lump of chalk. The sallow little man who fitted my breeches remarked that the buff Bedford cord which I had selected was "a very popular one". As he put the finishing touch with his chalk he asked me to stand up in the stirrups. Whereupon he gazed upon his handi-work and found it good. "Yes, that's a beautiful seat," he remarked serenely. I wondered whether he would say the same if he could see me landing over a post-and-rails on Hark-away. The artist responsible for my coat was a taciturn and deferential Scotchman, stout, bald, and blond. He, too, seemed satisfied that the garment would do him credit. My sole regret was that I hadn't yet been asked to wear the Hunt button. Downstairs in the dignified and reposeful reception room the presiding presence was warming himself in front of a bright fire. As he conducted me to the door I observed with secret awe some racing colours in a glass case on the wall. In after years I recognized them as being Lord Rosebery's.

Craxwell & Co. was a less leisurely interior. As might have been expected, there was an all-pervading odour of leather, and one was made to feel that only by a miracle could they finish up to time the innumerable pairs of top-boots for which they had received orders. The shop bristled and shone with spurs; and whips and crops of all varieties were stacked and slung and suspended about the walls. Pace was indicated everywhere and no one but a hard-bitten thruster could have entered without humility. A prejudiced mind might have imagined that all Craxwell's customers belonged to some ultra-insolent, socially snobbish, and libertine breed of military Mohocks. But the percentage, I am sure, was quite a small one, and my boots, though awkward to get into at first, were close-fitting and high in the leg and altogether calculated to make me feel that there were very few fences I would not cram my horse at. In outward appearance, at least, I was now a very presentable fox-hunter.

Stephen Colwood had advised me to patronize those particular places, and it was no fault of his that I was still a comparative greenhorn. Anyhow, young Mr. Craxwell (who looked quite as much a gentleman as the self-satisfied sportsmen I saw in his shop) was kind enough to tell me that I had "a very good leg for a boot".

*   *   *

By the time I had put my bowler hat under my seat in the grand circle at Queen's Hall I was in a state of unsporting excitement about Kreisler. The name itself was suggestive of eminence, and I was aware that he was a great violinist, though I did not know that he would afterwards become the most famous one in the world. I was also unconscious that I was incapable of discriminating between a good violinist and a second-rate one. My capacity for admiration was automatic and unlimited, and his photograph on the programme

117

made me feel that he must be a splendid man. I was influenced, too, by the audience, which showed its intensity of expectation by a subdued hubbub of talk which suddenly ceased altogether and was swept away by the storm of clapping which greeted the appearance of Kreisler.

That he was an eminent violinist was obvious, even to me, before he had played a single note of the Handel Sonata with which the concert began. There was something in the quiet and confident little swing of his shoulders as he walked on to the platform; something about the way he bowed with his heels together; something about his erect and dignified attitude while the accompanist flattened the pages of the music on the piano; this "something" impressed me very much. Then with a compact and self-possessed nod he was ready, and his lofty gaze was again on the audience.

During the serenely opening bars of the accompaniment both the bow and the violin were hanging from his left hand, and the inevitable gesture with which he raised the instrument to his chin seemed to sustain the rhythm of my excitement which reached its climax as I heard the first calm and eloquent phrase. The evergreen loveliness of the sonata unfolded itself, and Kreisler was interpreting it with tenderness and majesty. For him the concert was only one in that procession of recitals which carried him along on his triumphant career. But I knew then, as I had never known before, that such music was more satisfying than the huntsman's horn. On my way home in the train my thoughts were equally divided between the Kreisler concert and my new hunting things. Probably my new boots got the best of it.

Sitting by the schoolroom fire after tea on the last Saturday in November, I cleaned my almost new pipe (for I had taken to smoking, though I hadn't enjoyed it much so far) with a white pigeon's feather from the lawn.

I had got home early after a rotten half-day with the Dumborough. I'd had four days with them since the opening meet, and it was no use pretending that I'd enjoyed myself. Apart from the pleasure of wearing my self-consciously new clothes I had returned home each day feeling dissatisfied. It wasn't so much that the Hunt seemed to spend most of its time pottering round impenetrable woodlands as that the other subscribers appeared to be unwilling to acknowledge my existence except by staring me into a state of acute awareness of my ignorance of what was being done and how to do it. There was also the problem of Harkaway, who demonstrated more clearly every time I took him out that his stamina was insufficient for a hard day's hunting. It was only his courage which kept him going at all; in spite of Dixon's efforts in the stable the old horse was already, as he ruefully remarked, looking "properly tucked-up", and the long distances to the meets were an additional hardship for him.

As I lit my pipe I felt that I ought to be blissfully reconstructing the day's sport. But there seemed to be no blissful details to reconstruct. The hounds had run fairly well for about half an hour, but very little of it had been in the open. And I had been so busy hanging on to my excitable horse that I had only a hazy recollection of what had happened, except that Bill Jaggett had damned my eyes for following him too closely over the only jumpable place in a fence. Bill Jaggett was, to my mind, one of the horrors of the Hunt. He was a hulking, coarse-featured, would-be thruster; newly rich, ill-conditioned, and foul-mouthed. "Keep that bloody horse well out of my way," was a specimen of his usual method of verbal intercourse in the hunting-field. What with the vulgarly horsey cut and colour of his clothes and the bumptious and bullying manners which matched them, he was no ornament to the Dumborough Hunt; to me he was a positive incubus, for he typified everything that had alarmed and repelled me in my brief experience of fox-hunting. Except for the violent impression he made on my mind I should have said nothing about him; but even now I cannot remember his behaviour without astonishment. He was without exception the clumsiest and most mutton-fisted horseman I have ever observed. No horse ever went well for him, and when he wasn't bellowing at his groom he was cursing and cropping the frothing five-year-old which was carrying his fifteen stone carcass. (He usually rode young horses, since he flattered himself that he was "making" them to sell at a profit; but as he was short-sighted he frequently fell on his head and gave me the satisfaction of watching him emerge from a ditch, mud-stained and imprecating.) He took no interest in anything except horses and hunting, and it was difficult to believe that he had ever learnt to read or write.

He was one of a small contingent who fancied themselves as hard riders. Owing to the character of the country they always had to be looking for something to jump, whether the hounds were running or not, and they were often in trouble with Lord Dumborough for "larking" over unnecessary fences. In this they were conspicuous, for the other followers of the Hunt were a pusillanimous lot of riders, and there was always a queue of them at the gaps, over which they bobbed and bounced like a flock of sheep. Musing on my disappointing experiences, I decided that next week I would go and have a day with the Potford Hounds who were no further off than the Dumborough. They were said to be short of foxes, but Dixon had heard that their new Master had been showing good sport.

*   *   *

Elaborate arrangements had to be made for my day with the Potford. The distance to the meet was nearly fourteen miles, and Dixon decided that the best plan was for him to ride Harkaway over the night before. This outing was very much to his taste, and it was easy to imagine him clattering importantly into the yard at the Bull Inn with Harkaway's rug rolled on the saddle in front of him, and doing everything that was humanly possible to make the old horse comfortable in the strange stable. It is equally certain that, over his glass of beer, in the evening, he would leave no doubt in the minds of the gossips in the bar-parlour that his young gentleman was a very dashing and high-class sportsman. All this he would do with the sobriety and reticence of an old family servant; before going to bed he would take a last look at Harkaway to see whether he had finished up his feed.

Driving myself to the meet in the soft, cloudy morning, I enjoyed feeling like Mr. Sponge on his way to look at a strange pack. The only difference was that Sponge was a bold and accomplished rider and I was still an experimental one. But my appearance, I hoped, would do Dixon no discredit, and on the seat beside me was my newest acquisition, a short leather hunting-crop with a very long lash to it. The length of the lash, though extremely correct, was an embarrassment. The crop had only arrived the previous day, and I had taken it out on to the lawn and attempted to crack it. But I was unable to create the echoing reports which hunt servants seemed to produce so effortlessly, and my feeble snappings ended with a painful flick on my own neck. So I resolved to watch very carefully and see exactly how they did it. Big swells like Bill Jaggett never lost an opportunity of cracking their whips when they caught sight of a stray hound. I couldn't imagine myself daring to do that or shout "Get along forrid" in such tremendous tones; but it would be nice to feel that I could make the welkin ring with my new crop if I wanted to. I had yet to learn that the quiet and unobtrusive rider is better liked by a huntsman and his assistants than the noisy and officious one.

I wondered whether I should know any of the people out with the Potford, and wished I had made a better job of tying my white stock that morning. Tying a stock was very difficult, especially as I didn't know how to do it. Mr. Gaffikin's was wonderful, and I wished I knew him well enough to ask him how the effect was produced.

I was keen to see what the new Master of the Potford was like. Dixon had heard quite a lot about him. His name was Guy Warder, and he was a middle-aged man who hunted the hounds himself and did everything as cheaply as possible. He bought the most awful old screws for next to nothing at Tattersalls, made his stablemen ride them all the way down from London to save the expense of a horse-box, and brought them out hunting next day. It seemed that the Hunt was already divided into factions for and against him, and it was doubtful whether he would be allowed to hunt the country another season. It was said that he was a bad rider and always held on to the pommel of his saddle when jumping his fences. It was also rumoured that he sometimes got very drunk. People complained that he was slow, and often drew the coverts on foot. But he was popular with the farmers, and had been killing an abnormal number of foxes.

There he was, anyhow, sitting low down in the saddle among his hounds on a patch of grass in front of the Bull Inn. He was a dumpy little man with a surly red face, and he wore a coat that had once been scarlet and was now plum-coloured.

He was on a good-looking horse, but the whips were mounted on under-bred and raw-boned animals which might well have been sent to the kennels for the hounds to eat. The hounds were dull-coated and hungry-looking. Evidently Mr. Guy Warder cared nothing for smartness.

Dixon saw me into the saddle with a quietly satisfied air and I rode out of the stable-yard. The first person I recognized was Bill Jaggett, who was hoisting himself on to the back of a slim, skittish, and startled-looking roan mare. He greeted me with a scowl and then remarked with a grunt, "You've brought your old skin over here, have you? Don't give him much rest, do you?" The sneer in his voice made me hate him more than ever, but I was too diffident and confused to reply.

With him was his boon companion, Roger Pomfret, a ginger-haired, good-for-nothing nephew of Lord Dumborough who blundered about the country on a piebald cob and vied with Jaggett in coarseness of language and general uncouthness. But Pomfret, who was impecunious and spent his spare time in dubious transactions connected with the Turf, had a touch of bumpkin geniality about him, and was an amiable and polished gentleman when closely compared with his unprepossessing associate, who, at that moment, was adjuring him (with the usual epithets) not to knock the guts out of that horse or he'd never lend him another (at the same time jogging his own mare unmercifully in the mouth and kicking her with one of his long spurs). "*Will* you stand still, you ——" but before the last word was out of his mouth the huntsman had shaken up his hounds with a defiant toot of the horn and was trotting down the road.

"The old rat-catcher doesn't allow much law, does he? It's only six minutes past eleven now!" remarked Pomfret, consulting his ticker with an oafish grin.

I dropped behind them, and was at once joined by Mr. Gaffikin, effusively cheerful, elbows well out, and a bunch of violets in his buttonhole. His friendliness revived my spirits, and he seemed to regard Jaggett and Pomfret as an excellent joke. "It's as good as a play when they start slanging one another," he said, eyeing their clumsy backs as they tip-tupped along.

He then told me, in an undertone, to keep pretty wide-awake to-day, as he'd heard that old Warder'd got something up his sleeve. He winked expressively. "I hear they've had one or two *very queer* foxes lately," he added. I wasn't sure what he meant, but I nodded sagaciously.

Nothing exciting happened, however, at the first covert. In accordance with his usual habit, the huntsman got off his horse and plunged into the undergrowth on foot.

"They say the old boy's got a better nose than any of his hounds," someone remarked.

In spite of my anxiety to avoid him, I found myself standing close behind Jaggett, who was bragging about a wonderful day he'd had "up at Melton" the week before. But I was feeling more at my ease now, and I was expressing this by swinging the lash of my crop lightly to and fro. The result was appalling. Somehow the end of it arrived at the rump of Jaggett's roan mare; with nervous adroitness she tucked in her tail with my lash under it. She then began kicking, and in my efforts to dislodge the lash I found myself "playing" Jaggett and his horse like a huge fish. The language which followed may be imagined, and I was flabbergasted with confusion at my clumsiness. When I had extricated my thong and the uproar had subsided to a series of muttered imprecations, I retreated.

To my surprise Mr. Gaffikin came up and congratulated me admiringly on the way I had "pulled Bill Jaggett's leg". He said it was the neatest thing he'd ever seen and he wouldn't have missed it for worlds. He slapped his leg in a paroxysm of amusement, and I modestly accepted the implication that I had done it on purpose. Guy Warder then emerged from his investigations of the undergrowth and blew his hounds out of covert.

"Where are you going now, Master?" shouted a sharp-faced man with a green collar on his cut-away coat.

"You'll find out when I get there," growled Warder, hunching his shoulders and trotting briskly down the lane.

Mr. Gaffikin explained that the green-collared man was a notoriously tardy and niggardly subscriber. Nevertheless, we were apparently making an unexpected excursion, and people were audibly wondering what the old beggar was up to now. Anyhow, I gathered that we were heading for the best bit of the vale country, though it had been expected that we would draw some big woods in the other direction. After a couple of miles he turned in at a gate and made for a small spinney. Word now came back from the first whip that "an old dog-fox had been viewed there this morning". Half-way across the field to the spinney the Master pulled up, faced round, and exclaimed gruffly, "I'd be obliged if you'd keep close together on this side of the covert, gentlemen." He then cantered off with his hounds and disappeared among the trees.

"Stick close to me," said Mr. Gaffikin in a low voice. "The old devil's got a drag laid, as sure as mutton."

He was right. A minute afterwards there was a shrill halloa; when we got round to the far side of the spinney there was the huntsman going hell for leather down the slope with his hounds running mute on one side of him. With my heart in my mouth I followed Mr. Gaffikin over one fence after another. Harkaway was a bold jumper and he took complete control of me. I can remember very little of what happened, but I was told afterwards that we went about four miles across the only good bit of vale in the Potford country. The gallop ended with the huntsman blowing his horn under a park wall while the hounds scrabbled and bayed rather dubiously over a rabbit-hole. There were only eight or ten riders up at the finish, and the credit of my being among them belonged to Harkaway. Jaggett, thank heaven, was nowhere to be seen.

Warder took off his cap and mopped his brow. Then he looked with grudging good humour at the remnant of his field and their heaving horses. "Now let the bastards say I don't go well enough!" he remarked, as he slipped his horn back in its case on his saddle.

III

My successful scramble across the Potford Vale obliterated all the dreariness and disappointment of my days with the Dumborough. My faith in fox-hunting had been reinforced in the nick of time, and I joggled home feeling a hero. Highly strung old Harkaway seemed to share my elation. His constitution was equal to a fast hunt, but he needed to be taken home early in the afternoon. The long dragging days in the Dumborough woodlands wore him out. Even now he had a dozen miles to go to his stable, but they seemed short ones to me for I was thinking all the way how pleased Dixon would be. For the first time in my career as an independent sportsman I had a big story to tell him.

In the light of my mature experience I should say that I had very little to tell Dixon, unless I had told him the truth. The truth (which I couldn't have admitted, even to my inmost self) was that my performance had consisted not so much in riding to hounds as in acting as a hindrance to Harkaway's freedom of movement while he followed Mr. Gaffikin's mare over several miles of closely-fenced country—almost pulling my arms out of their sockets in the process. Had I told the truth I'd have said that during that gallop I was flustered, uncomfortable, and out of breath; that at every fence we jumped I was all over the saddle; and that, for all I had known, there might have been no hounds at all, since they were always a couple of fields ahead of us, and we were, most of us, merely following the Master, who already knew exactly which way they would go.

I lay stress on these facts because it is my firm belief that the majority of fox-hunting riders never enjoy a really "quick thing" while it is in progress. Their enjoyment, therefore, mainly consists in talking about it afterwards and congratulating themselves on their rashness or their discretion, according to their temperaments. One man remembers how he followed the first whip over an awkward stile, while another thinks how cleverly he made use of a lucky lane or a line of gates. Neither of them was able to watch the hounds while they were running. And so it was with me. Had I been alone I should have lost the hounds within three fields of the covert where they started.

But my complacency had been unperturbed by any such self-scrutinies when I clattered into the stable-yard in the twilight, just as Dixon emerged from the barn with a sieve of oats and a stable-lantern. His quick eyes were all over the horse before I was out of the saddle.

"Going a bit short in front, isn't he?" was his first remark.

I agreed that he *was* going a bit queer. Dixon had seen in a moment what I had failed to notice in twelve miles. My feeling of importance diminished. I followed the two of them into the loose-box. Dixon's lantern at once discovered an over-reach on the heel of one of Harkaway's front feet. No reference was made to my having failed to notice it; and as we said, it was a clean cut, which was much better than a bruise. When asked whether it had been a good day, I replied "Topping", but Dixon seemed in no hurry to hear about it, and he went out to get the gruel. I stood silent while the old horse drank it eagerly—Dixon remarking with satisfaction that he'd "suck the bottom out of the bucket if he wasn't careful".

Unable to restrain myself any longer, I blurted out my news: "They ran slap across the vale for about twenty-five minutes; a five-mile point without a check. It must have been seven or eight miles as they ran!"

Dixon, who was already busy brushing the dried mud off Harkaway's legs, straightened himself with a whistle. "Did you see it all right?"

"The whole way; there were only ten up at the finish."

"Did they kill him?"

"No, he got into a rabbit-hole just outside Cranfield Park. The Master said it was no good trying to get him out as it was such a big place." Dixon looked puzzled.

"That's funny," he remarked. "They told me at the 'Bull' last night that he's a great one for terriers and digging out foxes. A lot of the subscribers complain about it. They say he's never happy unless he's got his head down a rabbit-hole!"

With a knowing air I told him that Mr. Gaffikin had said it was a drag.

"By Jingo! If it was a drag they must have gone like blazes!" I asserted that they *did* go like blazes.

"You must have jumped some big places."

There was a note of surprise in his voice which made me feel that I had been doing more than was expected of me. Could it be possible, I wondered, that Dixon was actually proud of his pupil? And, indeed, there must have been a note of jubilation in his voice when, as he bent down to brush the mud off Harkaway's hocks, he asked: "Did Mr. Gaffikin see him jumping?"

"Yes. I foll——I was close to him all the way."

Perhaps it was just as well that Harkaway, munching away at his feed, was unable to lift his long-suffering face and say what *he* thought about my horsemanship! Looking back at

128

that half-lit stable from the detachment of to-day, I can almost believe that, after I had gone indoors to my boiled eggs, Dixon and the old horse had a confidential chat, like the old friends that they were. Anyhow, the horse and his groom understood one another quite as well as the groom understood his master.

*   *   *

Aunt Evelyn did her best to come up to the scratch while I was talking big at the dinner-table. But the wonderful performances of Harkaway and myself during our exciting half-hour in the Potford Vale were beyond her powers of response, and her well-meant but inadequate interjections caused my narrative to lose a lot of its sporting significance. Anxiety for my safety overshadowed her enthusiasm, and when I was telling her how we jumped a brook (it was only a flooded ditch, really) she uttered an ill-timed warning against getting wet when I was hot, which nearly caused my narrative to dry up altogether.

Faithful Miriam made things no better by exclaiming, as she handed me a plate with two banana fritters on it, "You'll break your neck, sir, if you go out with them hounds much oftener!"

What was the good of trying to make them understand about a hunt like that, I thought, as I blundered up the dark stairs to the schoolroom to dash off a highly coloured account of my day for Stephen Colwood. He, at any rate, was an audience after my own heart, and the only one I had, except Dixon, whose appreciation of my exploits was less fanciful and high-flown. Writing to Stephen I was at once away in a world of make-believe; and the letter, no doubt, was a good example of what he used to call my "well-known sprightly insouciance".

Poor Stephen was living in lodgings in London, and could

only get home for a hunt on Saturdays. A wealthy neighbour had promised Parson Colwood an opening for his son if he could qualify as a chartered accountant, and this nauseating task occupied him five days a week. So my visualization of Stephen, exiled in a foggy street in Pimlico, made it doubly easy for me to scribble my lively account of a day which now seemed so delightfully adventurous.

Stephen's reply was a telegram asking me to stay at the Rectory for as long as I liked, and this was followed by a letter in which he announced that he'd got a month's holiday. "If your old nag's still lame I can get you some top-hole hirelings from Downfield for thirty-five bob a day, and I've ordered the Guv'nor to offer up prayers next Sunday forbidding the Almighty to send any frost to Sussex."

Aunt Evelyn considered this almost blasphemous; but she thought my visit to Hoadley Rectory an excellent idea, for Stephen was quite one of her favourites, and of the Rev. Colwood (whom she had met at a diocesan garden-party) she had the highest possible opinion. "Such a fine face! And Mrs. Colwood seemed a real fellow creature—quite one of one's own sort," she exclaimed, adding, "D'you mind holding his hind-legs, dear?" for she was preoccupied at the moment in combing the matted hair out of one of her Persian cats.

PART FIVE: AT THE RECTORY

^^

I

Stopping at every station, a local train conveyed me sedately into Sussex. Local and sedate, likewise, were the workings of my brain, as I sat in an empty compartment with the *Southern Daily News* on my knees. I had bought that unpretentious paper in order to read about the Ringwell Hounds, whose doings were regularly reported therein. And sure enough the previous day's sport was described in detail, and "Among the large field out" was the name, with many others, of "Mr. Colwood, junr." Although I had yet to become acquainted with the parishes through which Reynard had made his way, I read with serious attention how he had "crossed the Downfield and Boffham road, borne right-handed into Hooksworth Wood, turned sharply back, and worked his way over the country to Icklesfield", etc., etc., until "hounds ran into him after a woodland hunt of nearly three hours". The account ended with the following words: "If ever hounds deserved blood they did this time, as they had to work out nearly every yard of their fox's line."

Having read this through twice I allowed my thoughts to dally with the delightful prospect of my being a participator in similar proceedings next day. Occasionally I glanced affectionately at the bulging kit-bag containing those masterpieces by Craxwell and Kipward which had cost me more than one

131

anxious journey to London. Would Stephen approve of my boots, I wondered, staring out of the window at the reflective monochrome of flooded meadows and the brown gloom of woodlands in the lowering dusk of a heavily clouded December afternoon.

Whatever he might think of my boots, there was no doubt that he approved of my arrival when the fussy little train stopped for the last time and I found him waiting for me on the platform. I allowed him to lug my bag out of the station, and soon he had got it stowed away in the old yellow-wheeled buggy, had flicked his father's favourite hunter into a trot ("a nailing good jumper, but as slow as a hearse"), and was telling me all about the clinking hunt they'd had the day before, and how he'd enjoyed my account of the Potford gallop. "You've got a regular gift for writing, you funny old cock! You might make a mint of money if you wrote for *Horse and Hound* or *The Field*!" he exclaimed, and we agreed that I couldn't write worse than the man in the *Southern Daily*, whose "Reynard then worked his way across the country" etc. afterwards became one of our stock jokes.

In describing my friendship with Stephen I am faced by a difficulty which usually arises when one attempts to reproduce the conversational oddities of people who are on easy terms. We adopted and matured a specialized jargon drawn almost exclusively from the characters in the novels of Surtees; since we knew these almost by heart, they provided us with something like a dialect of our own, and in our care-free moments we exchanged remarks in the mid-Victorian language of such character-parts as Mr. Romford, Major Yammerton, and Sir Moses Mainchance, while Mr. Jorrocks was an all-pervading influence. In our Surtees obsession we went so far that we almost identified ourselves with certain characters on appropriate occasions. One favourite role which Stephen facetiously imposed on me was that of a young gentleman named Billy

Pringle who, in the novel which he adorns, is reputed to be very rich. My £600 a year was thus magnified to an imaginary £10,000, and he never wearied of referring to me as "the richest commoner in England". The stress was laid on my great wealth and we never troubled to remember that the Mr. Pringle of the novel was a dandified muff and "only half a gentleman". I cannot remember that I ever succeeded in finding a consistent role for Stephen, but I took the Surtees game for granted from the beginning, and our adaptation of the Ringwell Hunt to the world created by that observant novelist was simplified by the fact that a large proportion of the Ringwell subscribers might have stepped straight out of his pages. To their idiosyncrasies I shall return in due course: in the meantime I am still on my way to Hoadley Rectory, and Stephen is pointing out such fox-hunting features of the landscape as are observable from the high road while we sway companionably along in the old-fashioned vehicle.

* * *

"That's Basset Wood—one of our werry best Wednesday coverts," he remarked, indicating with the carriage-whip a dark belt of trees a couple of miles away under the level cloud-bars of a sallow sunset. He eyed the dimly undulating pastures which intervened, riding over them in his mind's eye as he had so often ridden over them in reality.

"We'll be there on Monday," he went on, his long, serious face lighting up as his gaze returned to the road before him. "Yes, we'll be drawing there on Monday," he chuckled, "and if we can but find a straight-necked old dog-fox, then I'll be the death of a fi'-pun'-note—dash my wig if I won't!"

I said that it looked quite a nice bit of country and asked whether they often ran this way. Stephen became less cheerful as he informed me that there was precious little reason for them to run this way.

"There's not a strand of wire till you get to the road," he exclaimed, "but over there"—(pointing to the left) "there's a double-distilled blighter who's wired up all his fences. And what's more, his keeper shoots every fox who shows his nose in the coverts. And will you believe me when I tell you, George my lad, that the man who owns those coverts is the same ugly-mugged old sweep who persuaded the Guv'nor to get me trained as a chartered accountant! And how much longer I'm going to stick it I don't know! Seven months I've been worriting my guts out in London, and all on the off-chance of getting a seat in the office of that sanctimonious old vulpicide."

I consoled him with a reminder that he'd spent most of August and September shooting and fishing in Scotland. (His father rented a place in Skye every summer.) And during the remainder of the drive we debated the deeply desirable and not impossible eventuality of Stephen's escape from chartered accountancy. His one idea was "to get into the Army by the back door". If only he could get into the Gunners he'd be happy. His elder brother Jack was in the Gunners, and was expecting to be moved from India to Ireland. And Ireland, apparently, was a fox-hunting Elysium.

"I really must have a chat with Colonel Hesmon about it. By the way, the dear old boy's asked us both to lunch to-morrow."

This led to a rhapsody about that absolutely top-hole performer Jerry, who had been given him by the Colonel after he'd won the Heavy Weight Race. My Harkaway on the other hand, was more a subject for solicitude, and I reluctantly confessed that he didn't seem up to my weight. It was a thousand pities, said Stephen, that I couldn't have bought that six-year-old of young Lewison's. "Given him for his twenty-first birthday by his uncle, who'd forked out £170 for him. But young Lewison couldn't ride a hair of the horse, though he was a nailing fine 'lepper' and a rare good sort at that. They sent him up to Tatts last week, and he went for £90, according to the paper. Gosh, what a bit of luck for the cove who got him so cheap!"

My appetite for horseflesh was stimulated by this anecdote, but I wondered what Mr. Pennett would say if I wrote and told him that I'd bought another ninety pounds' worth! For Mr. Pennett still refused to allow me more than £450 of my £600. The balance, he said, must be "invested for a rainy day".

*　　　*　　　*

Stephen's visionary contemplations of "being stationed at the Curragh and riding at Punchestown Races" were interrupted by our arrival at the Rectory. I had stayed there more than once in the summer, so I received a surly but not unfriendly salute from Abel, the grim little old groom with iron-grey whiskers who led our conveyance soberly away to the stable-yard. This groom was an old-fashioned coachman, and he had never been heard to utter a sentence of more than six words. His usual reply, when asked about the health of one of the horses, was either, "Well enough" or "Not over-bright". Stephen now reminded him (quite unnecessarily, and probably not for the first time) that two of the horses would be going out hunting on Monday. Abel grunted, "Got 'em both shod this afternoon," and disappeared round the corner of the shrubbery with the buggy.

There was only one thing against him, said Stephen, and that was that he hadn't a ghost of an idea how to trim their tails, which were always an absolute disgrace. "I've told him again and again to *pull* the hair out," he remarked, "but he goes on just the same, cutting them with scissors, and the result is that they come out at the opening meet with tails like chrysanthemums!"

From this it may be inferred that there were many things in the Rectory stable which fell short of Stephen's ideal. He and his brothers were always trying to bring "the old guv'nor" into line with what they believed to be the Melton Mowbray standard of smartness. There was also the question of persuading him to buy a motor car. But Parson Colwood was a Sussex man by birth and he valued his native provincialism more than the distant splendours of the Shires toward which his offspring turned their unsophisticated eyes. The Rectory, as I knew it then, had the charm of something untouched by modernity.

The Rev. Harry Colwood, as I remember him, was a composite portrait of Charles Kingsley and Matthew Arnold. This fanciful resemblance has no connection with literature, toward which Mr. Colwood's disposition was respectful but tepid. My mental semi-association of him with Arnold is probably due to the fact that he had been in the Rugby eleven somewhere in the 'sixties. And I have, indeed, heard him speak of Arnold's poem, *Rugby Chapel*. But the Kingsley affinity was more clearly recognizable. Like Kingsley, Mr. Colwood loved riding, shooting and fishing, and believed that such sports were congruous with the Christian creed which he unobtrusively accepted and lived up to. It is questionable, however, whether he would have agreed with Kingsley's Christian Socialism. One of his maxims was "Don't marry for money but marry where money is", and he had carried this into effect by marrying, when he was over forty, a sensible Scotch lady with a fortune of £1,500 a year, thereby enabling his three sons to be brought up as keen fox-hunters, game-shooters, and salmon-fishers. And however strongly the Author of his religion might have condemned these sports, no one could deny him the Christian adjectives gentle, patient, and just.

At first I had been intimidated by him, for the scrutinizing look that he gave me was both earnest and stern. His were eyes that looked straight at the world from under level brows, and there was strictness in the lines of his mouth. But the kindliness of his nature emerged in the tone of his voice, which was pitched moderately low. In his voice a desire for gaiety seemed to be striving to overmaster an inherent sadness. This undertone of sadness may have been accentuated as the result of his ripened understanding of a world which was not all skylarking and sport, but Stephen (who was a lankier and less regular-featured edition of his father) had inherited the same quality of voice. Mr. Colwood was a naturally nervous man with strong emotions, which he rigidly repressed.

When I arrived that afternoon both the Rector and his wife were attending some parochial function in the village. So Stephen took me up to the schoolroom, where we had our tea and he jawed to me about horses and hunting to his heart's content. He ended by asserting that he'd "sooner cheer a pack of Pomeranians after a weasel from a bath-chair than waste his life making money in a blinking office".

II

A tenor bell in Hoadley Church tower was making its ultimate appeal to those who were still on their way to morning service. While Stephen and I hurried hatless across the sloping cricket-field which divided the Rectory garden from the churchyard I sniffed the quiet wintry-smelling air and wondered how long Mr. Colwood's sermon would last. I had never been to his church before; there was a suggestion of embarrassment in the idea of seeing him in a long white surplice—almost as if one were taking an unfair advantage of him. Also, since I hadn't been to church with Aunt Evelyn for Heaven knew how long, I felt a bit of an outsider as I followed

Stephen up the aisle to the Rectory pew where his matronly mother was awaiting us with the solemnly cheerful face of one who never mumbled the responses but made them as though she meant every word. Stephen, too, had the serene sobriety of an habitual public-worshipper. No likelihood of his standing up at one of those awkward places when everyone kneels down when you don't expect them to.

As the service proceeded I glanced furtively around me at the prudent Sunday-like faces of the congregation. I thought of the world outside, and the comparison made life out there seem queer and unreal. I felt as if we were all on our way to next week in a ship. But who was I, and what on earth had I been doing? My very name suddenly seemed as though it scarcely belonged to me. Stephen was sitting there beside me, anyhow; there was no doubt about his identity, and I thought what a nice face he had, gentle and humorous and alight with natural intelligence. I looked from him to his father who had been in the background, so far, since the curate had been reading the service (in an unemphatic businesslike voice). But the Rector's eye met mine, which shied guiltily away, and my wool-gathering was interrupted. Even so might his gaze have alighted on one of the coughing village children at the back of the church.

My sense of unfamiliarity with what was going on was renewed when Colonel Hesmon's wizened face and bushy grey eyebrows appeared above the shiny brass eagle to read the First Lesson. This was not quite the same Colonel who had been in such a frenzy of excitement over the point-to-point race eight months ago, when he had exclaimed, over and over again, "I've told the boy that if he wins *I'll give him the horse!*"

The Colonel's voice was on church parade now, and he was every inch a churchwarden as well. He went through the lesson with dispassionate distinctness and extreme rapidity.

Since it was a long passage from Isaiah, he went, as he would have said, "a rattling good gallop". But the words, I thought, were incongruous ones when uttered by the Colonel. "And he will lift up an ensign to the nations from afar, and will hiss unto them from the end of the earth: and, behold, they shall come with speed swiftly: none shall be weary nor stumble among them; none shall slumber nor sleep; neither shall the girdle of their loins be loosed, nor the latchet of their shoes be broken: whose arrows are sharp, and all their bows bent, their horses' hoofs shall be counted like flint, and their wheels like a whirlwind: their roaring shall be like a lion, they shall roar like young lions: yea, they shall roar, and lay hold of the prey, and shall carry it away safe, and none shall deliver it. And in that day they shall war against them like the roaring of the sea: and if one look unto the land, behold darkness and sorrow, and the light is darkened in the heavens thereof. Here endeth the First Lesson." And the brisk little man turned over the leaves to a passage from Peter, arranged the gold-embroidered marker, and returned to his pew with erect and decorous demeanour.

Twenty minutes later Mr. Colwood climbed the pulpit steps to the strains of "O God our help in ages past". My own vocal contribution was inconspicuous, but I had a stealthy look at my watch, which caused Stephen, who was giving a creditable performance of the hymn, to nudge me with his elbow. The sermon lasted a laborious twelve minutes. The Rector had a nervous mannerism which consisted in his continually gathering up his surplice with his left hand, as if he were testing the quality of the linen with his fingers. The offertory was for a missionary society, and he took as his text: "*He that hath two coats, let him impart to him that hath none; and he that hath meat, let him do likewise.*" The results of the collection were handed to him on a wooden plate by the Colonel, who remarked afterwards at lunch that he "didn't mind saying that with the best will in the world he'd have preferred to give his half-sovereign to someone nearer home"—Stephen having already made his rather obvious joke—"Whatever the Guv'nor may say in his sermon about 'imparting', if I ever get a new hunting-coat I'm going to ruddy well keep my old one for wet days!"

The sun was shining when we emerged from the musty smelling interior. The Colonel, with his nattily rolled umbrella, perfectly brushed bowler hat, and nervously blinking eyes, paid his respects to Mr. Colwood with punctilious affability; then he shepherded Stephen and myself away to have a look round his stables before lunch. We were there in less than five minutes, the Colonel chatting so gaily all the way that I could scarcely have got a word in edgeways even if I had felt sufficient confidence in myself to try.

The Colonel had been a widower for many years, and like most lonely living people he easily became talkative. Everything in his establishment was arranged and conducted with elaborate nicety and routine, and he took an intense pride in his stable, which contained half a dozen hunters who stood in well-aired and roomy loose-boxes, surrounded by every luxury which the Colonel's care could contrive: the name of each horse was on a tablet suspended above the manger. Elegant green stable-buckets (with the Colonel's numerous initials painted on them in white) were arranged at regular intervals along the walls, and the harness-room was hung with enough bits and bridles to stock a saddler's shop. It was, as Stephen pointed out to me afterwards, "a regular museum of mouth-gear". For the Colonel was one of those fussy riders with indifferent hands who are always trying their horses with a new bit.

"I haven't found the key to this mare's mouth yet," he would say, as the irritated animal shook its head and showered everyone within range with flecks of froth. And when he got home from hunting he would say to his confidential old head-groom: "I think this mare's still a bit under-bitted, Dumbrell," and they would debate over half the bits in the harness room before he rode the mare again.

"Sunday morning stables" being one of his favourite cere-monies, the Colonel now led us from one loose-box to another, commenting affectionately on each inmate, and stimulated by the fact that one of his audience was a stranger. Each of them, apparently, was a compendium of unique equine qualities, on which I gazed with unaffected admiration, while Stephen chimed in with "Never seen the old chestnut look so fit, Colonel", or "Looking an absolute picture", while Dumbrell was deferentially at hand all the time to share the encomiums offered to his charges. The Colonel, of course, had a stock repertory of remarks about each one of them, including how they had won a certain point-to-point or (more frequently) why they hadn't. The last one we looked at was a big well-bred brown horse who stood very much "over at the knees". The Colonel had hunted him twelve seasons and he had an equivalently long rigmarole to recite about him, beginning with "I remember Sam Hames saying to me (I bought him off old Hames of Leicester, you know) —that horse is the most natural jumper I've ever had in my stable. And he was right, for the old horse has only given me one bad toss in twelve years, and that was no fault of his own, for he landed on the stump of a willow tree; it was at that rough fence just outside Clout's Wood—nasty place, too— you remember I showed it you the other day, Steve"; all of which Stephen had probably heard fifty times before, and had been shown the "nasty place" half a dozen times into the bargain. It was only when he heard the distant booming of the luncheon-gong that the Colonel was able to tear himself away from the brown horse's loose-box.

While going into the house we passed through what he

called "the cleaning room", which was a sort of wide corridor with a skylight to it. Along the wall stood an astonishing array of hunting boots. These struck me as being so numerous that I had the presence of mind to count them. There were twenty-seven pairs. Now a good pair of top-boots, if properly looked after and repaired, will last the owner a good many years; and a new pair once in three years might be considered a liberal allowance for a man who has started with two or three pairs. But the Colonel was nothing if not regular in his habits; every autumn he visited, with the utmost solemnity, an illustrious bootmaker in Oxford Street; and each impeccable little pair of boots had signalized the advent of yet another opening meet. And, since they had been impeccably cared for and the Colonel seldom hunted more than three days a week, they had consequently accumulated. As we walked past them it was as though Lord Roberts were inspecting the local Territorials, and the Colonel would have been gratified by the comparison to the gallant Field-Marshal.

It did not strike me at the time that there was something dumbly pathetic about those chronological boots with their mahogany, nut-brown, and salmon-coloured tops. But I can see now that they symbolized much that was automatic and sterile in the Colonel's career. He had retired from the Army twenty years before, and was now sixty-six, though active and well preserved. And each of those twenty years had been as stereotyped as his ideas. The notions on which he had patterned himself were part regimental and part sporting. As a military man he was saturated with the Balaclava spirit, and one could also imagine him saying, "Women and children first" on a foundering troopship (was it the *Warren Hastings* which went down in the early 'nineties?). But the Boer War had arrived seven years too late for him, and the gist of the matter was that he'd never seen any active service. And some-how, when one came to know him well, one couldn't *quite* imagine him in the Charge of the Light Brigade: but this may have been because, in spite of the dashing light-cavalry tone of his talk, he had served in a line regiment, and not at all a smart one either. (His affluence dated from the day when he had married where money was.)

As a sportsman he had modelled himself on what I may call the Whyte-Melville standard. His conversational behaviour echoed the sentiments and skylarking vivacities of mid-Victorian sporting novels and the coloured prints of a slightly earlier period. And yet one could no more imagine him participating in a moonlight steeplechase than one could visualize him being shot through the Bible in his breast pocket in a death or glory attack. Like many chivalrous spirits, he could never quite live up to the ideal he aimed at. He was always talking about "Brooksby", a hard-riding journalist who, in the Colonel's heyday, had written regularly for *The Field*. He had several volumes of these lively scribblings and he had read and re-read them in his solitary evenings until he knew the name of every gorse-covert and woodland in the Shires.

But, as Stephen might have said (if he'd been capable of relaxing his admirable loyalty to his god-father) "The dear old Colonel's always bucking about Leicestershire, but I don't suppose he's had half a dozen days there since he was foaled!" And when the Colonel asked one to dine at "the Club" ("You'll always find me in town in Ascot week, my dear boy") "the Club" (he had two) wasn't quite up to the standard he set himself, since instead of being that full-blown fogeydom "The Naval and Military", it had to face things out as merely ("Capital Club! Lot of nice young chaps there!") "the Junior".

On this special Sunday, however, I could still estimate the Colonel's importance as being equivalent to twenty-seven pairs of top-boots. In fact, I thought him a terrific swell, and it wouldn't have surprised me to hear that he'd won the Grand National when he was a gallant young subaltern. At luncheon (roast beef and apple tart) he was the most attentive of hosts, and by the time we had finished our port—("I think you'll find this a nice light-bodied wine. I get it through the Club.") —he had given most of his favourite anecdotes an airing. While the decanter was on its way round Stephen tackled him about the miseries of learning to be a chartered account-ant. The lament was well received, and when he said, "I've been wondering, Colonel, whether I couldn't possibly get into the Gunners through the Special Reserve," the idea was considered a capital one.

The Colonel's face lit up: "I tell you what, my boy, I'll write at once to an old friend of mine at the War Office. Excellent officer—used to be in the 'Twenty-Third'. Very useful man on a horse, too."

Warmed up by the thought of Stephen getting a commis-sion, he asked me whether I was in the Yeomanry. Reluctantly confessing that I wasn't, I added that I'd been thinking about it; which was true, and the thought had filled me with un-utterable alarm. When we rose from our chairs the Colonel drew my attention to the oil-paintings which adorned the walls. These were portraits of his past and present hunters— none of whom, apparently, "knew what it was to put a foot wrong". Among many other relics and associative objects which he showed us was a large green parrot which he "had bought from a sailor five-and-twenty years ago". He had taught the bird to ejaculate "Tear 'im and eat 'im", and other hunting noises. Finally, with a certain access of *grand seigneur* dignity, he waved to us from his front doorstep and vanished into the house, probably to write a letter to his old friend at the War Office.

At nine o'clock next morning my cold fingers were making their usual bungling efforts to tie a white stock neatly; but as I had never been shown how to do it, my repeated failures didn't surprise me, though I was naturally anxious not to disgrace the Rectory on my first appearance at a meet of the Ringwell Hounds. The breakfast bell was supplemented by Stephen's incitements to me to hurry up; these consisted in cries of "Get-along-forrid" and similar hunt-servant noises, which accentuated my general feeling that I was in for a big day. While I was putting the final touches to my toilet I could hear him shouting to the two Scotch terriers who were scuttling about the lawn: (he was out there having a look at that important thing, the weather.)

Fully dressed and a bit flurried, I stumped downstairs and made for the low buzz of conversation in the dining-room. Purposing to make the moderately boisterous entry appropriate to a hunting morning, I opened the door. After a moment of stupefaction I recoiled into the passage, having beheld the entire household on its knees, with backs of varying sizes turned toward me: I had entered in the middle of the Lord's Prayer. After a temporizing stroll on the lawn I re-entered the room unobtrusively; Stephen handed me a plate of porridge with a grin and no other reference was made to my breach of decorum.

After breakfast he told me that I'd no more idea of tying a stock than an ironmonger; when he had re-tied it for me he surveyed the result with satisfaction and announced that I now "looked ready to compete against all the cutting and thrusting soldier-officers in creation".

By a quarter past ten the Rector was driving me to the

meet in the buggy—the groom having ridden his horse on with Stephen, who was jogging sedately along on Jerry. The Rector, whose overcoat had an astrakhan collar, was rather reticent, and we did the five miles to the meet without exchanging many remarks. But it was a comfort, after my solitary sporting experiments, to feel that I had a couple of friendly chaperons, and Stephen had assured me that my hireling knew his way over every fence in the country and had never been known to turn his head. My only doubt was whether his rider would do him credit. We got to the meet in good time, and Mr. Whatman, a very large man who kept a very large livery-stable and drove a coach in the summer, was loquacious about the merits of my hireling, while he supervised my settlement in the saddle, which felt a hard and slippery one.

As I gathered up the thin and unflexible reins I felt that he was conferring a privilege on me by allowing me to ride the horse—a privilege for which the sum of thirty-five shillings seemed inadequate repayment. My mount was a wiry, nondescript-coloured animal, sober and unexcitable. It was evident from the first that he knew much more about the game than I did. He was what is known as a "safe conveyance" or "patent safety"; this more than atoned for his dry-coated and ill-groomed exterior. By the time I had been on his back an hour I felt more at home than I had ever done when out with the Dumborough.

The meet was at "The Five Bells", a wayside inn close to Basset Wood, which was the chief stronghold of fox-preservation in that part of the Ringwell country. There was never any doubt about finding a fox at Basset. Almost a mile square, it was well-rided and easy to get about in, though none too easy to get a fox away from. It was also, as Stephen remarked when we entered it, an easy place to get left in unless one kept one's eyes and ears skinned. And his face kindled at the delightful notion of getting well away with the hounds, leaving three parts of the field coffee-housing at the wrong end of the covert. It was a grey morning, with a nip in the air which made him hopeful that "hounds would fairly scream along" if they got out in the open and, perhaps for the first time in my life, I felt a keen pleasure in the idea of sitting down and cramming my horse at every obstacle that might come in our way.

In the meantime I had got no more than a rough idea of the seventy or eighty taciturn or chattering riders who were now making their way slowly along the main-ride while the huntsman could be heard cheering his hounds a little way off among the oaks and undergrowth. I had already noticed several sporting farmers in blue velvet caps and long-skirted black coats of country cut. And scarlet-coated Colonel Hesmon had proffered me a couple of brown-gloved fingers with the jaunty airified manner of a well-dressed absent-minded swell. He was on his corky little grey cob, and seemed to be having rather a rough ride. In fact the impetuous behaviour of the cob suggested that the Colonel had yet to find the key to his mouth.

An open space toward the top end of the wood formed a junction of the numerous smaller paths which were tributaries of that main channel—the middle-ride. At this point of vantage a few of the more prominent characters from among the field had pulled up, and since the hounds had yet to find a fox I was able to take a few observations of people who afterwards became increasingly familiar to me in my mental conspectus of the Ringwell Hunt. Among them was the Master, of whom there is little to be said except that he was a rich man whose resignation was already rumoured. His only qualification was his wealth, and he had had the bad luck (or bad judgment) to engage a bad huntsman. Needless to say the Master's perplexities had been aggravated by the criticisms and cavillings of subscribers who had neither the wealth, knowledge, nor initiative necessary for the office which this gentleman had found so ungrateful. Much of this I had already learned at the Rectory, where he was given his due for having done his best to hunt the country in handsome style. Sitting there that morning on a too-good-looking, well-bred horse, he seemed glum and abstracted, as though he suspected that most of his field would poke fun at him when his back was turned. One of his troubles was that he'd never learnt how to blow his horn properly, and his inexpert tootlings afforded an adequate excuse for those who enjoyed ridiculing him.

Chief among these was Nigel Croplady. When I first observed him he was sitting sideways on his compact short-tailed brown horse; a glossy top-hat was tilted over his nose. His supercilious, clean-shaven face was preoccupied with a loose-lipped inspection of his own left leg; his boot-tops were a delicate shell-pink, and his well-cleaned white "leathers" certainly justified his self-satisfied scrutiny of them.

"That blighter's always talking about getting a flying-start," remarked Stephen in an undertone, "but when hounds run he's the most chicken-hearted skirter in Sussex." I was able to verify this later in the day when I saw him go irresolutely at a small fence on a bank, pull his horse across it with a shout of " 'Ware wire!" and hustle away in search of a gate, leaving a hard-riding farmer to take it in his stride—the wire having been an improvisation of Croplady's over-prudent mind.

The group which I was watching also included two undemonstrative elderly men (both of whom, said Stephen, were fifty pound subscribers and important covert owners) and several weather-beaten ladies, none of whom looked afraid of a liberal allowance of mud and water.

The Rev. Colwood (who was on a one-eyed screw which

his soldier-son had picked up for seventeen pounds at a sale of Army remounts) now joined the group. He was sitting well forward in the saddle with the constrained look of a man who rather expects his horse to cross its front legs and pitch him over its head. Beside him, on a plump white weight-carrier, was a spare-built middle-aged man in a faded pink coat who scattered boisterous vociferations on everybody within hail. "Morning, Master. Morning, Mrs. Moffat. Morning, Nigel!" His beaming recognitions appeared to include the whole world in a sort of New Year's Day greeting. And, "Hallo, Stephen ole man," he shouted, turning in our direction so suddenly that his animal's rotund hind quarters bumped the Rector's horse on his blind side and nearly knocked him over. The collision culminated when he grabbed my hand and wrung it heartily with the words, "Why, Jack, my lad, I thought you were still out in India!" I stared at him astonished, while his exuberance became puzzled and apologetic.

"*Is* it Jack?" he asked, adding, with a loud laugh, "No, it's some other young bloke after all. But you're the living spit of Steve's elder brother—say what you like!"

In this way I became acquainted with one of the most popular characters in the Hunt. Arthur Brandwick was a doctor who had given up his small country practice some years before. "Always merry and bright" was his motto, and he now devoted his bachelor energies to the pursuit of the fox and the conversion of the human race to optimism.

A solemn purple-faced man, who had been eyeing me as if he also had his doubts about my identity, now came up and asked me for a sovereign. This was Mr. McCosh, the Hunt secretary, and it was my first experience of being "capped" as a stranger. I produced the gold coin, but he very civilly returned it when Stephen informed him that I was staying at the Rectory.

Just as these negotiations concluded, a chorus of excited

hallooings on the outskirts of the wood proclaimed that Reynard had been viewed by some pedestrians.

"Those damned foot people again! I'll bet a tenner they've headed him back!" sneered Croplady, whose contempt for the lower classes was only equalled by his infatuation for a title. (His family were old-established solicitors in Downfield, but Nigel was too great a swell to do much work in his father's office, except to irritate the clients, many of whom were farmers, with his drawling talk and dandified manners.)

"Come on, Snowball!" exclaimed Brandwick, shaking his corpulent white steed into a canter, and away he went along the main-ride, ramming his hat down on his head with the hand that held his whip and scattering mud in every direction.

"Chuckle-headed old devil! Mad as a hatter but as kind-hearted as they make 'em," said Stephen, watching him as he dipped in and out of the hollows with his coat-tails flapping over his horse's wide rump. And without any undue haste he started off along one of the smaller rides with myself and my hireling at his heels.

Everybody hustled away into the wood except the stolid secretary and two other knowledgeable veterans. Having made up their minds that the fox would stick to the covert, they remained stock-still like equestrian statues, watching for him to cross the middle-ride. They were right. Fox-hunting wiseacres usually are (though it was my wilful habit in those days to regard everyone who preferred going through a gate to floundering over a fence as unworthy of the name of sportsman).

Later on, while Stephen and I were touring the covert with our ears open, we overtook a moody faced youth on a handsome bay horse. "Hullo, Tony! I thought you'd parted with that conspicuous quad of yours at Tatts last week," exclaimed Stephen, riding robustly up alongside of him and giving the bay horse a friendly slap on his hind quarters.

Young Lewison (I remembered what Stephen had said about him and the expensive hunter which he "couldn't ride a hair of") informed us that the horse had been bought by a Warwickshire dealer and then returned as a slight whistler. "I'm sick of the sight of him," he remarked, letting the reins hang listlessly on the horse's neck.

Gazing at the nice-looking animal, I inwardly compared him with dear old Harkaway. The comparison was all in favour of the returned whistler, whose good points were obvious even to my inexperienced eyes. In fact, he was almost suspiciously good-looking, though there was nothing flashy about his fine limbs, sloping shoulders, and deep chest.

"His wind can't be very bad if you'd never noticed it," remarked Stephen, eyeing him thoughtfully, "and he certainly does look a perfect gentleman."

Meanwhile the horse stood there as quiet as if he were having his picture painted. "I wish to goodness someone would give me fifty pounds for him," exclaimed Lewison petulantly, and I had that queer sensation when an episode seems to have happened before. The whole scene was strangely lit up for me; I could have sworn that I knew what he was going to say before a single word was out of his mouth. And when, without a second's hesitation, I replied, "*I'll* give you fifty pounds for him," I was merely overhearing a remark which I had already made.

Young Lewison looked incredulous; but Stephen intervened, with no sign of surprise, "Damn it, George, you might do worse than buy him, at that price. Hop off your hireling and see what he feels like."

I had scarcely settled myself in the new saddle when there was a shrill halloa from a remote side of the covert. We galloped away, leaving Lewison still whoaing on one leg round the hireling, who was eager to be after us.

"Well, I'm jiggered! What an enterprising old card you

are!" ejaculated Stephen, delightedly slapping his leg with his crop and then leaning forward to listen for the defect in the bay horse's wind. "Push him along, George," he added; but we were already galloping freely, and I felt much more like holding him back. "Dashed if *I* can hear a ghost of a whistle!" muttered Stephen, as we pulled up at a hunting-gate out of Basset Wood.

"We're properly left this time, old son." He trotted down the lane and popped over a low heave-gate into a grass field. My horse followed him without demur. There wasn't a trace of the hunt in sight, but we went on, jumping a few easy fences, and my heart leapt with elation at the way my horse took them, shortening and then quickening his stride and slipping over them with an ease and neatness which were a revelation to me.

"This horse is an absolute dream!" I gasped as Stephen stopped to unlatch a gate.

But Stephen's face now looked fit for a funeral. "They must have run like stink and we've probably missed the hunt of the season," he grumbled.

A moment later his face lit up again. "There's the horn— right-handed—over by the Binsted covers!" And away he went across a rushy field as fast as old Jerry could lay legs to the ground.

A lot of hoof-marks and a gap in a big boundary fence soon showed us where the hunt had gone. We were now on some low-lying meadows, and he said it looked as if we'd have to jump the Harcombe brook. As we approached it there was a shout from downstream and we caught sight of someone in distress. A jolly faced young farmer was up to his arm-pits in the water with his horse plunging about beside him.

"Hullo, it's Bob Millet and his tubed mare!" Stephen jumped off Jerry and hurried to the rescue.

"I'm having the devil's own job to keep the water out of

my mare," shouted Millet, who didn't seem to be worrying much about getting soaked to the skin.

"Haven't you got a cork?" inquired Stephen.

"No, Mr. Colwood, but I'm keeping my finger on the hole in her neck. She'll be drowned if I don't."

This peculiar situation was solved by Stephen, who held the mare by her bridle and skilfully extricated her after several tremendous heaves and struggles.

We then crossed the brook by a wooden bridge a few hundred yards away—young Millet remarking that he'd never come out again without his cork. Soon afterwards we came up with the hounds, who had lost their fox and were drawing the Binsted covers without much enthusiasm. Colonel Hesmon commiserated with us for having missed "quite a pretty little dart in the open". If he'd been on his brown mare, he said, he'd have had a cut at the Harcombe brook. "But this cob of mine won't face water", he remarked, adding that he'd once seen half the Quorn field held up by a brook you could have jumped in your boots.

*   *   *

The huntsman now enlivened the deflated proceedings by taking his hounds to a distant holloa on the other side of the brook. A man on a bicycle had viewed our fox returning to Basset Wood. The bicyclist (Stephen told me as we passed him in the lane where he'd been providing the flustered huntsman with exact information) was none other than the genius who reported the doings of the Hunt for the *Southern Daily News*. In the summer he umpired in county cricket matches, which caused me to regard him as quite a romantic personality.

While they were hunting slowly back to the big wood on a very stale line, young Lewison reappeared on my hireling. Looking more doleful than ever, he asked how I liked Cockbird. Before I had time to answer Stephen interposed with "He makes a distinct noise, Tony, and his wind's bound to get worse. But my friend Sherston likes the feel of him and he'll give you fifty."

I concealed my surprise. Stephen had already assured me that the whistle was so slight as to be almost undetectable. He had also examined Cockbird's legs and pronounced them perfect. Almost imperceptible, too, was the wink with which Stephen put me wise about his strategic utterance, and I met Lewison's lack-lustre eyes with contrived indifference as I reiterated my willingness to give him fifty. Internally, however, I was in a tumult of eagerness to call Cockbird my own at any price, and when my offer had been definitely accepted nothing would induce me to get off his back. We soon arranged that Mr. Whatman's second horseman should call for the hireling at Lewison's house on his way back to Downfield.

"We'll send you your saddle and bridle to-morrow," shouted Stephen, as Cockbird's ex-owner disappeared along the lane outside Basset Wood. "Tony never thinks of anything except getting home to his tea," he added.

We then exchanged horses, and though the hounds did very little more that afternoon, our enthusiasm about my unexpected purchase kept our tongues busy; we marvelled more and more that anyone could be such a mug as to part with him for fifty pounds. As we rode happily home to the Rectory, Cockbird jogged smoothly along with his ears well forward. Demure and unexcited, he appeared neither to know or care about his change of ownership.

*   *   *

"Mr. Pennett can go to blazes!" I said to myself, while I was blissfully ruminating in my bath before dinner. Stephen then banged on the door and asked if I intended to stay in there all night, so I pulled the plug out, whereupon the water began to run away with a screeching sound peculiar to that particular bathroom. (Why is it that up-to-date bathrooms have so much less individuality than their Victorian ancestors? The Rectory one, with its rough-textured paint and dark wooden casing, had the atmosphere of a narrow converted lumber-room, and its hot-water pipes were a subdued orchestra of enigmatic noises.)

While the water was making its raucous retreat my flippant ultimatum to the family solicitor was merged in a definite anxiety about paying for Cockbird. And then there was (an additional fifteen guineas) the question of my subscription to the Ringwell.

"Of course you'll enter him for our point-to-point," Stephen had said while we were on our way home. "He's a lot faster than Jerry, and he'll simply walk away with the Heavy Weights. Send in your sub. and start qualifying him at once. You've only got to bring him out eight times. He's done nothing to-day, so you can have him out again on Wednesday."

The idea of my carrying off the Colonel's Cup had caused me delicious trepidations. But now, in the draughty bathroom and by the light of a bedroom candle, I was attacked by doubts and misgivings. It was easy enough for Stephen to talk about "qualifying" Cockbird; but how about my own qualifications as a race-rider? The candle flickered as if in ominous agreement with my scruples. There was a drop of water on the wick and the flame seemed to be fizzling toward extinction. Making it my fortune-teller, I decided that if it went out I should fall off at the first fence. After a succession of splutters it made a splendid recovery and spired into a confident survival.

*   *   *

At the dinner-table the Rector glowed with austere geniality while he carved the brace of pheasants which represented
a day's covert-shooting he'd had with Lord Dumborough—
"a long-standing annual fixture of mine", he called it. During
our day's hunting we had only caught occasional glimpses of
him. But he had got away from Basset Wood with the
hounds, and had evidently enjoyed himself in his reticent way.
We discussed every small detail of our various experiences.
Kind Mrs. Colwood kept up with the conversation as well as
could be expected from an absentee who hadn't ridden since
she was quite a girl. She was interested and amused by hearing
all about who had been out and what they had said, but she
obviously found some difficulty in sharing her husband's
satisfaction about the clever way in which "Lord Nelson"
(the one-eyed horse) had popped over a stile with an awkward take-off and a drop on the landing-side. She must have
endured many anxious hours while her family were out hunting, but her pinnacle of perturbation had been reached when
Stephen rode in the Hunt Races—an ordeal which (unless
Jerry went lame) was re-awaiting her the next April. She
could never be induced to attend "those horrible point-to-
points" which, as she often said, would be the death of her.

On this particular evening my new horse was naturally the
main topic, and his health was drunk in some port which had
been "laid down" in the year of Stephen's birth. After this
ceremony the Rector announced that he'd heard for certain
that the Master was sending in his resignation.

"Here's to our next one," he added, raising his glass again,
"and I hope he'll engage a first-rate huntsman."

I assumed a sagacious air while they deplored the imperfec-
tions of Ben Trotter, and the way he was for ever lifting his
hounds and losing his head. Stephen remarked that whatever
those humanitarian cranks might say, there was precious little
cruelty to foxes when they were being hunted by a chap like

Ben, who was always trying to chase his fox himself and never gave his hounds a chance to use their noses. The Rector sighed and feared that it was no use pretending that the Ringwell was anything but a cold-scenting country. We then adjourned to the study, where we soon had our own noses close to the ordnance map. At this moment I can see Mr. Colwood quite clearly. With a slight frown he is filling his pipe from a tin of "Three Nuns" mixture; on the wall behind him hangs a large engraving of "Christ leaving the Praetorium".

IV

Early in the afternoon of the following Thursday I journeyed homeward in the jolting annex of a horse-box. Although it was a sort of fifth-class compartment I felt serenely contented as I occasionally put my hand through the aperture to stroke Cockbird's velvet nose. He appeared to be a docile and experienced railway traveller, and when he stepped out of the box at Dumbridge Station he had an air of knowing that he'd saved himself a twenty-mile walk. The porters eyed him with the respect due to such a well-bred animal. Having arranged for my kit-bag to be conveyed to Butley on the carrier's van, I swung myself into the saddle which I had borrowed from the Colwoods. It was a mellow afternoon for mid-winter, and our appearance, as reflected in the Dumbridge shop-windows, made me feel what, in those days, I should have called "a frightful nut". Cockbird's impeccable behaviour out hunting on the previous day had increased my complacency, and it was now an established fact that I had got hold of a top-hole performer with perfect manners.

Nobody at home was aware of what I'd been up to down in Sussex, and Dixon got the surprise of his life when we clattered into the stable-yard. So far as he was concerned it was the first really independent action of my career. When I arrived he was having his tea in his cottage over the coach-house; I could hear him clumping down the steep wooden stairs, and I sat like a statue until he emerged from the door by the harness room with his mouth full of bread and butter. The afternoon was latening, but there was, I think, a quietly commemorative glow from the west. He stood with the sunset on his face and his final swallowing of the mouthful appeared to epitomize his astonishment. Taken aback he undoubtedly was, but his voice kept its ordinary composure. "Why, what's this?" he asked. I told him.

*   *   *

Aunt Evelyn behaved like a brick about Cockbird. (How was it that bricks became identified with generous behaviour?) Of course she admired him immensely and considered it very clever of me to have bought him so cheap. But when it came to writing out the cheque for him I was obliged, for the first time in my life, to ask her to lend me some money. She promised to let me have it in a few days.

Next morning she went to London, "just to do a little Christmas shopping at the Army and Navy Stores". I was in the drawing-room when she returned. I heard the dog-cart drive up to the front door, and then Aunt Evelyn's voice telling Miriam how tired she felt and asking her to make some tea. I didn't bother to get up when she came into the room, and after replying to my perfunctory inquiry whether she'd had a good day she went to her bureau and fussed about with some papers. Somewhat irritably I wondered what she was in such a stew about as soon as she'd got home. Her quill-pen squeaked for a short time and then she came across to the arm-chair where I was sitting with Edmund Gosse's *Father and Son* on my knee.

"There, dear. There's the money for your horse, and the Hunt subscription as well." She placed a cheque on the arm of the chair. "It's your Christmas present," she explained. It was so unexpected that I almost forgot to thank her. But I had the grace to ask whether she could really afford it.

"Well, dear," she said, "to tell the truth, I *couldn't*. But I *can* now." And she confessed that she'd sold one of her rings for seventy-five pounds up in London. "And why not?" she asked. "I'm so delighted at your having taken up hunting again; it's such a healthy hobby for a young man, and Dixon's almost beside himself—he's so pleased with the new horse. And after all, dear, I've got no other interest in the whole world except you."

Miriam then appeared with the tea-tray, and soon afterwards I went upstairs to gloat over my good fortune.

PART SIX: THE COLONEL'S CUP

~~~~~~

I

By the end of February I had made further progress in what I believed to be an important phase of my terrestrial experience. In other words (and aided by an exceptionally mild winter) I had averaged five days a fortnight with the hounds. I had, of course, confided in Dixon my intention of entering Cockbird for the Ringwell HeavyWeight Race. My main object now seemed to be to jump as many fences as possible before that eventful day arrived. Meets of the Dumborough had been disregarded, and a series of short visits to the Rectory had continued the "qualifying" of Cockbird. ("Qualifying" consisted in drawing the Master's attention to the horse during each day's hunting; and I did this more than conscientiously since Stephen and I were frequently shouted at by him for "larking" over fences when the hounds weren't running.)

The problem of Harkaway's lack of stamina had been solved by Dixon when he suggested that I should box him to the Staghound meets. He told me that they generally had the best of their fun in the first hour, so I could have a good gallop and bring the old horse home early. This took me (by a very early train from Baldock Wood) to a new and remote part of the country, and some of the fun I enjoyed there is worth a few pages of description.

The Coshford Vale Stag Hunt, which had been in existence as a subscription pack for about half a century, had been kept on its legs by the devoted efforts of a group of prosperous hop-farmers and a family of brewers whose name was a household word in the district. *Gimling's Fine Ales* were a passport to popularity, and the genial activities of Mr. "Gus" Gimling, who had been Master for more years than he cared to count, had kept the Hunt flourishing and assured it of a friendly reception almost everywhere in the country over which it hunted (described in the scarlet-covered Hunting Directory as "principally pasture with very little plough"). This description encouraged me to visualize an Elysium of green fields and jumpable hedges; but the country, although it failed to come up to my preconceived idea of its charms, included a nice bit of vale; and in those days there was very little wire in the fences.

I need hardly say that, since stags were no longer indigenous to that part of England, the Coshford stag-hunters kept theirs at home (in a deer paddock a few miles from the kennels). The animal which had been selected to provide the day's sport was carried to the meet in a mysterious-looking van, driven by the deerkeeper, a ruddy faced Irishman in a brown velveteen jacket who had earned a reputation for humorous repartee, owing to the numerous inquiries of inquisitive persons on the roads who asked him what he'd got in that old hearse of his.

Provincial stag-hunts are commonly reputed to be comic and convivial gatherings which begin with an uproarious hunt-breakfast for the local farmers. Purple faced and bold with cherry brandy, they heave themselves on to their horses and set off across the country, frequently falling off in a ludicrous manner. But the Coshford sportsmen, as I knew them, were businesslike and well-behaved; they were out for a good old-fashioned gallop. In fact, I think of them as a somewhat serious body of men. And since the field was mainly composed of farmers, there was nothing smart or snobbish about the proceedings.

I need hardly say that there was no levity in my own attitude of mind when I set out for my first sample of this new experiment in sportsmanship. In spite of talking big to Dixon the night before, I felt more frightened than light-hearted. For I went alone and knew no one when I got there. Dixon had talked to me about Harry Buckman, who acted as amateur huntsman and was well known as a rider at hunt races all over the country. That was about all I'd got to go on, and I gazed at Buckman with interest and admiration when he tit-tupped stylishly past me at the meet with his velvet cap cocked slightly over one ear. Buckman was a mixture of horse dealer and yeoman farmer. In the summer he rode jumpers in the show ring. His father had hunted a pack of harriers, and it was said that when times were bad he would go without his dinner himself rather than stint his hounds of their oatmeal.

Roughly speaking, young Buckman's task as huntsman was twofold. Firstly, he was there to encourage and assist the hounds (a scratch pack—mostly dog-hounds drafted from foxhound kennels because they were over-sized) in following the trails of their unnaturally contrived quarry; secondly, he had to do everything he could to prevent his hounds from "pulling down" the deer. With this paradoxical but humane object in view he had once jumped a railway gate; by this feat of horsemanship he arrived in the nick of time and saved the deer's life. Fast hunts were fairly frequent, but there were slow-hunting days when scent was bad and the Coshford subscribers were able to canter along at their ease enjoying a pretty bit of hound-work. Sometimes the uncarted animal got clean away from them, and there was a special interest attached to a meet when they drew for an outlying deer.

My first day with the Staghounds was on Christmas Eve and I find the following entry in my diary: "*Coshford; Packman's Green*. Perfect hunting day; came on wet about 2.30. Turned out at Hazelpits Farm and ran well to Wissenden, then on by Chartley Church and Henhurst down the hill and on towards Applestead. Took deer ('Miss Masterful') about 2. Nine-mile point. Harkaway in good form. Took a toss over a stile toward the end. Very nice country, especially the first bit." From this concise account it may seem as if I had already mastered the Coshford topography, but I suspect that my source of information was a paragraph in a local paper.

I cannot remember how I made myself acquainted with the name of the deer which provided the nine-mile point. But in any case, how much is taken for granted and left unrecorded in that shorthand description? And how helpful it would have been now if I had written an accurately observed and detailed narrative of the day. But since the object of these pages is to supply that deficiency I must make my reminiscent deductions as best I can. And those words from my diary do seem worth commenting on—symbolic as they are of the equestrian equilibrium on which my unseasoned character was trying to pattern itself. I wrote myself down that evening as I wanted myself to be—a hard-bitten hunting man, self-possessed in his localized knowingness and stag-hunting jargon. The words might well have been penned by a middle-aged sheep-farmer, or even by Mr. "Gus" Gimling himself. "Took a toss over a stile" is the only human touch. But taking tosses was incidental to the glory of being a hard rider. What I ought to have written was—that I couldn't make up my mind whether to go at it or not, and the man behind me shouted "go on if you're going", so I felt flustered and let Harkaway rush at it anyhow and then jerked his mouth just as he was taking off, and he didn't really fall, but only pecked badly and chucked me over his head and then stood quite still waiting for me to scramble up again, and altogether it was rather an inglorious exhibition, and thank goodness Stephen wasn't there to see it. For though Stephen and I always made a joke out of every toss we took, it wouldn't have suited my dignity if he'd told me in cold blood that I was still a jolly rotten rider—the tacit assumption being that my falls were entirely due to my thrusting intrepidity.

It will be noticed that no mention is made of the method by which "Miss Masterful" was "taken", although I had witnessed that performance for the first time in my life. As far as I can recollect, Miss M. having decided that the show had lasted long enough, plunged into a small pond and stood there with only her small head appearing above the muddy water. Raucous ratings and loud whip-crackings restrained the baying hounds from splashing in after her, and then genial Mr. Gimling, assisted by one of the whiskered wiseacres of the hunt (in a weather-stained black coat which came nearly down to his knees, white cord breeches, black butcher-boots, and very long spurs), began to get busy with a long rope. After Miss M. had eluded their attempts several times they succeeded in lassooing her head and she was persuaded to emerge from the pond. She was then frog-marched away to a farm building, where she awaited the arrival of her conveyance, which was cruising about the country and usually put in an appearance much earlier than might have been expected.

It can also be inferred from my diary that the weather "came on wet" as soon as I'd started my ten-mile ride back to the railway-station and Harkaway's horse-box, and that the supporters of the Coshford Hunt departed in different directions wishing one another a merry Christmas and a happy New Year. It may also be inferred that poor Miss Masterful sweated and shivered in the barn with heaving sides and frightened eyes. It did not occur to me to sympathize with her as I stood at the entrance to watch them tie her up. I only wondered how far I was from the station and my poached eggs for tea. Any sympathy I had was reserved for Harkaway, who looked as if he'd had more galloping than was good for him. But when I was jogging back by Chartley Church, with my coat collar turned up and the rain soaking my knees, I chuckled to myself as I thought of an amusing incident which had happened earlier in the day.

We were galloping full-tilt along a road just outside a cosy village. An angry-faced old parson was leaning over his garden gate, and as we clattered past he shook his fist at us and shouted "Brutes! Brutes!" in a loud unclerical voice. Excited and elated as I was, I turned in the saddle and waved my whip derisively at him. Silly old buffer! And what a contrast to that jolly sporting parson in a low-crowned top-hat who went so well and came up and talked to me so nicely while Miss Masterful was being hauled out of the pond!

I have analysed the orthodox entry in my diary more fully than I had intended. But how lifelessly I recover the breathing reality of which those words are the only relics. The night before hunting: the anxious wonderings about the weather; lying awake for a while with busy thoughts about to-morrow that grow blurred with the beginning of an untroubled sleep. And then Miriam battering on the door with "it's twenty to seven, sir", and the first look at the quiet morning greyness, and the undefinable feeling produced by the yellow candle-light and the wintry smelling air from the misty garden. Such was the impermanent fabric as it unfolded: memory enchants even the dilatory little train journey which carried my expectant simplicity into the freshness of a country seen for the first time. All the sanguine guesswork of youth is there, and the silliness; all the novelty of being alive and impressed by the urgency of tremendous trivialities.

The end of February became the beginning of March, and this unavoidable progression intensified my anticipations of the date in April which meant so much to me. Cockbird had done his eight qualifying days without the slightest mishap or the least sign of unsoundness. He was so delightfully easy to handle that my assurance as a rider had increased rapidly. But in the period of preparation Dixon and I, between us, carried a large invisible load of solicitude and suspense. Our conversational demeanour was jauntily portentous. But when I was alone with myself and indoors, I often felt so nervous that the month-long remoteness of the point-to-points became almost unbearable. My confidence in Cockbird's ability to carry off the Colonel's Cup served only to magnify my imaginations of what might go wrong in the race through my own lack of experience.

I consoled myself with day-dreams in which I won in every way that my limited racing repertory could contrive. There was cantering home an easy winner; and there was winning cleverly by half a length; and there was coming up with a rush to score sensationally in the last stride. Easy winner lacked intensity; I would have preferred something more spectacular and heroic. But this was difficult to manage; I couldn't win with my arm in a sling unless I started in that condition, which would be an anti-climax. On the whole I was in favour of a fine finish with Stephen, although even this seemed inappropriate because Jerry was believed to be much slower than Cockbird, and could only hope to win if I fell— a thought which reduced my suppositions to reality.

Meanwhile Cockbird existed unperturbed, munching large feeds of crushed oats (with which Dixon mixed some water, for he had an idea that this was good for his wind) and doing three hours' steady work on the road every day. Once a week we took him to a ten-acre field on a hillside, which a well-disposed farmer allowed us to use for gallops. Round and round we went with set and serious faces (Dixon riding Harkaway) until we had done three presumptive miles up and down hill. When we pulled up Dixon would jump off, and I would jump off to stand meekly by the horses' snorting heads while he fussed round Cockbird with as much solemnity and solicitude as if he were a Grand National favourite. And, so far as we were concerned, "the National" (which was to be run ten days before the Ringwell Heavy Weight Race) was quite a secondary affair, though we sometimes talked about it in an offhand way which might have led a stranger to suppose that either of us might slip up to Liverpool to see it, provided that we could spare the time. Neither of us doubted that Cockbird himself could "get round Aintree" if asked to do so. He was, we agreed, a regular National stamp of horse, and though I had never seen an Aintree fence, I was quite sure that no fence was too big for him.

On some such afternoon (for we always went out in the afternoon, though before breakfast would have been more correct, but it would have made the day so long and empty), on some such afternoon, when Cockbird had done his gallop to our mutual satisfaction and we were jogging quietly home, with the sun making haloes on the fleeces of the sheep who watched us pass—on some such afternoon, I repeat, I was reminded of the old days when I was learning to ride the cob Sheila, and of how I used to ask Dixon to pretend to be Mr. MacDoggart winning the Hunt Cup. Such a suggestion now would have struck both of us as unseemly; this was no time for such childish nonsense as that (though, when one came to think of it, twelve years ago wasn't such a very long time and "the twenty hop-kilns" were still down there in the valley to

167

remind me of my childish excitement about them). But the thought passed through my mind, and at the same moment the warning whistle of a train going along the Weald would remind me of that interrogative railway journey which the three of us would be making in not much more than two weeks' time—was it really as near as that now?

The thought of Mr. MacDoggart's remote victories at Dumborough Races made me wish that I could ask Dixon for some first-hand information about race-riding. But although he had once worked in a racing-stable, he'd never had an opportunity of riding in a race. And I was shy of asking him questions which would expose my ignorance of things which, for some reason, I supposed that I ought to have known; so I had to make the best of such hints as he dropped me.

And then there was the difficulty of dress, a subject on which he never offered advice. Desperately in need of information, I asked myself what I was to wear on my head. Stephen had worn some sort of cap last year, but the idea of buying a jockey-cap seemed somehow ludicrous. (I remembered the old brown corduroy one I wore on my first day with the Dumborough.)

On this particular afternoon I had shortened my stirrups by several holes. I had observed, in some steeplechasing photographs in an illustrated paper, that the jockeys rode with their knees ever so much higher than mine. This experiment caused me to feel important and professional but less secure in the saddle. And when Cockbird made a sudden swerve (quite needlessly alarmed by a blackbird that flew out of the hedge which we hugged so as to make the field as large as possible) I almost lost my balance; in fact I nearly fell off. Dixon said nothing until we were on our way home, and then he merely remarked that he'd never believed in riding very short. "They always say that for a point-to-point there's nothing like sticking to the old-fashioned hunting seat." I took the hint, which was a wise one.

Much depended on Cockbird; but much more depended on me. There were moments when I felt acutely conscious of the absolute nullity of my past as a race-rider. It wasn't easy to discuss the event when one was limited by a tacit avowal that one had no idea what it would feel like. The void in my experience caused circumlocutions. My only authority was Stephen, whose well-known narrative of last year's race I was continually paraphrasing. The fact that the Ringwell country was so far away added to the anxious significance of my attempt. How could we—humble denizens of an inglorious unhunted region—hope to invade successfully the four-day-a-week immensity which contained the Colonel and his coveted Cup?

Such was the burden of my meditations while I lugged the garden roller up and down the tennis lawn after tea, while the birds warbled and scolded among the laurels and arbutuses in the latening March twilight and Aunt Evelyn tinkled Handel's "Harmonious Blacksmith" on the piano in the drawing-room.

III

It will have been observed that, in the course of my career as a sportsman, I was never able to believe that I could do a thing until I had done it. Whatever quality it was which caused this tentative progress toward proficiency, it gave intensity to everything that I did. I do not claim that it was unusual—this nervousness of mine about my first point-to-point race. On the contrary, I am sure that it was a normal and exemplary state of mind. Anyone who cares to do so is at liberty to make fun of the trepidations which a young man carries about with him and conceals. But there is a risk in such ridicule. As I remember and write, I grin, but not unkindly, at my distant and callow self and the absurdities which constitute his chronicle. To my mind the only thing that matters is the resolve to do something. Middle-aged retrospection may decide that it wasn't worth doing; but the perceptions of maturity are often sapless and restrictive; and "the thoughts of youth are long, long thoughts", even though they are only about buying a racing-cap.

A week before the races I went to London and bought a cap with a jutting peak; it was made of black silk, with strings that hung down on each side until they had been tied in front. I had remarked, quite casually, to Stephen, that I supposed a top-hat was rather uncomfortable for racing, and he had advised me about the cap, telling me to be sure to get one which came well down over my ears, "for there's nothing that looks so unworkmanlike as to have a pair of red ears sticking out under your cap". Whereupon he pulled one of mine, which, as he said, were big enough to catch any wind there was.

I also bought a weight-cloth. The Heavy Weight Racers had to carry fourteen stone, and after Dixon had weighed me and my hunting saddle on the old weighing machine in the harness room, we came to the conclusion that, assuming our antiquated machine to be accurate, I should be required to carry twelve pounds of lead.

"Thank heaven it wasn't thirteen," I thought, as I went into the stable to give Cockbird a few well-washed carrots.

He certainly was looking an absolute picture, though Dixon said he'd like to get a shade more of the meat off him. As he nipped playfully at my sleeve I marvelled at my good fortune in being the possessor of such unparalleled perfection.

With an access of elation I ran back to the house in a hail-storm. The sun was out again by the time I was upstairs brushing my hair for luncheon. I got out my new cap and tried it on before the glass. Then Miriam bumped into the room with a can of hot water, and as I hadn't time to snatch it off I stood there with the strings hanging down, looking, no doubt, a bit of a fool.

"Oh, sir, you did give me a turn!" she ejaculated, "I'd hardly have known you in that there jockey-cap!" She added that I'd be the death of them all before I'd done.

During luncheon Aunt Evelyn remarked that she did so hope it wouldn't be wet for the point-to-points. She had never seen one in her life, but she had once been to Dumborough Races, which she considered dangerous. Fortunately for her peace of mind, she still visualized a point-to-point as a sort of paper-chase, and I said nothing to counteract this notion, although I did not want to minimize the grandeur of next week's events. Aunt Evelyn's intense love of horses made Cockbird the object of an admiration which almost equalled my own. This, combined with her unshakeable faith in Dixon, gave her a comfortable feeling that I was quite safe on Cockbird. But when Miriam, rather tactlessly, blurted out, "Mr. George hasn't half got a lovely jockey-cap!" she showed symptoms of alarm.

"Oh, I do hope the jumps won't be very big!" she exclaimed. To which I replied, somewhat boastfully, that I meant to get over them whatever they might be like.

"I'm going over to walk round the course with Stephen on Sunday. He says it's a course that wants knowing," I said, helping myself to some more tapioca pudding.

Stephen had warned me that I shouldn't be able to stay at the Rectory for the Races, because his mother was already "in such a muck-sweat about it" that the topic was never touched on in her presence. So I bicycled to Dumbridge, took the slow train which explored Sussex on Sunday mornings, got out at a wayside station, and then bicycled another seven miles to the course. (The seven-mile ride saved me from going on to Downfield and changing on to the branch line which went to the station close by the course.) These exertions were no hardship at all on that dusty spring day; had it been necessary, I would gladly have bicycled all the whole thirty miles from Butley and back again. Nothing in my life had ever appeared more imperative than that I should walk round that "three and a half miles of fair hunting country" and memorize each obstacle in the sequence. I wanted to carry home in my cranium every inch of the land over which Cockbird wou I strenuously hoped, stride with his four legs.

In the meantime I had plenty to occupy my mind pleasantly as I pedalled seriously along the leafless lanes. I already knew that part of the Ringwell country moderately well; I could identify most of the coverts by their names, and I ruminated affectionately on the rainy February days when I had gone round and through them in a hot and flustered gallop with the mud from the man in front of me flying past my head. Eagerly I recognized the hedges and heavegates which I had jumped, and the ruddy faces of the Ringwell sportsmen accompanied my meditations in amicable clusters.

Memories within memories; those red and black and brown coated riders return to me now without any beckoning, bringing along with them the wintry smelling freshness of the woods and fields. And how could I forget them, those evergreen country characters whom once I learnt to know by heart, and to whom I have long since waved my last farewell (as though at the end of a rattling good day)? Sober-faced squires, with their civil greetings and knowing eyes for the run of a fox; the landscape belonged to them and they to the homely landscape. Weather-beaten farmers, for whom the activities of the Hunt were genial interludes in the stubborn succession of good or bad seasons out of which they made a living on their low-lying clay or wind-swept downland acres.

These people were the pillars of the Hunt—the landowners and the farmers. The remainder were merely subscribers; and a rich-flavoured collection of characters they were, although I only half-recognized them as such while I was with them.

There was loquacious old Mr. Dearborn; formerly a none-too-successful stockbroker, and now a gentleman of leisure, who enjoyed himself on a couple of spavined screws which (he continually asserted) were worth at least a couple of hundred apiece and as clever as cats, though he'd never given more than thirty pounds for a horse, and rarely went as high as that; both of them, as Stephen said, looked lonely without a gig behind them. Old Dearborn jabbered his way through the days, attaching himself to one group of riders after another until a fox was found; at the end of a good hunt he would always turn up again, puffing and blowing and purple in the face, but voluble with enthusiasm for the way his horse had got over "one of the ugliest places you ever saw in your life". However tedious he may have been, the Ringwell field wouldn't have been the same without him.

Many an exuberant voice and lively countenance I could revive from that vanished cavalcade. But I can't help thinking that the best man of them all was "Gentleman George", as we called him. George was a grey-haired groom; Mr. Clampton, his middle-aged master, was "something in the City"—a natty untalkative little man, who came out in queerly cut clothes and a low-crowned hat. Mr. Clampton kept three stout-hearted weight-carriers, but he seldom hunted more than one day a week. George put in as many days as possible; he called it "keeping the guv'nor's 'osses well in work". No day was too long and no fence too hairy for George and the guv'nor's 'osses. At the most remote meets he would trot up—his fine-featured open face subdued to the decorum of servitude and a jolly twinkle for ever lurking in his keen eyes. (He was a man who could condense more meaning into a single wink than most political speakers can put into a peroration.) Always he had his free and easy hail for the hunt-servants (to whom he could generally give some useful information during the day); for the gentry he reserved a respectful rap of his hat-brim and a sonorous "Mornin', sir". However curt his utterances were, the tones of his voice seemed to imply the underlying richness and vigour of his vitality. He knew every inch of the country backwards, and the short-tailed grey who was his favourite had done fourteen seasons with those hounds since Mr. Clampton first bought him as a five-year-old from a farm in County Waterford.

The great joke about George was his method of acting as second horseman when his worthy master was out hunting. This, of course, should have meant that he kept as much as possible to the roads and handed the horse over to his employer as soon as the first horse had done as much galloping and jumping as was considered good for him. Not so George, who was seldom more than two fields away from hounds, however hard they ran. Times without number I have seen him come crashing through some black-looking fence and then turn to shout back at the irresolute Mr. Clampton, "Shove 'im at it, sir; there's a big old ditch on the landing side!" And at the end of a gallop, when both horses were smoking hot, he would dismount with the utmost gravity and exchange horses with his master, who had even been known to go home first, leaving his privileged retainer to knock holes in the fences in a late afternoon hunt.

In him I seem to be remembering all that was warm-hearted and exhilarating in my days with the Ringwell, for he showed a special interest in Stephen Colwood and myself, and was never so well contented as when he was showing us the way over an awkward place or giving us the benefit of his ripe experience and intimate knowledge. There was some-

174

thing noble about him. And so (I choose to think) it was for "Gentleman George" that I kept the kindliest of my meditations as I was bicycling to the point-to-point course.

*　　　*　　　*

It was peaceful and pleasant to be squatting on a gate and opening the package of sandwiches that Miriam had made me. The gate opened on to a boggy lane which ran through Cruchett's Wood—a well-known covert. But Cruchett's Wood was beginning to look more idyllic than sporting now; it was dotted with primrose bunches, and the wild anemones were numerous. Although I saw them with placid appreciation my uppermost thought was that the country was drying up nicely; deep going was believed to be a disadvantage to Cockbird, who was supposed to possess a turn of speed which he would have more chance of showing if the ground were dry.

The early afternoon was quiet and Sunday-like as I sat with half a ham-sandwich in my hand; a saffron butterfly fluttered aimlessly along the hedge; miles away the grey-green barrier of the downs overlooked the inactive Weald, and I thought I'd rather like to be up there, by the old windmill on Ditchbury Beacon.

Discarding this unsportsmanlike notion I went on my way; half an hour later my uncompanioned identity had been merged in my meeting with Stephen and we were very deliberately inspecting the first few fences. There was a stake-and-bound hedge on a bank which we didn't much like the look of. While we were still planted in front or it the cheery voice of Arthur Brandwick hailed us with "That's a place where you'll have to take a pull at your old horse, Steve." With him was Nigel Croplady, wearing white gaiters and puffing a cigar; his somewhat supercilious recognition of my existence made me feel that I had no business to be there at all. Croplady was on the Point-to-Point Committee; he had helped to plan out the course and had supervised the making up and trimming of the fences.

"I'm not at all sure we oughtn't to have made the course a bit stiffer," he remarked.

Brandwick replied that he wouldn't be saying that if he were having a bump round it himself.

Croplady expressed regret that he wasn't able to ride the horse he'd entered for the Heavy Weights. "That infernal knee of mine went groggy again while I was playing golf on Thursday. But I've got 'Boots' Brownrigg to ride him for me, so he ought to be in the picture all right."

I gathered that "Boots" Brownrigg was in the "Blues" and had "ridden a clinking good finish at the Guards' Meeting at Hawthorn Hill the other day".

Brandwick told us that he'd asked Roger Pomfret to ride his young horse. "He's a mutton-fisted beggar; but the horse is a bit nappy, and young Roger'll be the man to keep him going at his fences."

Every syllable they uttered made my own private aspirations more preposterous and perishable: my optimism was at a very low ebb as we plodded across a wet pasture to the next obstacle, which had a wide ditch on the take-off side.

"There's another place where there'll be trouble for somebody!" Brandwick's jolly voice seemed to be glorying in the prospect of horses refusing and riders shooting up their necks, or even over their ears. He turned to me. "Let's see, you're running that nice-looking bay of yours, aren't you?"

I replied, "Yes, I'm having a ride."

Croplady became knowledgeable about the entries, which had long been a subject for speculation between Stephen and myself. "Quite a hot lot for the Heavy Weights this year. Two of those Cavalry thrusters who keep their nags in Downfield. They're always rather an unknown quantity."

Stephen remarked that the Colonel's Cup was well worth

winning, and Croplady agreed that it was a much better pot than the Light Weight one, and must have cost the old boy five-and-twenty quid at least.

Silent and disheartened, I longed to be alone again; the presence of the other two made it impossible for me to talk naturally to Stephen, and I couldn't help feeling that they regarded me as an entry which could be ruled out of all serious consideration. The whole affair had become bleakly detached from my previous conception of it. I was just a greenhorn. What chance had I got against Brownrigg of the "Blues", or those ferociously efficient Cavalry officers? Bicycling back to the station with only just time to catch the train, I visualized myself refusing the first fence and colliding with Roger Pomfret, who was associated in my memory with all my most timorous experiments with the Dumborough.

Aunt Evelyn found me an uncommunicative companion that evening; and it wasn't easy to talk to Dixon about the course when I went to the stable next morning. "I hear there's a very hot lot entered for the Heavy Weights," I said, as I watched him polishing away at Cockbird's glossy coat. My tone was, perhaps, a shade extenuatory. I couldn't bring myself to speak of Brownrigg of the "Blues".

Dixon straightened himself and passed his hand along Cockbird's back. "Don't you worry about that. I'll bet our horse gives some of 'em a shaking up!" he replied.

Cockbird gave a playful hoist of his hind quarters and then snatched a mouthful of hay from his rack. I wished that the confidence of my confederates was a little more infectious.

IV

The races were to be on Wednesday. After exercising our minds on the problem of how best to convey Cockbird to the course by two o'clock on that afternoon, we decided against his spending the previous night in Downfield. I suggested that he would probably sleep better in his own stable, which struck me at the time as being improperly expressed, though it was necessary that he should lie down and shut his eyes like everybody else who has something important to do next day. In this connection I should like to mention an odd fact, which is that when I dream about horses, as I often do, they usually talk like human beings, although the things they say, as in most dreams, are only confused fantasias on ordinary speech.

Anyhow, it was arranged that Dixon should ride Cockbird to Dumbridge on Wednesday morning, box him to Downfield put him up at Whatman's "Hunting and Livery Stables" for two or three hours, and then jog him quietly out to the course, which was about four miles from Downfield. In the meantime I was to ride Harkaway to Dumbridge (I felt that this ride would be better for me than if I drove in the dog-cart), catch a later train, and find my way out to the course as best I could. The bag holding my coat, boots, cap, spurs, and weight-cloth would go by the carrier. (I mention these details because they did seem so vastly important at the time.)

Cockbird's night's rest was, I imagine, normal, and it didn't occur to me to speculate about Dixon's. My own slumbers were what I should then have considered inadequate; that is to say, I lay awake for a couple of hours and then slept like a top until Miriam called me at eight.

I came down to breakfast reticent and self-conscious. Patient Miriam's anxiety that I should eat a good breakfast wasn't well received, and Aunt Evelyn's forced cheerfulness made me feel as if I were going to be hanged in the afternoon. She had never made any reference to the possibility of her going to see the Races. I have no doubt that she was as sensitive to the precarious outcome of the adventure as I was. For me the whole day, until my race started, was pervaded by the sinking sensation which is commonly called being in a blue funk. But when the stable-boy (his face clearly showing his awareness that he was at close quarters with momentous happenings) had led Harkaway out of the stable, and I had mounted and was trotting through the village, I was conscious of being as fit as I'd ever been in my life, and of being in some way harmonious with the mild, half-clouded April morning which contained me.

The morning tasted good; but it had only one meaning: it was the morning of the point-to-points. To have understood the gusto of that physical experience would have been to destroy the illusion which we call youth and immaturity—that unforeseeing actuality which retrospection can transmute into a lucid and orderly emotion. The April morning, as I see it now, symbolized a stage which I had then reached in my earthly pilgrimage.

But whatever "bright shoots of everlastingness" my body may have felt, my ordinary mind manifested itself only by instructing me to feel in my coat pocket for the half-sheet of notepaper on which I had written "This is to certify that Mr. G. Sherston's bay gelding Cockbird has been fairly and regularly hunted with the Ringwell Hounds"; to which the M.F.H. had appended his signature, adding the figures of the current hunting season, which I had carelessly omitted. This document had to be shown at the scales, although when I actually got there the Clerk of the Scales forgot to ask me for it. When I was making sure that it was still in my pocket I was still under the misapprehension that unless I could produce it in the weighing tent I should be disqualified from riding in my race.

In the middle of the village I met John Homeward and his van. He was setting out on his monotonous expedition to the county town, and I stopped for a few words with him. His

179

benevolent bearded face made me feel more confident, and so did his gruff voice when he took a stumpy clay pipe out of his mouth to wish me luck.

"I've asked Tom to put half a crown on for me," he said; "it'll be a great day for Butley if you win!" His blunt nod, as I left him sitting under the shadow of his hooded van, was a send-off which stiffened my faltering ambition to prove myself worthy of being the owner of Cockbird.

Remembering how I'd bicycled off to the Ringwell Meeting twelve months before, I thought how flabbergasted I should have been if I'd been told that I should be riding in a race there next year. And in spite of that persistent sinking sensation, I was thankful that, at any rate, I had got as far as "having a bump round". For whatever might happen, I was much superior to any of the spectators. Taking my cap off to two elderly ladies, the Miss Pattons, who passed me on their tricycles with bobs and smiles, I wondered whether it was going to rain. Perhaps the sun came out to show that it was going to be a fine afternoon. When I was on the main road I passed Joey, the lizard-faced stone-breaker, who looked up from his flint-hammering to salute me with a grin.

*   *   *

The sun was still shining when I got to the course; but it was now less easy to believe that I had engaged myself to contribute to the entertainment which was attracting such a crowd of cheerful country folk. I felt extraneous and forlorn. Everyone else seemed intent on having as good a time as possible on such a lovely afternoon. I had come briskly out from Downfield on a two-horse char-a-banc which was waiting outside the station. The journey cost half a crown. Several of my fellow-passengers were "bookies" and their clerks, with their name-boards and giant umbrellas; their jocosities accentuated the crudity of the impact on my mind made by the realistic atmosphere of racing. I did my best to feel as much like a "gentleman-rider" as I could, and to forget that I was making my first appearance in a race.

The air smelt of trodden turf as I lugged my bag (loaded with fourteen one-pound lead weights) into the dressing-room, which was in a farm building under some elms on the crest of the rising ground which overlooked the sparsely flagged course. After dumping the bag in a corner of the dry-mud floored barn, I went out to look for Cockbird and Dixon. They were nowhere to be seen, so I returned to the dressing-room, reminding myself that Dixon had said he wouldn't bring "our horse" out there any earlier than he was obliged to, since it would only excite him; I also realized that I should get "rattled" myself unless I kept quiet and reserved my energies for three o'clock.

The first race was run at two, and mine was the third event on the card, so I bought that absorbing document and perched myself on an old corn-bin to peruse it. "*Riders are requested to return their number-cloths to the Clerk of the Scales immediately after each race.*" I had forgotten that number-cloths existed, so that was news to me. "*These Steeplechases are held subject to National Hunt Rules as to corrupt and fraudulent practices.*" A moment's reflection convinced me that I need not worry about that admonition; it was sufficiently obvious that I had a clean sheet under National Hunt Rules, though it flattered me to feel that I was at last within their jurisdiction.

After these preliminaries I looked inside the card, at the entries. Good heavens, there were fourteen in my race! Several of the names I didn't know. Captain Silcock's "Crumpet". Mr. F. Duckwith's "Grasshopper". Those must be the soldiers who hunted from Downfield. Mr. G. Bagwell's "Kilgrubbin III". That might be—yes, of course, it was—the fat little man on the weedy chestnut, who was always refusing small timber out hunting. Not much danger from him as long as I kept well out of his way at the first fence, and probably he, and several of the others, wouldn't go to the post after all. My own name looked nice.

A blue-jowled man in a yellow waistcoat hurried in, exclaiming, "Can anybody lend me a weight-cloth?" I glanced at my bag and resolved that nothing would induce me to lend him mine (which had yet to receive its baptismal instalment of sweat). Several riders were now preparing for the first race, but no one took any notice of me until ginger-haired Roger Pomfret came in. He had been inspecting the fences, and he wiped his fleshy red face with his sleeve as he sat down and started rummaging in his bag. Tentatively I asked him what he thought of the course. I was quite glad to see someone I knew, though I'd have preferred to see someone else. He chucked me a surly nod, which he supplemented with— "Course? I don't mind telling you, this something course would break the heart of a blank buffalo. It's nothing but twists and turns, and there isn't a something fence you could go fast at without risking your something neck, and a nice hope I've got on that blank sketchy jumper of Brandwick's!"

Before I could think of an answer his boon companion in blasphemy, Bill Jaggett, came in (embellished with a brown billycock hat and black and white check breeches). Jaggett began chaffing him about the something unhealthy ride he was going to have in the Heavy Weights. "I'll lay you a tenner to a fiver you don't get round without falling," he guffawed. Pomfret took the bet and called him a pimply faced bastard into the bargain.

I thought I might as well get dressed up: when I had pulled my boots on and was very deliberately tucking the straps in with the boot-hook, Stephen strolled in; he was already wearing his faded pink cap, and the same elongated and anxious countenance which I had seen a year ago. No doubt my own face matched his. When we'd reassured one another about the superlative fitness of our horses he asked if I'd had any lunch, and as I hadn't he produced a bar of chocolate and an orange, which I was glad to get. Stephen was always thoughtful of other people.

The shouts of the bookies were now loudening outside in the sunlight, and when I'd slipped on my raincoat we went out to see what we could of the Light Weight Race.

*   *   *

The first two races were little more than the clamour and commotion of a passing procession. The "Open Race" was the main excitement of the afternoon; it was run "in colours", and there were about a dozen dashing competitors, several of them well-known winners in such events.

But everything connected with this contest reached me as though from a long way off, since I was half-stupefied by yawning nervousness. They appeared to be accomplishing something incredible by galloping round the course. I had got to do it myself in half an hour; and what was worse, Dixon was relying on me to put up a creditable performance. He even expected me to give the others "a shaking up". Stephen had ceased to be any moral support at all: in spite of his success last year he was nearly as nervous as I was, and when the field for the Open Race had filed out of the hurdle-guarded enclosure, which did duty as the paddock, he disappeared in the direction of Jerry and I was left to face the future alone.

Also, as far as I knew, my horse hadn't yet arrived, and it was with a new species of alarm that I searched for him after I had seen the race start; the paddock and its environs now looked unfriendly and forsaken.

I discovered my confederates in a quiet corner under a hay-rick. They seemed a discreet and unassuming pair, but Dixon greeted me with an invigorative grin. "I kept him away from the course as long as I could," he said confidentially; "he's as quiet as a sheep, but he knows what he's here for; he's staled twice since we got here." He told me that Mr. Gaffikin was about and had been looking for me. "He says our horse stands a jolly good chance with the going as good as it is."

I said there was one place, in and out of a lane, where I'd have to be careful.

We then escorted Cockbird to the paddock; by the time we were there and I'd fetched my weight-cloth, the Open Race was over and the spectators were trooping back again. Among them was Mr. Gaffikin, who hailed me companionably with "Hullo, old chap; jolly sporting of you to be having a ride!" and thereafter took complete charge of me in a most considerate manner, going with me to the weighing tent with the weight-cloth over his arm, while I, of course, carried my saddle.

The winner of the Open Race was weighing in when we arrived, and I stepped diffidently on to the machine immediately after his glorified and perspiring vacation of the seat. Mr. Gaffikin doled out a few leads for me to slip into the leather pouches on the dark blue cloth until I tipped the scale at fourteen stone. The Clerk of the Scales, an unsmiling person with a large sallow face—he was a corn-merchant—verified my name on the card and handed me my number-cloth and armlet; my number was seven; under less exacting conditions I might have wondered whether it was a lucky number, but I was pushed out of the way by Pomfret. Arthur Brandwick (in a grey bowler) was at his elbow, talking nineteen to the dozen; I caught a glimpse of Stephen's serious face; Colonel Hesmon was with him, behaving exactly the same as last year, except that, having already "given the boy the horse", he could no longer say that he was going to do so if he won the race.

While Dixon was putting the last testing touches to Cockbird's straps and buckles, the little Colonel came across to assure me that if Jerry didn't win there was no one he'd rather see first past the judge's waggon than me. He added that he'd taken a lot of trouble in choosing the Cup—"very nice goblet shape—got it from Stegman & Wilks—excellent old firm in the City". But his eye wandered away from Cockbird; his sympathies were evidently strongly implicated in Jerry, who was as unperturbed as if he were being put into a brougham to fetch someone from the station.

Near him, Nigel Croplady was fussing round his horse, with quite a crowd round him.

The terrific "Boots" Brownrigg was puffing a cigarette with apparent unconcern; his black cap was well over his eyes and both hands were plunged in the pockets of a short blue overcoat; from one of the pockets protruded a short cutting whip. His boots were perfection. Spare built and middle-sized, he looked absolutely undefeatable; and if he had any doubts about his own abilities he concealed them well.

Stifling another yawn, I did my best to imitate his demeanour. The bookies were bawling "Two to one bar one". Cockbird, stimulated by publicity, now began to give himself the airs of a real restive racehorse, chucking his head about, flattening his ears, and capering sideways in a manner which caused the onlookers to skip hastily out of range of his heels.

"I say, that's a classy looking quad!" exclaimed a youth who appeared to have purchased the paddock. He consulted his card, and I overheard his companion, as they turned away, saying something about "his jockey looking a bit green". "We'd better back Nigel's horse. They say he'll win for a cert."

For want of anything else to do at this critical moment I asked Dixon whether he'd put Homeward's half-crown on. He said, "Yes, sir; Mr. Gaffikin's man has just done it for me, and I've got a bit on for myself. *It's a good thing;* they're laying five to one about him. Mr. Stephen's horse is at two's."

Mr. Gaffikin chimed in with "Mikado's a hot favourite. *Two to one on,* all along the line!" Mikado was Croplady's horse.

Mr. Gaffikin then tied the strings of my cap in a very tight bow; a bell jangled and a stentorian voice shouted. "Now, then, gentlemen, I'm going down to the post." The blue sky suddenly went white; my heart bumped; I felt dazed and breathless. Then Mr. Gaffikin's remote voice said, "Let me give you a leg up, old chap"; I grabbed hold of the reins, lifted an awkward foot, and was lifted airily on to the slippery saddle: Cockbird gave one prance and then stood still; Dixon was holding him firmly by the head. Pressing my knees into the saddle I overheard Mr. Gaffikin's ultimate advice. "Don't go in front unless you can help it; but *keep well with 'em.*" They both wished me luck and released me to my destiny.

I felt as if I'd never been on Cockbird's back before; everything around me appeared unreal and disconnected from all my previous experience. As I followed Stephen out of the paddock in a sort of equestrian trance I caught sight of his father's face, pale and fixed in its most strenuous expression; his eyes followed his son, on whose departure he was too intent to be able to take in anyone else. We filed through a gate under some trees: "Gentleman George" was standing by the gate; he stared up at me as I passed. "That's the 'oss for my money," was all that he said, but his measured tone somehow brought me to my senses, and I was able to look about me when we got down to the starting place.

But even then I was much more a passenger than a resolute rider with his wits about him to "pinch" a good start. There were seven others. I kept close to Stephen. We lined up uneasily; while the starter (on his dumpy grey cob) was instructing us to keep the red flags on the right and the white flags on the left (which we already knew) I noticed Pomfret (on a well-bred, excitable brown), and Brownrigg (Croplady's bright chestnut looking very compact) already stealing forward on the side furthest from him.

When he said "Go", I went with the others; albeit with no sense of initiative. The galloping hoofs sounded strange. But Cockbird felt strong under me and he flicked over the first fence with level and unbroken stride; he was such a big jumper and so quick over his fences that I had to pull him back after each one in order to keep level with Jerry, who was going his best pace all the way. One of the soldiers (in a top-hat) was making the running with Brownrigg and Pomfret close behind him. At the awkward fifth fence (the one on a bank) Pomfret's horse jumped sideways and blundered as he landed; this caused Pomfret to address him in uncomplimentary language, and at the next obstacle (another awkward one) he ran out to the left, taking one of the soldiers with him. This, to my intense relief, was the last I saw of him. I took it at a place where a hole had been knocked in it in the previous races. The next thing I remember was the brook, which had seemed wide and intimidating when I was on foot and had now attracted a small gathering of spectators. But water jumps are deceptive things and Cockbird shot over this one beautifully. (Stephen told me afterwards that he'd "never seen a horse throw such an enormous lep".) We went on up a long slope of firm pasture-land, and I now became aware of my responsibility; my arms were aching and my fingers were numb and I found it increasingly difficult to avoid taking the lead, for after jumping a couple more fences and crossing a field of light ploughland we soared over a hedge with a big drop and began to go down the other side of the hill. Jerry was outpaced and I was level with Mikado and the Cavalry soldier who had been cutting out the work. As Stephen dropped behind he said, "Go on, George; you've got 'em stone-cold."

We were now more than three parts of the way round, and there was a sharp turn left-handed where we entered on the last half-mile of the course. I lost several lengths here by taking a wide sweep round the white flag, which Brownrigg almost touched with his left boot. At the next fence the soldier went head over heels, so it was just as well for me that I was a few lengths behind him. He and his horse were still rolling about on the ground when I landed well clear of them. Brownrigg looked round and then went steadily on across a level and rather wet field which compelled me to take my last pull at Cockbird. Getting on to better ground, I remembered Mr. Gaffikin's advice, and let my horse go after him. When I had drawn up to him it was obvious that Cockbird and Mikado were the only ones left in it. I was alone with the formidable Brownrigg. The difference between us was that he was quite self-contained and I was palpitating with excitement.

We were side by side: approaching the fourth fence from the finish he hit his horse and went ahead; this caused Cockbird to quicken his pace and make his first mistake in the race by going too fast at the fence. He hit it hard and pecked badly; Brownrigg, of course, had steadied Mikado for the jump after the quite legitimate little piece of strategy which so nearly caused me to "come unstuck". Nearly, but not quite. For after my arrival at Cockbird's ears his recovery tipped me half-way back again and he cantered on across the next field with me clinging round his neck. At one moment I was almost in front of his chest. I said to myself, "I *won't* fall off", as I gradually worked my way back into the saddle. My horse was honestly following Mikado, and my fate depended on whether I could get into the saddle before we arrived at the next fence. This I just succeeded in doing, and we got over somehow. I then regained my stirrups and set off in urgent pursuit.

After that really remarkable recovery of mine, life became lyrical, beatified, ecstatic, or anything else you care to call it. To put it tersely, I just galloped past Brownrigg, sailed over the last two fences, and won by ten lengths. Stephen came in a bad third. I also remember seeing Roger Pomfret ride up to Jaggett in the paddock and inform him in a most aggressive voice that he'd got to "something well pay up and look pleasant".

Needless to say that Dixon's was the first face I was aware of; his eager look and the way he said, "Well done", were beyond all doubt the quintessence of what my victory meant to me. All else was irrelevant at that moment even Stephen's unselfish exultation and Mr. Gaffikin's loquacious enthusiasm. As for Cockbird, no words could ever express what we felt about him. He had become the equine equivalent of Divinity.

*   *   *

Excited as I was, an inward voice cautioned me to control my volubility. So when I had weighed in and returned with my saddle to find a cluster of knowing ones casting an eye over the winner, I just waited soberly until Dixon had rubbed him down, mounted, and ridden serenely out of sight. The Colonel was on the spot to congratulate me on my "nailing good performance" and, better still, to give Dixon his due for having got Cockbird so fit. Those few lofty minutes when he was making much of his horse were Dixon's reward for all the trouble he had taken since Cockbird had been in his charge. He had needed no such incentive, but he asked for nothing more. While he was on his way back to Downfield he may also have thought to himself how he had made me into a good enough rider to have got round the course without a catastrophe. (He had yet to hear full details of the race—including my peculiar acrobatics toward the end, which had been witnessed by no one except the rider of Mikado, who had been kind enough to tell Croplady that he never saw such a thing in his life, which was, I hoped, intended as a compliment.)

When I had watched Dixon's departure I found that public interest was being focused on the Yeomanry Team Race. I was glad to slip away by myself: a few fields out in the country I relaxed my legs on a five-barred gate and contemplated my achievement with as much mental detachment as I could muster. Even in those days I had an instinct for getting the full flavour of an experience. Perhaps I was fortunate in not yet having become aware that the winner of the last race is forgotten as soon as the next one starts.

Forty minutes later I had claimed my cup. (There was no ceremony of presentation.) Having crammed the ebony pedestal into my kit-bag I came out into the paddock with the cup in my other hand. It was convenient to carry, for it had handles to it.

Good-natured Arthur Brandwick came up and offered me a lift back to Downfield. While he was patting me on the back I caught sight of a figure which seemed somehow familiar. A loose-built ruddy-faced young sportsman was talking to a couple of jovial whiskered farmers; he sat on a shooting-stick with his thin neatly gaitered legs straightened; a brown felt hat was tipped well over his blunt nose, for the five o'clock sun was glaring full in his eyes. I wondered who it was he reminded me of. Brandwick answered my unspoken question.

"D'you twig who that is?" I shook my head. "Well, take another good look at him. It's our new Master, and a hell of a good lad he is, from all I've heard. Up till a month ago everyone thought the country'd have to be hunted by a Committee next season. There was something fishy about every one of the coves who'd applied for the Mastership. And then this chap wrote and offered to hunt the hounds himself and put up fifteen hundred a year if we guaranteed him another two thousand. Hardly a soul knew about it till to-day. We're lucky to get him. He's been hunting a good rough country in Ireland the last two seasons and showing rare sport. He's run across for a couple of days to look at us." As we walked away the new Master turned his head and favoured us with a slow and rather blank stare.

"What did you say his name was?" I asked, when we were out of earshot. Brandwick informed me that his name was Milden—Denis Milden—and I knew that I'd known it all the time, though I hadn't set eyes on him since I was eleven years old.

*　　　*　　　*

Aquamarine and celestial were the shoals of sunset as I hacked pensively home from Dumbridge. The Colonel's Cup clinked and joggled against my saddle. Time was irrelevant. But I was back at Butley by eight o'clock, and Cockbird, who had returned by an earlier train, was safe and sound; a little uneasily he wandered around his loose-box, rustling the deep straw, but always going back to the manger for another mouthful of clover-hay. Dixon serenely digested triumph with his tea; presently he would go out to the "Rose and Crown" to hand Homeward his multiplied half-crown and overawe the gossips with his glory.

Absolved and acquiescent was the twilight as I went quietly across the lawn and in at the garden door to the drawing-room. Aunt Evelyn's arm-chair scrooped on the beeswaxed floor as she pushed it back and stood up with her bottle of smelling-salts in her hand. For the first time since my success I really felt like a hero. And Miriam served the dinner with the tired face of a saint that seemed lit with foreknowledge of her ultimate reward. But at that time I didn't know what her goodness meant.

At the end of our evening, when they had gone upstairs with my highly coloured history of the day in their heads, I strolled out into the garden; for quite a long time I stared at the friendly lights that twinkled from the railway station and along the dark Weald. I had brought something home with me as well as the Cup. There was this new idea of Denis Milden as Master. For I hadn't forgotten him, and my persistent studying of *Horse and Hound* and *The Hunting Directory* had kept me acquainted with his career as an amateur huntsman since he had left Oxford. A dog barked and a train went along the Weald . . . the last train to London, I thought. . . .

Going back to the drawing-room, I lit a pair of candles which made their miniature gold reflections on the shining surface of the massive Cup. I couldn't keep my eyes away from it. I looked round the shadowed room on which all my childhood and adolescence had converged, but everything led back to the talisman; while I gazed and gazed on its lustre I said to myself, aloud, "It can't be true that it's really there on the table!" The photograph of Watts's "Love and Death" was there on the wall; but it meant no more to me than the strangeness of the stars which I had seen without question, out in the quiet spring night. I was secure in a cosy little universe of my own, and it had rewarded me with the Colonel's Cup. My last thought before I fell asleep was, "Next season I'll come out in a pink coat."

192

PART SEVEN:
DENIS MILDEN AS MASTER

I

All through an extra fine summer I often wondered how the new Master was getting on in the Ringwell country. But I was almost entirely ignorant of what a Master of Hounds does with himself between April and September. I saw next to nothing of Stephen, who was at Aldershot, learning how to be a Special Reserve officer in the Royal Field Artillery.

My own energies were mainly expended on club cricket matches. I managed to play in three or four matches every week; I was intent on keeping my batting average up to twenty runs per innings, which I found far from easy, though

I had one great afternoon when I compiled a century for Butley against some very mediocre village bowling. Those long days of dry weather and white figures moving to and fro on green grounds now seem like an epitome of all that was peaceful in my past. Walking home across the fields from Butley, or driving back in the cool of the evening after a high-scoring game on the county ground at Dumbridge, I deplored my own failure or gloated over one of my small successes; but I never looked ahead, except when I thought about next winter's hunting. The horses were out at grass; and so, in a sense, was I.

Now and again I accompanied Aunt Evelyn to a garden-party where, as a rule, I competed in a putting tournament, which was a favourite mode of entertainment at the time. Solemnly round someone's garden I putted, partnered, perhaps, by a major's wife or a clergyman's daughter. At Squire Maundle's I won a magnifying glass, and on another occasion I carried off a carriage clock. Aunt Evelyn, who preferred croquet, was extremely pleased, and my leisurely conquests among herbaceous borders and yew hedges accentuated the unique pride I had in my racing Cup. In an exciting match play final on Captain Huxtable's mossy and evergreen-shaded lawn I just failed to capture an ivory paper knife.

One week-end in July Stephen came to stay with us. Artillery life had caused no apparent change in him. We indulged in cheerful nostalgia for the chase. After sniffing the trussed hay in the stable-barn we contemplated Cockbird and Harkaway in the paddock. We sighed for a nice moist winter morning. Stephen was hoping to get "attached" to some Gunners who were conveniently stationed in the Ringwell country. He could tell me nothing about the new Master, except that he was already reputed to be a tireless worker and very well liked by the farmers. For his benefit I unearthed my early impressions of Denis Milden as I had seen him when he was staying at Dumborough Castle as a boy. Already Milden was a very great man in our minds.

My memory of that summer returns like a bee that comes buzzing into a quiet room where the curtains are drawn on a blazing hot afternoon.

*   *   *

By the middle of September Dixon had got the horses up from grass. Cricket matches were out of season, but there hadn't been a spot of rain since the end of June. Robins warbled plaintively in our apple orchard, and time hung rather heavy on my hands. The Weald and the wooded slopes were blue misted on sultry afternoons when I was out for a ruminative ride on one of my indolent hunters. Hop-picking was over early that year and the merry pickers had returned to the slums of London to the strains of the concertina or accordion. I was contemplating an expedition to the West End to order a short-skirted scarlet coat and two pairs of white breeches from Kipward & Son; Craxwell was to make me a pair of boots with mahogany coloured tops. I intended to blossom out at the opening meet as a full-fledged fox-hunter.

The autumn was a period of impatience. I longed for falling leaves and the first of November. The luminous melancholy of the fine September weather was a prelude rather than an elegy. I was only half in love with mists and mellow fruitfulness. I did not dread the dark winter as people do when they have lost their youth and live alone in some great city. Not wholly unconscious of the wistful splendour, but blind to its significance, I waited for cub-hunting to end. Europe was nothing but a name to me. I couldn't even bring myself to read about it in the daily paper. I could, however, read about cubbing in the Midlands; it was described at some length every week in the columns of *Horse and Hound*. Any other interests I had are irrelevant to these memoirs, and were in any case subsidiary to my ambition as a sportsman.

Disapproving Mr. Pennett had left me severely alone since the previous winter, and for the time being my income seemed adequate.

Toward the end of the month Stephen asked me to stay at the Rectory. He had escaped from Aldershot and was about to join his new brigade, which was quartered in the Ringwell country. Both his brothers were still serving their country in foreign parts.

The first morning I was there we got up at four o'clock, fortified ourselves with boiled eggs and cocoa, and set off on bicycles to a cubbing meet about eight miles away. The ground was still as hard as a brick, and we had decided to save the horses' legs for later on and see what we could "from our flat feet". Cock-crowing dimness became daylight; the road was white and dry, but the air smelt of autumn. I saw Milden again, in the glinting rays of a quiet scarlet-orbed sunrise; he was on a compact little roan horse; among his hounds outside some gryphoned lodge-gates he leant forward in diplomatic conference with a communicative keeper. The "field" consisted of a young lady with a cockaded groom and a farmer on an unclipped and excited four-year-old. A few more riders turned up later on when the hounds were chivvying an inexperienced cub up and down a wide belt of woodland. After the first invigorating chorus in the early morning air had evoked our enthusiasm the day soon became sultry: pestered by gnats and flies we panted to and fro, and then followed the hunt to another big covert.

By ten o'clock we had both of us lost our early ardour; they had killed a cub and now a brace had gone to ground in a warren. Stephen told me that the Master was mad keen on digging out foxes, which in that and many other parts of the country were too plentiful for good sport later in the season.

While cheering his hounds up and down the woods he had several times passed us; but he was engrossed in his job and scarcely gave us a glance

When we arrived at the rabbit-warren I could at first see nothing of him but the back of his old mulberry coat; his head and shoulders were half underground; he had just put a terrier in and was listening intently for muffled subterranean barkings. Stephen got into conversation with Will, the first whip, who was an old friend of his, since he'd been second whip under the previous huntsman (the ineffectual Ben Trotter). I didn't dare to hope that Milden would remember me, but when he straightened himself and swivelled a jolly red face in my direction I gazed at him with humble expectancy.

I drew his face blank; for his eyes travelled on toward the first whip and he exclaimed, with the temporary Irish brogue which he had acquired while he was hunting the Kilcurran Hounds, "They're a tarrible long time bringing those spades, Will!"

Whereupon he picked up his heavy-thonged crop and whistled some baying and inquisitive bitches away from the rabbit-hole, addressing them in the unwriteable huntsman's lingo which they appeared to understand, judging by the way they looked up at him. "Trinket . . . good ole gal . . . here; Relic; Woeful; Bonnybell; get along bike, Gamesome . . . good little Gamesome"—with affectionate interpolations, and an aside to Will that that Windgall was entering first rate and had been right up in front all the morning . . . "throwing your tongue a treat, weren't ye, little Windgall?" Windgall jumped up at him and flourished her stern.

Soon afterwards the second whip rode through the undergrowth encumbered with spades, and they took their coats off in the dappling sunshine for a real good dig. The crunch of delving spades and the smell of sandy soil now mingled with the redolence of the perspiring pack, the crushed bracken that the horses were munching, and the pungent unmistakeable odour of foxes. However inhumane its purpose, it was a kindly country scene.

Well enough I remember that September morning, and how, when I offered to take a turn with one of the spades, Denis Milden looked at me and said, "Haven't I seen ye somewhere before?" I answered shyly that perhaps he'd seen me at the point-to-points. It seemed providential when Will reminded him that I'd won the Hunt Heavy Weights. Milden casually remarked, "That must be a good horse of yours."

Emboldened by this, I asked whether by any chance he remembered meeting me out with the Dumborough nearly fourteen years before. But for the life of him he couldn't recollect that. "Ye see I've seen such a tarrible lot of new people since then!" he remarked cheerily, pushing his blue velvet cap up from a heated brow. Nevertheless, I toiled back to the Rectory well satisfied with the way I'd managed to remind him of my undistinguished identity, and Stephen exulted with me that the new Master was such an absolutely top-hole chap. "Not an atom of swank about him." It is quite possible that we may both of us have talked with a slight Irish accent when we were telling the attentive Rector all about it during luncheon.

II

October arrived; the drought broke with forty-eight hours' quiet rain; and Dixon had a field day with the new clipping machine, of which it is enough to say that the stable-boy turned a handle and Dixon did the rest. He had decided to clip the horses' legs this season; the Ringwell was a bad country for thorns, and these were naturally less likely to be overlooked on clipped legs, which also were more sightly and dried quicker than hairy ones.

"Only bad grooms let their horses get cracked heels", was one of his maxims. "Only lazy grooms wash the mud off with water" went without saying.

We often spoke about the new Master, who was already the sum and substance of my happy hunting-ground thirty miles away. Dixon remembered him distinctly; he had always considered him the pattern of what a young gentleman ought to be. Frequently I wished Aunt Evelyn's sedate establishment could be transplanted into that well-foxed and unstagnant county. For one thing it was pretty poor fun for Dixon if I were to be continually boxing Cockbird and Harkaway to Downfield or staying at the Rectory; but Dixon seemed satisfied by the bare fact of my being a hunting man.

Resplendent in my new red coat, and almost too much admired by Aunt Evelyn and Miriam, I went off to the opening meet by the early train from Dumbridge to Downfield. Half an hour's ride took me to the kennels, where I joined an impressive concourse, mounted, in vehicles, and on foot. The sun shone after a white frost, and everyone was anxious to have a look at the new Master. My new coat was only a single spot of colour among many, but I felt a tremendous swell all the same. Familiar faces greeted me, and when we trotted away to draw Pacey's Plantation, old Mr. Dearborn bumped along beside me in his faded red coat and blue and white spotted bird's-eye cravat. "This horse ought to have one of you young chaps on his back!" he exclaimed. "Jumps too big for an old buffer like me; never known him put a foot wrong, clever as a cat—(*hold up, will you!*)" . . . his clever hunter having tripped badly on some stones.

He presented me to an affable person on the other side of him—Mr. Bellerby, of Cowslake Manor. Mr. Bellerby was mounted on a fidgety, ewe-necked, weak-middled, dun-coloured mare. He had a straggling sandy beard and was untidily dressed in new clothes which looked all wrong. He seemed to have put them on in a hurry—baggy black coat half-unbuttoned—spurs falling back from loose-fitting, patent-leather boots, starched stock with a horseshoe pin insecurely inserted—badly cut white corduroy breeches; and an absurdly long cane hunting-crop without a thong. He had a mackintosh coat rolled up and strapped on the back of his saddle. He wore moss-green worsted gloves, and his mare's bridle had a browband of yellow and black striped patent leather.

Mr. Dearborn remarked, when we lost sight of him in the crowd outside the covert, that he was a queer fish to look at, but a very warm man in Mincing Lane. "Made a pile of money out in the East; just come to live in our country; built a billiard-room on to his house, I hear; sort of man who might be good for a fifty pound subscription. Fear he's no horseman, however. That dun of his gallops like a train till she gets near a fence, and then digs her toes in. I know all about her, for he bought her in the summer from a neighbour of mine. Pity he didn't ask my advice. I'd have let him have this one for a hundred and twenty. Absolute patent-safety, this one; jump a house if you asked him to!"

Now it so happened that the new owner of Cowslake Manor provided the liveliest incident that I remember out of that day, which was "badly served by scent" as the local scribe reported in the paper. A fox was found in Pacey's Plantation (it was hinted that he'd been put there by Mr. Pacey, a hard-riding farmer who believed in showing the foot people some fun on an opening day). The majority of the field hustled round the outside of the covert, but I thought to be clever and went through by a grassy ride. A short distance in front of me galloped Mr. Bellerby; his hat bounced on his back, suspended by its string, and he was manifestly travelling quicker than he had intended. Someone in front pushed through the gate out of the Plantation, and while we neared it the open gate was slowly swinging back again. It was uncertain which would win, Mr. Bellerby or the gate. I stole past him on his near side, got there just in the nick of time, and retarded the gate with my left hand. Mr. Bellerby bolted through the aperture, narrowly avoiding the gatepost with his right knee. It was an easily managed exploit on my part, since I had Cockbird well under control, and, as usual, he understood what we were about every bit as well as his owner. Mr. Bellerby continued his involuntary express journey across a ridge-and-furrow field, bore down on a weak hedge, swerved, shot half-way up his mare's neck, and came to a standstill while Cockbird was taking the fence in his stride.

After Mr. Pacey's fox had got into a drain half a mile further on, Mr. Bellerby reappeared and besieged me with his gratitude. He really didn't know how to thank me enough or how to congratulate me in adequate terms on what he persisted in describing as my "magnificent feat of horsemanship". It was, he asserted, the most alarming experience he'd ever had since he was run away with down a steep hill in a dogcart years ago in Surrey; he recalled his vivid emotions on that appalling occasion. "Shall I jump out, I thought, or shall I remain where I am? I jumped out! I shall never forget those awful moments!"

Embarrassed by his effusive acknowledgments I did my best to avoid him during the rest of the day, but he was constantly attaching himself to me, and everybody who happened to be near us had to hear all about my marvellous feat of horsemanship.

"Not a second to spare! I really think Mr. Sherston saved my life!" he ejaculated to Sir John Ruddimore, a stolid and rather exclusive landowner who followed the hounds very sedately with an elderly daughter. The local big-wig listened politely to the story; but I felt a fool, and was much relieved when I saw the back of Mr. Bellerby as he tit-tupped away to Cowslake Manor after pressing me to accept a cheroot about eight inches long out of a crocodile-skin case.

I returned to Butley without having exchanged a word with Milden. Whenever I saw him his face was expressionless and he seemed to be unaware of anything except his hounds and what they were doing. Nigel Croplady, however, referred to him by his christian name and led one to suppose that he had been indispensable to him since he had taken the country. But Croplady, I am afraid, was just a little bit of a snob.

For several weeks Milden remained eminently unapproachable, although I diligently went out with his hounds, enlarging my equestrian experience by taking a full thirty-five bobs' worth out of Whatman's hard-legged hirelings. My moneysworth included several heavy falls on my hat, but I took rather a pride in that, since my sole intention was to impress the Master with my keenness. Up to Christmas the hounds showed very moderate sport; scent was bad, but I overheard a lot of grumbling (mainly from unenterprising riders) about Milden being such a slow huntsman. Certainly he seemed in no hurry, but I was always quite satisfied, myself, as long as I had done plenty of jumping by the end of a day.

And our amateur huntsman, as I afterwards discovered, knew exactly what he was doing. As soon as he took over the country he had asserted his independence by getting rid of the Ringwell dog-pack, on which the members had always prided themselves so much. To the prudent protestations of the Committee he replied bluntly that although the doghounds were all right to listen to in the woods, they were too slow for words on the unenclosed downs, and too big and cloddy for the cramped and strongly fenced vale country. He added that Ben Trotter had got them into terrible bad habits and he wasn't going to waste his time teaching them how to hunt.

Shortly afterwards he had bought five-and-twenty couple of unentered bitches at Rugby Hound Sales; so that, when the Ringwell-bred puppies came in from walk, he began the season with no less than thirty-seven couple of unentered hounds. To those people who properly understood hunting his patient methods must have been a welcome contrast to the harum-scarum, hoicking, horn-blowing "which way'd'e go?" performances of the late huntsman.

Denis Milden refused to lift his hounds unless he was obliged to do so, and in this way he taught them to hunt on a catchy scent without looking for help. They learned to keep their noses down, and day after day Milden watched them worrying out the barely workable line of a fox who was half an hour ahead of them; he was deaf to the captious comments of his field and the loudly offered information of would-be helpers who knew which way his fox had gone. The result of this procedure was that after Christmas, when scenting conditions improved, the light-boned bitches began to hunt like blazes; in fact, as he said, "they fairly screamed along", and of the two packs he really couldn't make up his mind which was the better—the big bitches or the little bitches. When the big bitches had pushed an old dog-fox out of Basset Wood and killed him after a fast fifty minutes with only one check, a six-mile point over all the best of the Monday country, the little bitches went one better with a really beautiful hunt from one of the big gorse coverts on the hills. The grumbling contingent now forgot that they'd ever uttered a word of criticism, and for the moment were unable to exercise their grumbling aptitude at all. But the real wiseacres, such as Sir John Ruddimore and Fred Buzzaway, nodded conclusively to one another, as though agreeing that it was only what they'd been expecting all the time.

Fred Buzzaway, whose name has just cropped up casually, was a totally different type of sportsman from that reticent local magnate Sir John Ruddimore (of Rapworth Park). Always fond of a joke, Fred Buzzaway was a blue-jowled dog-faced bachelor, who habitually dressed as though it were going to be a pouring wet day. Bowler hat well down over his ears; dark whipcord coat and serviceable brown breeches; tight and skimpy stock; such was his rig-out, wet or fine. I see him now, splashed with mud, his coat collar turned up, and his head bent against the driving rain. His boots were usually muddy owing to his laudable habit of getting off his horse as often as possible to give it a rest, and during a slow hunt he was often to be seen leading his mount and even running beside it. He was an active man on his feet, and when he wasn't riding to hounds he was following a pack of foot-harriers. Stag-hunting he despised. "Jackasses hunting a carted jackass", he called it. In his youth Buzzaway had been called to the Bar. His friends always said that when he got there he asked for a bottle of "Bass" and never went back again after he had discovered his mistake. From this it may be inferred that he had a wholesome belief in good liquor.

"Beer goes well with beagling," he would remark, "but after a fox-hunt I feel the need for something stronger."

Few of my fox-hunting acquaintances seem to have been taciturn, but Buzzaway, I am inclined to think, outwent them all in consistent chattiness. He enjoyed airing his observations, which were shrewd and homely. He was one of those men whose personal conviction as to which way the hunted fox has gone is only equalled by their expert knowledge, at the end of a gallop, of the ground he went over. His intimacy with minor local topography was unsurpassed by anyone I knew. Even when he had been out with some neighbouring pack, he could reel off the parish names like clockwork. When asked what sort of a day he'd had, he would reply:

"Found in Clackett's Copse, ran a couple of rings, and then out by Hogstye, over the old fosse-way, and into Warthole Wood, where he tried the main-earths and went on into Cuddleswood Park; along the Banks and into Hawk's Rough, back by the Banks into the Park, left-handed by Warthole Wood . . ." and so on, until one could almost have believed that he'd been riding the fox himself instead of one of his low-priced and persevering hunters.

As might be imagined, he was by no means difficult to get to know. At first I was rather scared by the noises he made whenever I was anywhere near him: either he was hustling along close behind me, shouting "Forrard on", or else he was cracking his whip at a straggling hound, or bawling "Hold up" to his horse at a jump, and I felt that I should be the next one to get shouted at. But I soon discovered what a cheery customer he was, and I became one of his best listeners. Needless to say, he was on easy terms with the Master, and it was in his company that I made my first step toward knowing Milden well.

Buzzaway was one of the privileged (or pushful) people who were sometimes to be seen riding along a road beside the huntsman, although Milden's manner was abstracted and discouraging to conversation. More than once I had overtaken the hounds on their way to a meet, but I had always kept unobtrusively at the rear of the procession, which included three second-horsemen, one of them carrying a terrier in a bag. I was so shy that I scarcely ventured to say good-morning when I passed Milden at the meet. But one day in the middle of December I stayed out to the very end on one of Whatman's hirelings; as a rule I started back to Downfield a bit earlier, to catch my train, but it was getting dark early and the hounds had been running hard in the big woods all day, changing foxes several times. Milden was standing up in his stirrups and blowing his horn; the first whip was counting the hounds with little wags of his crops as though conducting a string band. Buzzaway was taking a long pull at his flask, and everyone else had gone home. Will announced that they were all there except Purity.

"Blast that Purity!" muttered Milden, whereupon Purity emerged penitently from the shades of the covert and the cavalcade moved off along the lane.

So it came about that I found myself riding mutely along in the middle of the pack with Buzzaway and the Master. In front of us "Toprail", the hunting correspondent of the *Southern Daily*, wobbled along on his bicycle and accumulated information from the second whip, a melancholy young man named Bill Durrant, whose existence was made no merrier by the horses he had to ride, especially the one he was on—a herring-gutted piebald which, as he had been heard to complain, was "something crool over timber".

"Well, Master," remarked Buzzaway, "you were devilish unlucky when that fresh fox got up in Cowleas Wood! I viewed your hunted fox going back to Danehurst Hatch, and he looked so beat I could almost have caught him myself."

Milden tucked his horn into the case on his saddle. "Beat, was he? We'll catch him next time, never you fear. And we'll hunt *you* when we get short of foxes. I'll be bound you'd leave a good smell behind you!"

Buzzaway grinned with as much pleasure as if he'd been paid the most graceful of compliments. Jabber, jabber, jabber went his tongue, undiscouraged by the inadequate response it met with. And considering the amount of shouting he'd done during the day, it wasn't to be wondered at that Milden was somewhat silent and preferred to munch a large brown biscuit which he produced from his pocket in a twist of paper. Later on, however, he turned to me and asked if I'd got far to go. When he heard that I lived thirty miles away in the next county he said I "must be desperate keen, to come all that way", and my heart glowed with gratitude. But this was nothing compared with what I felt when he continued, "I tell you what, I can put you up at the Kennels any time you like, when you're having a day with us. It's terrible quiet there of an evening, and I'd be glad of someone to talk to. Just drop me a card the day before, and bring your horse as well if you like; or you can find your way out from Downfield somehow if you're on one of Whatman's screws." He tickled my hireling's neck with the end of his crop. "They earn their keep all right, don't they? That poor old sod was out the day before yesterday, I know, for some silly blighter from the barracks landed slap in the middle of my hounds on him. I wish some of those soldiers weren't quite so mad on jumping. It's the only thing they come out for!"

We got to Clumpton crossroads and he said good-night. Buzzaway and I trotted briskly on toward Downfield in a drizzle of rain. I could scarcely believe that I had been invited to stay at the Kennels, and I listened absent-mindedly to my companion's account of a day he'd had with the Cotswold last season when staying with his brother. Ordinarily I should have found this interesting, but the only information I gathered was that though the Cotswold was a niceish country for watching hounds work, the Ringwell needed brains as well as boldness and he asked for nothing better. I then parted from him and clattered into Whatman's cobbled yard.

III

It was close on Christmas, but the weather remained mild, and in the following week I wrote a concise letter offering myself as a guest at Ringwell after Wednesday's hunting—the meet being only a few miles from the Kennels. At home I said not a word about my sudden elevation in the sporting world, and I allowed Aunt Evelyn to take it for granted that I was going to Hoadley Rectory. After I had actually been to the Kennels I could talk about it, but not before. It was too important an event for casual conversation, and even Dixon was kept in the dark about it. Aunt Evelyn had shown the right amount of interest in Denis Milden, remembering him as such a nice-looking boy, and remembering also how she had come across his people in Northamptonshire when she was a girl—a well-known sporting family who had a large place near, she thought, Daventry. I sometimes wished that my own family was like that, for the architecture of my exist-ence seemed meagre, and I wanted to be strongly connected with the hunting organism which at that time I thought of as the only one worth belonging to. And it *was* (though a limited one) a clearly defined world, which is an idea that most of us cling to, unless we happen to be transcendental thinkers.

Staying at the Kennels was the most significant occasion my little world could offer me, and in order that he might share my sublunary advancement I took Cockbird with me. In reply to my reserved little note I received a cheery letter from Denis: he would be delighted to see me and gave detailed instructions about my bag being called for and taken out to the Kennels from Downfield. He told me to be sure to bring a rug for my horse as he was "terrible short of clothing". My belongings were to be conveyed to the Kennels on the "flesh-cart", which would be in Downfield that day. I was surprised that he should take so much trouble, for I had yet to learn how methodical and thorough he was in everything which he undertook.

I remember nothing of that day's hunting; but the usual terse entry in my diary perpetuates the fact that the meet was at "The Barley Mow". "Found in Pilton Shaw and Crump-ton Osiers, but did little with either as scent was rotten. Weather very wet in afternoon; had quite a good hunt of nearly two hours from Trodger's Wood; hounds were stopped in Basset Wood at 4.25." The concluding words, "Stayed at the Kennels", now seem a very bleak condensation of the event. But it did not occur to me that my sporting experiences would ever be called upon to provide material for a book, and I should have been much astonished if I could have foreseen my present efforts to put the clock back (or rather the calendar) from 1928 to 1911.

Yet I find it easy enough to recover a few minutes of that grey south-westerly morning, with its horsemen hustling on in scattered groups, the December air alive with the excitement of the chase, and the dull green landscape seeming to respond to the rousing cheer of the huntsman's voice when the hounds hit off the line again after a brief check. Away they stream, throwing up little splashes of water as they race across a half-flooded meadow. Cockbird flies a fence with a watery ditch on the take-off side. "How topping," I think, "to be alive and well up in the hunt"; and I spurt along the sound turf of a green park and past the front of a square pink Queen Anne house with blank windows and smokeless chimneys, and a formal garden with lawns and clipped yew hedges sloping to a sunk fence. A stone statue stares at me, and I wonder who lived there when the house was first built. "I am riding past the past," I think, never dreaming that I shall one day write that moment down on paper; never dreaming that I shall be clarifying and condensing that chronicle of simple things through which I blundered so diffidently.

But the day's hunting is ended, and I must watch myself jogging back to the Kennels, soaked to the skin but quietly satisfied in my temporary embodiment with the Hunt establishment; beneath a clean-swept sky, too, for the rain-clouds have gone on with the wind behind them. Soon we are passing the village green; a quarter of a mile from the Kennels, Denis Milden blows a long wavering blast to warn the kennel-man and the head-groom that we are almost home. When we turn in at a gate under some trees there are men waiting with swinging stable-lanterns, which flicker on their red jerseys, outside the long range of portable loose-boxes which Denis has put up. He and his whips are quickly off their horses and into the kennel-yard among the jostling hounds. He has told me to find my way indoors and get my tea and a bath. Cockbird is led into a loose-box under the superior eye of Meeston the head-groom, a gruff, uncommunicative man in a long, dirty white kennel-coat. Cockbird gives his head a shake, glad to be rid of his bridle. Then he lowers it, and I pull his ears for a while—an operation which most horses enjoy when they are tired. The place is pervaded by a smell of oatmeal and boiled horseflesh, and the vociferations of the hounds accompany me as I tread stiffly through the darkness to a wicket-gate, and so to the front door of the old wood-built huntsman's house—"the wooden hutch", as we used to call it.

*　　　*　　　*

Welcomed by barks from an elderly Aberdeen and a slim white fox-terrier with a black head, I followed an expressionless young man-servant up the narrow staircase to my room, which was furnished with the bleakest necessities. The house creaked in the wind, and the geyser in the bathroom seemed likely to blow up at any moment. I was downstairs again and had finished my tea before Denis came in from the kennels. However late and wet he returned, he always saw his hounds fed, and it was usually about an hour before he was inside the house. No professional huntsman ever worked harder than he did, and he invariably rode to the meet and home again with his hounds.

Sitting in the poky little living-room on the ground floor, I was surrounded by all his significant personal belongings. There were a few photographs, mostly in silver frames, of his contemporaries at Eton and Oxford, all in hunting or racing clothes; the walls were hung with monotonously executed portraits of horses which he had owned, and there was one large group of four hounds which had won a first prize at Peterborough Hound Show. There was also a coloured drawing of himself winning a University Steeplechase. A few standard sporting books (including Lindsay Gordon's poems, and the leather-backed volumes of the *Foxhound Kennel Stud-Book*) filled a small bookcase. The letters and papers on his writing-table were very tidily arranged. On the sideboard were racing-cups and a huge silver tray "presented by the members of the Kilcurran Hunt as a testimony of their appreciation of the sport he had shown them during his Mastership". There were several foxes' masks among the pictures, with place and date of death in small white lettering: one or two brushes were tucked behind picture frames, and a fox's pad was mounted as the handle of a paper knife. Finally (and there was only just enough room for it) an upright piano with a pianola apparatus attached to it, demonstrated that he was fond of a bit of music. A record of Dvorak's "New World" Symphony appeared to be his only link with Europe. But he had the advantage of me as regards foreign travel, since he had once been to Budapest to play in a polo tournament. (He told me this at dinner, when we were saying how superior the English were to all foreigners.)

It was after half-past six when he came in. He seemed to take me for granted already, but he assured me once again that he was "terrible pleased to have someone to talk to". He threw off his wet hunting coat and slipped into a ragged tweed jacket which the silent servant Henry held out for him. As soon as he had swallowed a cup of tea he lit his pipe and sat down at his writing-table to open a pile of letters. He handed me one, with a grimy envelope addressed to "Mr. Milden, The Dog Kennels, Ringwell". The writer complained that a fox had been the night before and killed three more of his pullets, and unless he could bring the dogs there soon there wouldn't be one left and they'd really have to start shooting the foxes, and respectfully begging to state that he was owed fifteen shillings by the Hunt for compensation. Many of Denis's letters were complaints from poultry keepers or from small farmers whose seeds or sown ground had been ridden over when the land was wet. I asked what he did with these, and he replied that he sent them on to old McCosh, the Hunt secretary. "But when they look like being troublesome I go over and talk to them myself."

I found afterwards that he had a great gift for pacifying such people, to whom the Hunt might have been an unmitigated nuisance if it hadn't been an accepted institution. The non-hunting farmers liked to see the Hunt, but they disliked the marks it left on their land. The whole concern depended on the popularity and efficiency of the Master, and the behaviour of the people who hunted. Denis Milden's predecessor in the Mastership had been too lavish with indiscriminate five-pound notes; consequently the petitioners for compensation had begun to regard the Poultry and Damage Fund as a regular friend in need, and complaints from poultry farmers were far too frequent. To hear Denis talk about them one might have thought that hens were the enemies of society instead of being the providers of that universally respected object, the egg.

Watching him open those letters was an important step in my sporting education. Until then I had not begun to realize how much there was to be done apart from the actual chivvying of the foxes. Thenceforward I became increasingly aware that a successful day's hunting was the result of elaborate and tactful preparations, and I ceased to look upon an angry farmer with a pitchfork as something to be laughed at. In the meantime I wished he would go upstairs and change his wet clothes.

But he sat there in his muddy boots for almost an hour, writing letters in his careful calligraphy and filling in his diary—a log-book of details such as which horses had been out, where foxes had been found, and so on.

It was eight-thirty by the time he'd had his bath and was shouting from the top of the stairs to Mrs. Timson, the buxom grey-haired cook: "Mrs. Timson! Tell Henry to put that dinner on."

When that dinner had been put on and eaten (there was a large joint of beef, I remember) he asked me to play some music. I treadled away at the pianola, while he dozed in a shabby arm-chair with Moll, the fox-terrier, on his knees, and a litter of newspapers at his carpet-slippered feet. I had ambled to the end of a musical comedy arrangement ("*The Geisha*" I think it was) and was bundling the perforated music-roll back again with reverse motion when he suddenly heaved himself out of the chair, yawned, remarked that he'd give anything to be able to play the piano properly, whistled to the dogs, and turned them out into the night for an airing. He then lit a couple of candles, extinguished the unshaded oil-lamp, led the way upstairs, and hoped I'd sleep all right. All this sounds humdrum, but I have since then spent many a much duller evening with people who were under the impression that they were talking brilliantly. I have never cared greatly about highly sophisticated persons, although some of them may seek to enlarge their intellectual experience by perusing my modest narrative.

Lying awake that night I listened to the wind which was making queer noises round the flimsily constructed house. Once or twice there was an outburst of hound music from the kennels. Through the thin partition wall I could hear the grunts and snores of the stablemen, whose dormitory was next to the spare room. The blind on my window flapped. I thought how different staying at Ringwell Kennels was from what I'd expected. Yet it seemed exactly like what it ought to be. I wondered whether old Cockbird was asleep out in his loose-box. Thought what an odd character the head-groom looked, and how surprised Stephen would be when I told him all about my visit. Meditated on the difference between Denis hunting the hounds (unapproachable and with "a face like a boot") and Denis indoors—homely and kind and easy to get on with; would he really want me to come and stay with him again, I wondered. And then I fell into so sound a sleep that the stablemen on the other side of the partition wall failed to awake me when they got up at some unearthly hour and went down the dark stairs with their clumping boots to begin their work in the damp December morning.

IV

I must pass rather rapidly through the remainder of that season and the one which followed it. While Denis continued to show splendid sport, my own achievements included learning to identify the majority of the hounds by their names. This I did mainly while "walking out" with them on non-hunting days. The road by the Kennels had wide green borders to it, and along these we used to loiter for an hour or two at a time; the full-fed bitches, their coats sprinkled with sulphur, were continually being spoken to by name, and in this way I silently acquired information. I cannot say that I ever became anything of a judge of their shape and make, or that my knowledge has since proved profitable; but I knew Brightness from Brevity, Ramble from Roguery, and Wavelet from Watercress, and this enabled me to show an intelligent interest and to share the Master's enthusiasm for his favourites; I could speciously agree that, although Tempest was a beautiful bitch to look at, she was by no means what she might be when it came to hunting. Peerless, on the other hand, was worthy of her appellation, and frequently hit off the line when the others were at a loss to know which way their fox had gone across a bit of cold ploughland.

My regular visits to the Kennels, and the facility with which I echoed the Master's ideas and opinions, bolstered up my self-complacence and gave me a certain reflected importance among the members of the Hunt, which I should otherwise have lacked. I now wore the Hunt button and was regarded as being "in the know"; people like Colonel Hesmon and Fred Buzzaway would ask me whether I could tell them where the meets were likely to be the week after next. A few words of praise from Denis were, however, what I most wanted. Opportunities for earning his approval were not numerous; but now and again, when he was on a sticky jumper and I happened to be with him in a run, he would shout "Go on, George". Probably there was a big brambly hedge to be got over, and I would cram at it, not caring whether I took a heavy fall so long as I had the privilege of giving him a lead; the bigger the hole I made in the hedge the better pleased he was. He was a strong and patient horseman, and since the country was for the most part rough and "trappy" and the going deep on the heavy clay soil, he rode very deliberately at the fences. While everyone else was fully occupied in keeping with the hounds at all, Denis never seemed to have half his mind on the horse he was riding. His eyes were on the hounds, and he went over the country, as we used to say, "as if it wasn't there".

During January and February in his first season I had many good days with the Ringwell, riding anything I could hire or borrow when I hadn't one of my own to bring out. Stephen hunted regularly from his barracks, and shared my appreciation of Denis. He was ready, he said, to knock anyone off his horse who uttered a word of criticism against the huntsman.

His main ambition in life being to hunt a pack of hounds himself, he appointed himself a sort of amateur second whipper-in, and he was never so happy as when Denis asked him to watch the end of a covert or stop some hounds when they had divided and a few couple were away on the line of a second fox. Stephen called me a lucky old devil to be staying at the Kennels so often. He liked soldiering well enough, but the horses were his real interest. The guns, he said, were nothing but a nuisance, and he, for one, had no wish to chuck shells at anyone.

During the month of March my movements were restricted by the Coal Strike. There were no trains, and I missed some of the best hunts of the season. But I had a few days with the Dumborough and made myself conspicuous by jumping every fence I could find.

Dixon, who had been rather out of it, now came in for the solemnities of preparing Cockbird for the point-to-points. I ran him in a few "Open" races, but found that he couldn't go quite fast enough, though he jumped faultlessly and once finished third in a field of a dozen. Thanks to his reliability I was beginning to have quite a high opinion of myself. The Ringwell Races were late in April that year. Denis rode his best horse in the Heavy Weights and beat me by three lengths. His victory seemed to me quite appropriate, and everyone wanted him to win. It had never occurred to me that I should finish in front of him. Good-natured Mr. Gaffikin was there again to give me a leg-up, and he praised me for my improved handling of my horse. He assured me that if I'd won the Race two years running I should never have been able to get my hat on again—a remark which appeared to cause him extreme satisfaction, for he repeated it more than once, with a lady-killing laugh. (The inference was that I should have suffered from "a swelled head".)

I saw very little of Denis during that summer, which was a

wet one, and bad for my batting average. Having made only fifteen runs in my last seven innings I was glad enough to put away my cricket-bag, and by the second week in September I was back at the Kennels for a prolonged stay. There was a new lot of horses, and Denis, who badly needed someone to talk to, always had a spare one for me to ride.

* * *

Ringwell cubbing days are among my happiest memories. Those mornings now reappear in my mind, lively and freshly painted by the sunshine of an autumn that made amends for the rainy weeks which had washed away the summer. Four days a week we were up before daylight. I had heard the snoring stable-hands roll out of bed with yawns and grumblings, and they were out and about before the reticent Henry came into my room with a candle and a jug of warm water. (How Henry managed to get up was a mystery.) Any old clothes were good enough for cubbing, and I was very soon downstairs in the stuffy little living-room, where Denis had an apparatus for boiling eggs. While they were bubbling he put the cocoa-powder in the cups, two careful spoonfuls each, and not a grain more. A third spoonful was unthinkable.

Not many minutes afterwards we were out by the range of loose-boxes under the rustling trees, with quiet stars overhead and scarcely a hint of morning. In the kennels the two packs were baying at one another from their separate yards, and as soon as Denis had got his horse from the gruff white-coated head-groom, a gate released the hounds—twenty-five or thirty couple of them, and all very much on their toes. Out they streamed like a flood of water, throwing their tongues and spreading away in all directions with waving sterns, as though they had never been out in the world before. Even then I used to feel the strangeness of the scene with its sharp exuberance of unkennelled energy. Will's hearty voice and the crack of his whip stood out above the clamour and commotion which surged around Denis and his horse. Then, without any apparent lull or interruption, the whirlpool became a well-regulated torrent flowing through the gateway into the road, along which the sound of hoofs receded with a purposeful clip-clopping. Whereupon I hoisted myself on to an unknown horse—usually an excited one—and set off higgledy piggledy along the road to catch them up. Sometimes we had as many as twelve miles to go, but more often we were at the meet in less than an hour.

The mornings I remember most zestfully were those which took us up on to the chalk downs. To watch the day breaking from purple to dazzling gold while we trotted up a deep-rutted lane; to inhale the early freshness when we were on the sheep-cropped uplands; to stare back at the low country with its cock-crowing farms and mist-coiled waterways; thus to be riding out with a sense of spacious discovery—was it not something stolen from the lie-a-bed world and the luckless city workers—even though it ended in nothing more than the killing of a leash of fox-cubs? (for whom, to tell the truth, I felt an unconfessed sympathy). Up on the downs in fine September weather sixteen years ago. . . .

It is possible that even then, if I was on a well-behaved horse, I could half forget why we were there, so pleasant was it to be alive and gazing around me. But I would be dragged out of my day dream by Denis when he shouted to me to wake up and get round to the far side of the covert; for on such hill days we often went straight to one of the big gorses without any formality of a meet. There were beech woods, too, in the folds of the downs, and lovely they looked in the mellow sunshine, with summer's foliage falling in ever-deepening drifts among their gnarled and mossy roots.

*   *   *

"What you want is a good, hard, short-legged horse well up to your weight and able to get through the mud and do a long day," remarked Denis one afternoon in October.

We had been out from seven till four, with a good long spell of digging to finish up with. Having said this he settled himself in his chair, lit his pipe, and applied his mind to the Racing Intelligence in *The Sportsman* with an air of having settled the matter once and for all. The sort of horse he had described was the sort of horse everyone in the Ringwell country wanted; but Denis was never afraid of uttering an honest unvarnished exactitude.

I suggested that such a horse might cost more money than I could conveniently afford.

"Put a fiver on Michaelmas Daisy for the Cambridgeshire. She's at 100 to 8. I'm having a tenner on each way myself," he replied, without turning his head.

Although I'd never had more than half a sovereign on a horse in my life, and that was only at point-to-points, I risked two pounds ten shillings each way, and Michaelmas Daisy did it by half a length.

Soon afterwards Denis took me to see a dealer on the other side of the country, and there we found the very horse I wanted. The dealer (an amusing Irishman whose deportment I must for once decline to describe) was anxious to oblige the M.F.H. and knocked ten pounds off the price. Sunny Jim was mine for ninety pounds. He was a short-tailed, corky-looking bay with a habit of grinding his teeth as he jogged along the roads. And that is really all I intend to say about him, except that he was well worth the money and approved of by Dixon as a real old-fashioned sort. I could just manage fifty pounds out of my own money, so my fortuitous forty pounds saved the situation. Harkaway was now transferred to Aunt Evelyn's dogcart, where he conducted himself with dignity and decorum.

The opening meet therefore, found me prosperous and complacent, exhibiting my new horse to the Rev. Colwood, Buzzaway, "Gentleman George", and all the rest of my Ringwell friends, and successfully competing with Stephen and his brother officers from the barracks. But a couple of weeks before Christmas the continuity of things was abruptly fractured by an event which caused a terrible to-do among the supporters of the Ringwell Hounds, myself included. Just as we had all settled down to a record-breaking season, the Master handed in his resignation. A lawn-meet at Rapworth Park was rendered positively funereal by the announcement, and Mr. McCosh, the stolid purple-faced Hunt secretary, swallowed a stiff brandy and soda as if a posset of poison was the sole solution for the blow which had made him so huffy.

It had been a recognized fact that for Denis Milden the Ringwell country was only a stepping-stone to higher things. Nobody had hoped that he would remain with a provincial hunt for ever. But this was sudden. He had sometimes talked to me about his prospects of getting a better country, but he could be as dumb as a post when he had a motive for silence, and he had given me no inkling of a change before the morning when he came down to breakfast with a letter in his hand and informed me that he'd been elected Master of the Packlestone. He said it with satisfied sobriety, and I did my best to seem delighted. Now the Packlestone Hunt, as I knew well enough, was away up in the Midlands. And the Midlands, to put it mildly, were a long step from Butley. So Denis, as I might have expected, was to be translated to a region which I couldn't even visualize. It meant that he was going out of my existence as completely as he had entered it. Every time I returned to the Kennels I found greater difficulty in making my voice sound convincing while I conjectured to him about the attractive qualities of his new country.

In the meantime, as if to tantalize the Ringwellites, the

bitches excelled themselves. The only consolation was that he couldn't take them with him. A new Master was secured, but no one felt much confidence in him or the future. The less they knew about him the more they shook their heads over his inevitable fallibilities. Already it was rumoured that he was the slowest amateur huntsman in England; and now he was proposing to hunt the hounds himself two days a week.

When I discussed Denis Milden's departure with people out hunting they often assumed that I should be going with him. I replied guardedly that I hadn't thought about it yet, although the truth was that I had thought of little else. I had to acclimatize myself to the disconsolate idea of a Ringwell country where I should once again be reduced to the status of a visiting nonentity. But one evening when Denis was un-usually bright and communicative (after a good day in the nice bit of grass country close to the Kennels) he turned his blunt kindly face in my direction (he was at his writing-table with a lot of letters to answer), and remarked: "I'll have to get you up to Packlestone somehow. It's too sad for words to think of leaving you behind!" When he said that I knew that he intended me to go with him. And Denis had a habit of getting his own way.

PART EIGHT:
MIGRATION TO THE MIDLANDS

~~~~~~~~~~~~~~~~~~~~~~~~~~~~~~~~~~~~~

I

When Dixon arrived at the Packlestone Kennels in the middle of October, with my four hunters and a man under him, he was realizing an ambition which must often have seemed unattainable. To break away from Butley for a season in a country which adjoined such notable names as the Quorn, the Pytchley, and Mr. Fernie's—well might he have wondered how it had been brought about! But there we were and Aunt Evelyn had been left to drive through a lonely winter with Harkaway and the stable-boy—now nearly

222

eighteen and promoted to the dignity of wearing Dixon's top-hat and blue livery coat.

From the moment when Denis had first suggested my going with him, I had made up my mind to do it. Nevertheless, the fact remained that I couldn't afford it. I was putting myself in a false position in more ways than one: financially, because I should be spending my whole year's income in less than six months; and socially, because the people in the Packlestone Hunt quite naturally assumed that I was much better off than I really was. I had discussed it all with Denis in April. Denis was good at making fifteen shillings do the work of a pound, and he was fond of talking about money. But when I divulged my exact income he gravely admitted that the pecuniary problem was no easy one to solve. He found it a terrible tight fit himself; it had been costing him over two thousand a year out of his own pocket to hunt the Ringwell country, and the Packlestone would be an even more expensive undertaking. When we had worked it out on paper— so much a week for my own keep while living with him in the huntsman's house, so much for keep of horses, so much for my two men's wages, and so on—the total came to more than ten pounds a week. And I had to buy two more horses into the bargain; for, as he said, I couldn't have any fun with less than four, "and it absolutely defeats me how you're going to get four days a week even then".

"I'll have one good season, anyhow, whatever happens afterwards!" I exclaimed. All that I needed, at that juncture, was a miraculous doubling of my income.

The mental condition of an active young man who asks nothing more of life than twelve hundred a year and four days a week with the Packlestone is perhaps not easy to defend. It looks rather paltry on paper. That, however, was my own mental position, and I saw nothing strange in it, although I was well aware of the sort of things the family

223

solicitor would be saying if he were permitted to cast his eye over the half-sheet of paper on which Denis had figured out my probable expenditure. Aunt Evelyn, however, cordially approved of my project, and after consultations with Stephen (who thought it a magnificent effort) and the delighted Dixon, I bought a couple of horses in April and May, and then settled down to a summer of strict economizing. Cricket matches, at any rate, were an inexpensive occupation.

Of my new horses one was a bit of a gamble. He was a very good-looking chestnut who "roared like a bull". He had the reputation of being a wonderful performer, and I bought him, rather recklessly, for forty-three guineas, at the end of a sale at Tattersalls, after the horse I'd hoped to buy had gone for double the price I was able to bid for him. A vet. from the Ringwell country drew my attention to the handsome chestnut, assuring me that he'd heard from a safe quarter that he was a remarkable jumper. Throughout the summer Dixon and I contemplated him and speculated on his problematical capabilities (which proved to be in accordance with the information given me by the vet.).

My other new horse was the result of a chance ride in a point-to-point. He was a well-bred old horse, a great stayer, and a very bold jumper. After I had ridden him in two races, in both of which he finished strongly, though not fast enough to win, his owner offered to let me have him for thirty pounds admitting that he found him too much of a handful out hunting. I was already aware that the old chestnut had a very hard mouth, but I took him gladly and he carried me well and kept my weight down by causing me considerable exertions by his impetuous behaviour.

When Dixon brought the horses up from benighted Butley I had already been at Packlestone the best part of a month, riding Denis's horses out cub-hunting, getting to know my way about the country, and becoming acquainted with a few of the local characters, most of whom were extremely civil to me on account of my close connection with their new Master. I did my best to live up to my too conspicuous position, mainly by saying as little as possible and looking as knowledgeable as I knew how. My acclimatization to the new conditions was made easier by the fact that not many people came out cubbing before the middle of October. We clattered out in the misty mornings to disturb the important fox coverts and the demesnes of influential personages in the Hunt, and I learned to recognize the new faces in more or less segregated instalments.

On one occasion we went to a place about twenty miles from the Kennels, had two days' routing up the cubs, and spent two nights in a large country house. The owner was away, probably at some German spa: the furniture was draped in dust-sheets, and I remember that we had our dinner in a little housekeeper's room. To be there with Denis and his hounds gave me an agreeable feeling of having got into a modernized Surtees novel (though there was little evidence of modernity in what we did and saw). Less agreeable, I remember, was our sixteen-mile ride home on a grilling September afternoon, with the famous Packlestone dog-hounds, who found the dust and heat rather more than they could manage after a long morning.

Life at the Kennels appeared to me almost perfect, especially when I was sitting with Denis in the little room in the huntsman's house and discussing the new country in all its aspects. My approach to the country had been uncritical and eagerly expectant. Once I was settled there I saw it entirely through the eyes of Denis. If he found anything amiss I at once assumed that I had already taken the imperfection into account. For instance, several of the artificial gorse coverts, he said, were very thin; and no right-minded fox would remain in some of the small woods when once the leaves were off and the vegetation had died down. I shook my head and agreed that a lot of the coverts wanted looking after. Several new gorse coverts ought to be planted in the Friday country, which was the best part for riding over. And then there was the wire, which was deplorably prevalent in places, though well marked with red boards in the hedges. In the kennels, too, there was much to be attended to.

The Packlestone country was hunted four days a week. Its character was varied—cow-pastures and collieries being the extremes of good and bad. In some districts there were too many villages, and there were three or four biggish industrial towns. This abundance of population seemed to me an intrusion, and I wished I could clear every mean modern dwelling out of the hunt. For the most part, however, it appeared to be a paradise of jumpable fences, and compared with the well-wooded Ringwell region it was a tip-top country. For the first time in my life I was able to sit down and jump a dozen clear fences without pulling up. In fact, as Denis said, it was a place where I could jump myself silly. Also it had the charm of freshness, and I have always thought that a country becomes less enjoyable as one gets to know it better; in a strange country a twisting hunt seems like a straight one. But this is a truism which applies to many things in life besides riding to hounds.

Foxes were plentiful, except in parts of the Friday country; but there was no shortage anywhere as regards rich-flavoured Surteesian figures. Coming, as I did, from afar, and knowing nothing of their antecedents and more intimate aspects, I observed the Packlestone people with peculiar vividness. I saw them as a little outdoor world of country characters and I took them all for granted on their face value. How privileged and unperturbed they appeared—those dwellers in a sporting Elysium! Half-conscious of the sense of security and stability which they inspired, I watched them and listened to them with a comfortable feeling that here was something which no political upheaval could interrupt.

There was, however, one discordant element in life which I vaguely referred to as "those damned socialists who want to stop us hunting". Curiously enough, I didn't connect socialists with collieries, though there had been a long coal strike eighteen months before. Socialists, for me, began and ended in Hyde Park, which was quite a harmless place for them to function in. And I assured Denis that whatever the newspapers might say, the Germans would never be allowed to attack us. Officers at the barracks were only an ornament; war had become an impossibility. I had sometimes thought with horror of countries where they had conscription and young men like myself were forced to serve two years in the army whether they liked it or not. Two years in the army! I should have been astonished if I'd been told that socialists opposed conscription as violently as many fox-hunting men supported the convention of soldiering.

II

The Packlestone fox-hunters prided themselves on being hail-fellow-well-met—quite a happy family, in fact—though a large one, for there were always between a hundred and a hundred and fifty riders at a Monday meet. The Mondays, which were in the middle of the Hunt, attracted all the regular followers, whereas on Fridays there was a cutting and thrusting contingent from two adjoining hunts, and these people were rightly regarded as outsiders by the true-blue Packlestone residents.

During my October days new faces continually added themselves to the covert-side crowd, and by the time when I began to ride my own horses the fields were fairly representative, and I very soon found myself included in the friendliness for which the Hunt had a reputation, though it was some time before I could say that I felt at home, especially when I was on my old chestnut, who fairly pulled my arms out.

On a bright morning late in October, composed though slightly self-conscious on Cockbird's back outside Olton Gorse, I could look around me and identify the chief supporters of the Hunt. Prominent, owing to his official capacity, was the Field-Master, Bertie Hartby, a keen-faced man whose appointment by Denis had caused a certain amount of controversy. It was said that Hartby was always in too much of a hurry, but there he was, anyhow, intent on doing his best to keep the field in order.

Near him was a highly important personage, Captain Harry Hinnycraft, who for a vast number of years had been Honorary Secretary of the Hunt. "Dear old Captain Harry", as the young ladies called him (for on them he was wont to turn an appreciative eye), was by no means an easy old gentleman to please unless it suited him to be amiable. His unqualified approval of the new Master was balanced by an unconcealed prejudice against his Field-Master, who was, he asserted to all and sundry, "as wild as a hawk", varying this with "mad as a hatter". Compromise was a word of which Captain Hinnycraft had never mastered the meaning; massive and white-moustached on his magnificent weight-carriers, he had always ridden about the Packlestone country with the air of a monarch. He belonged to the old school of country gentlemen, ruling his estate with semi-benevolent tyranny and turning his back on all symptoms of social innovation. Under his domination the Packlestone country had been looked after on feudal system lines. His methods of dealing with epistolary complaints from discontented farmers was to ignore them; in verbal intercourse he bullied them and sent them about their business with a good round oath. Such people, he firmly believed, were put there by Providence to touch their hats and do as they were told by their betters. As might be expected, he had conventional eighteenth-century ideas about what constituted masculine gallantry and sprightly conversation. Captain Harry defied all criticism because he was a complete anachronism. And as such he continued beyond his eightieth year, until he fell into a fishpond on his estate and was buried by the parson whose existence he had spurned by his arrogance.

It may well be wondered how the Hunt had survived the despotism of this old-world grandee, with whom previous Masters had been obliged to co-operate (as "best Master we've ever had" while they reigned, and "good riddance of bad rubbish" when they resigned and left him to find someone to replace them).

An explanation of the continued prosperity of the Packlestone was largely to be found in Mrs. Oakfield of Thurrow Park, a lady who made friends wherever she went. Since her childhood she had been intimately associated with the Hunt, for her father had been Master for more than twenty years. From her large and well-managed estate she set an example of up-to-date (though somewhat expensive) farm-management, and every farmer in the country (except a few stubborn Radicals) swore by Mrs. Oakfield as the feminine gender of a jolly good fellow. As a fine judge of cattle and sheep they respected her; and to this was added her reputation for boundless generosity. The Packlestone farmers were proud to see Mrs. Oakfield riding over their land—as well they might be, for it was a sight worth going a long way to see. A fine figure of a woman she was, they all agreed, as she sailed over the fences in her tall hat and perfectly fitting black habit with a bunch of violets in her buttonhole. This brilliant horsewoman rode over the country in an apparently effortless manner: always in the first flight, she never appeared to be competing for her prominent position; quick and dashing, she was never in a hurry; allowing for the fact that she was very well mounted and knew the country by heart, she was undoubtedly a paragon of natural proficiency. John Leech would have drawn her with delight. I admired Mrs. Oakfield enormously; her quickness to hounds was a revelation to me, and in addition she was gracious and charming in manner. Whether she bowed her acknowledgement to a lifted hat at the meet or cantered easily at an awkward bit of timber in an otherwise unjumpable hedge, she possessed the secret of style. Needless to say, she was the only person in the Hunt who knew how to manage Captain Harry, who always spoke of her as "a splendid little woman". Which brings me back to my original explanation as to how the behaviour of that intractable old gentleman failed to cause as much trouble as one might have expected.

While Captain Hinnycraft lived and bulked big in the middle of the Monday country, all roads in the Wednesday district converged on Mrs. Oakfield at Thurrow Park. Fashionable Friday contained several good-sized estates and many important fox-preservers and staunch supporters, but no predominant personage. Saturday, however, had its unmistakable magnate in Sir Jocelyn Porteus-Porteous of Folesford Hall. The Saturday country was the least popular of the four divisions. Well-wooded, hilly, and sporadically blemished by collieries, it was considered very sporting by those who lived in it. A Saturday hunt was a scrambling, cramped, hound-musical affair, much enjoyed by middle-aged enthusiasts on slow horses. A minor feature which I remember was an abundance of holly trees, which contributed a cosy old-fashioned Christmas atmosphere to my impression of Saturdays. Sunny Jim, my short-tailed, short-backed, short-legged, clever performer, round Saturdays much more to his liking than the other days, with their cut and laid fences, big ditches, and quick bursts across pasture and arable. I was very fond of Jim and I always gave him half of the apple which I produced from my pocket early in the afternoon. He was an artful old customer, and sometimes when he heard me munching my apple he would halt and turn his head to receive his portion. He did this one day when I was loitering with a slack rein along one of the spacious green rides which ventilated the Folesford home coverts. The august presence of Sir Jocelyn happened to be just behind me; his amusement at Sunny Jim's intelligent behaviour is a lucky little stroke of reminiscence, for it is not easy to describe him without seeming a shade discourteous to Porteus-Porteous. (Note the majestic variation in spelling.)

No one could meet Sir Jocelyn and remain blind to the fact that he had a pompous manner. And when he was in the middle of the park at Folesford, with its chain of woodlands and superabundance of foxes and pheasants, he seemed just a little larger than life-size. (He was pardonably proud of the concordant profusion of those sporting incompatibles, the fox and the pheasant.) His ancestral seat (the Porteous family had sat there since Plantagenet times) was, if I remember rightly, a Gothic nucleus with Tudor and Jacobean additions. Unwelcome, from the picturesquely feudal point of view, were the rows of industrial habitations which had cropped up outside his grandiose gateway. These, with the unsightly colliery chimneys, were a lucrative element in his existence, since they represented mineral royalties for the owner of the estate. Nevertheless, his attitude toward such plebeian upstarts was lofty and impercipient: not having been introduced to them, he had not the pleasure of their acquaintance, so to speak. Sir Jocelyn was a short, thick-set, round-legged man with regular features and a moustache. It would be unfair to accuse him of looking complacent, for how could any man look otherwise than comfortable and well satisfied when he had inherited such an amply endowed existence? There was hauteur in his manner, but it was not unkindly, though it was accentuated by his unconscious habit of punctuating his utterances with regularly recurrent sniffs. In this connection I am unable to resist the temptation to reproduce a memorable remark which he once made to me out hunting.

That winter he gave a ball for the coming-out of his eldest daughter. (Mrs. Oakfield gave one in the same week—an intensely exciting week for the graceful nymphs, dashing sparks and diamonded dowagers of the Hunt.)

"When did you last give a ball at Folesford, Sir Jocelyn?" I politely asked him, gazing bashfully at one of his dangling top-boots.

"We have no record [sniff] of any ball at Folesford [sniff]," was his rejoinder.

Why there had never been any balls at Folesford I am still at a loss to understand. But the fact remained. It was [sniff] so. . . And Sir Jocelyn, as I have taken trouble to indicate, was the king of the Saturday country.

III

Anything like an adequate inventory of the Packlestone subscribers is beyond the scope of my narrative—pleasant though it would be to revive so many estimable and animated equestrians. Warm-hearted memory creates a crowded gathering when one has both the dead and the living to draw upon. I have no doubt that the Packlestone field (and its similitude elsewhere) still survives in its main characteristics. Nevertheless, I adhere protectively to my sense of its uniqueness as it was when I was a unit in its hurry of hoofs and covert-side chatter. I can believe in the present day existence of intrepid young ladies, such as were the two Miss Amingtons, who would have perished rather than see someone else jump a big fence without having a cut at it themselves on their game and not over-sound horses.

But are there still such veterans as those who went so well when I was there to watch them? Grey-bearded Squire Wingfield was over seventy, but he took the fences as they came and held his own with many a would-be thruster forty years younger. And there were two or three contemporaries of his who got over the country in a way which I remember with astonishment. Compared with such *anno Domini* defying old birds, jolly Judge Burgess (who came from London as often as his grave duties permitted) was a mere schoolboy. The Judge had returned to the hunting-field at the age of fifty, after thirty years' absence, and he had evidently made up his mind to enjoy every minute of it as he bucketed along on a hollow-backed chestnut who, he affirmed, knew a dashed sight more about hunting than his learned owner.

Regretfully I remember how incapable I was of appreciating many of the ripe-flavoured characters whom I encountered with such regularity. Obvious enough was the newly-rich manufacturer who lived in a gaudy multi-gabled mansion, and asked me, "'Ow many 'orses do *you* reckon to keep?" as he ambled along on a good-looking and confidential grey for which he had given a mint of money. Much more interesting, as I see him now, was Mr. Jariott, an exquisitely polite silver-haired gentleman, who lived alone in a shallow-roofed white-faced house in a discreetly undulating park. As owner of several good coverts, small and easy to get away from, he was a punctilious preserver of foxes. It was said that he knew all his foxes by name, and mourned the loss when one of them was killed. But he would have been horrified if his coverts had been drawn blank, and so far as I could hear, such a thing had never happened. The cut of his clothes

233

was soberly stylish and old-fashioned, and he was shy and sparing in his utterances. I was told that he bred a certain sort of shooting-dog and knew more about that breed than any other man in England. I have an idea that the dogs were golden brown, silky-haired, and elegant. I was only inside his house once, when the hounds met there: the interior left an impression of being only half lived in; I imagined Mr. Jariott as its attentive but lonely inhabitant, and the windows looked vacantly out on the pleasant park from the box-like building.

Not far from Mr. Jarriott's house there was a strip of woodland named Lady Byron's Covert. Years afterwards I discovered that the poet had lived at that house for a short time with that "moral Clytemnestra", his wife, who remained there in her aggrieved seclusion long after his departure to Italy. My knowledge of this seems to explain the impression of haunting unhappiness which the house made on my mind. I should like to know what old Mr. Jariott thought about it all.

Among the younger generation in the Packlestone Hunt the brothers Peppermore were far the most conspicuous, as they would have been in any sporting community. Jack and Charlie Peppermore were both under twenty-five and had already broken most of their bones. They were well known as amateur race-riders. Jack, the younger of the two, was in temporary retirement from racing, for he had cracked his skull in a hurdle race at the end of the previous winter. This did not prevent him from hunting, and he was usually to be seen out on some borrowed horse which had proved itself completely beyond the control of its owner. Charlie was rather more particular about what he rode, and was, correspondingly, a more reticent character. These brothers did and said pretty well what they pleased in the Packlestone Hunt; ungovernable as their exploits often were, they were always forgiven, for they were brilliant riders and had all the qualities which make a young man popular in sporting circles. They were reckless, insolent, unprincipled, and aggressively competitive; but they were never dull, frequently amusing, and, when they chose, had charming manners. In fact, they disarmed criticism, as do all people whom one cannot help admiring. And they were the last people in the world to expect excuses to be made for them. To me, at that time, they were the epitome of a proficiency and prestige to which I could not even aspire. As I remember them now they were desperately fine specimens of a genuine English traditional type which has become innocuous since the abolition of duelling. But if they were to some extent survivals from a less civilized age, they were also the most remarkable light-weight sparks I had ever seen, and as they treated me with amiable tolerance I considered myself fortunate in knowing them. Nor have I ever altered that opinion. For in their peculiar way the Peppermores were first-rate people, and I felt genuinely sorry when I read in an evening paper, a year or two ago, that Charlie Peppermore had fallen at the first fence in the Grand National when riding the favourite.

To say that the brothers were competitive is to put it mildly. Whenever it was a question of getting there first, they were absolute demons of energy, alertness, and pugnacious subtlety. In the hunting-field, however, they had little opposition to compete against, and in a fast hunt they were undefeatable. Denis Milden's arrival on the scene of their supremacy reminded them that they must look to their laurels; but Denis showed no awareness of the competitive spirit; his only purpose was to hunt the hounds, and the Peppermores very soon recognized this and did all they could to help him. To have aroused their animosity would have been no joke. Once when I was at a race meeting I happened to be standing beside Charlie Peppermore when an inferior amateur rider fell off, rather ignominiously, at a plain fence in front of the enclosure. The horse went on alone and the jockey scrambled to his feet and as he walked past us on the other side of the rails Charlie Peppermore laughed. It was the most insulting, contemptuous laugh I'd ever heard. Then he turned to me and drawled: "How I hate that man! I've been waiting years to see him break his neck."

Of the two, Denis liked Jack the better, and one Saturday in the middle of November Jack was invited to dinner, with two other young sportsmen who lived not many miles away. This was an uncommon event at the Kennels, and Mrs. Timson rolled up her sleeves and prepared a more than usually solid repast. When we came in from hunting Denis got out two bottles of champagne, and some full-bodied port. As a rule we drank water, and the quantity of champagne and port I had consumed in my whole life could easily have been contained in half a dozen bottles of each fluid.

"I'm afraid drink isn't too good for old Jack since that accident of his," remarked Denis, rubbing his forehead dubiously.

He then told the inscrutable Henry to "get that dinner on at eight o'clock" and went upstairs to dress—the occasion demanding the special effort of a dinner jacket.

Jack arrived alone in his father's brougham—a means of conveyance which seemed vaguely improbable. Peppermore senior had been a well-known figure on the Turf, and he still owned a few steeplechasers which his sons trained and rode. But he had become heavy and uncommunicative with middle age, and now devoted himself almost entirely to looking after his farms and house property (and putting the brake on his sons' transactions with bookmakers). Jack was the mainspring of the party, and his drawling voice kept us all amused with a continuous flow of chaff and chatter. I wish I could remember a single word of it, but as I am unable to do so I can only say that I made one with the other guests in compliant appreciation while Denis was an attentive host, and the champagne promoted conviviality in moderation.

After dinner we moved into the other room, which was even smaller. A decanter of port quickly became empty, and a certain rowdiness began to show itself among the company, though there was nothing to be rowdy about and very little space to be rowdy in. When Henry brought in the replenished decanter Jack picked up a small tumbler and filled it. From his demeanour it appeared that the competitive spirit was asserting itself. A few minutes afterwards he threw a chair across the room and the other young men felt it incumbent on them to imitate him. He then refilled his glass with port, standing in the middle of the room, drank it straight off, and collapsed on the floor. The little room was overheated by a roaring fire, and the air was heavy with cigar smoke. The other two guests were a bad colour, and I went to the front door to get a breath of the frosty air.

When I returned Denis was looking after the prostrate Jack; he was, I remember, making a hissing sound, as if he were grooming a horse, and I thought what a kind-hearted chap he was. He told me to go and order Jack's carriage. I went to the kitchen, and informed them in subdued tones that Mr. Peppermore was very drunk. The coachman grinned and went out to put his horse in.

I then became aware that I was very drunk myself, and soon afterwards Denis gently assisted me up the steep stairs to my room. I was glad, next morning, that I hadn't got to go out hunting. This was the first occasion on which I was authentically intoxicated.

To give a detailed account of my doings during that winter would be to deviate from my design. It may be inferred, however, that I enjoyed myself wholeheartedly and lived in total immunity from all intellectual effort (a fact which may seem rather remarkable to those who recognize a modicum of mental ability in the writing of these memoirs). For more than six months I perused nothing except newspapers; my pen was employed only in a weekly scribble to Aunt Evelyn, and in copying out hound pedigrees for Denis, who had discovered that the Packlestone pedigree books had not been kept with quite that precision which was proper for such essential registers. In this manner I acquired an exact knowledge of the ancestries of Vivian, Villager, Conquest, Cottager, and various other eloquent veterans whose music had made the ploughman pause with attentive ear on many a copse-crowned upland.

Odd enough it seems now, that detached and limited segment of my human experience, when I was so completely identified with what I was doing and so oblivious to anything else. Coming in at the end of a long day, I would find Dixon giving the horses their evening feed, or brushing the mud off the horse I had ridden in the morning. Dixon was entirely in his element now, and he had the intense satisfaction of going out as my second horseman. Dignified and discreet he rode about with the other grooms, catching an occasional glimpse of me as I popped over a fence into a lane or cantered across a field toward a covert. My broken-winded chestnut had turned out to be a wonderful hunter; I could trot him up to a high post and rails in absolute assurance that he would hop over it like a deer, and on such occasions he made me look a much better rider than I really was. In spite of all the hard work he had to get through, Dixon was permanently happy that winter. He was breathing the same air as the renowned Peppermores, whose steeplechasing successes made them heroic in his eyes; and every day he was within speaking distance of Denis Milden, for whom he had a corresponding admiration. When Denis came to my loose-box and told Dixon that the horses were looking fine, Dixon was more delighted than he knew how to say; and, of course, as befitted a "perfect gentleman's servant", he said almost nothing at all.

This was all very pleasant; but when the afternoons began to lengthen and I had just paid another bill for forage I was forced to look ahead and to realize that the end of the winter would find me in no end of a fix. Fix wasn't the word for it as I thought of what Mr. Pennett's face would look like when I told him that I was £300 in debt. "Out-running the constable" was the phrase which would leap to his lips as sure as eggs were eggs. It was certain that I should be obliged to sell two of the horses at the end of the season. I couldn't afford to keep them even if there had been room for them all in Aunt Evelyn's stable, which there wasn't (two of them had been put up in the village in the previous autumn).

Faced by the prospect of intensive economy in the summer and with no apparent hope of another season in the Midlands, my exodus from the Kennels meant disconsolate exile from all newly discovered delights. Even Denis had to admit this, but he had already more than enough to occupy his mind. The Packlestone people, too, were so pleasant to me, and so unaware of my inadequate resources, that I was frequently reminded of my forlorn future. Quite a number of them would be going to London for the season, or had houses there already, and when they hoped to see something of me in the summer I felt a very passable imitation of an impostor. Those prosperous and well-appointed lives had no connection with my economical future at Butley.

239

Nevertheless, I had visions of Mayfair in June, and all the well-oiled ingredients of affluence and social smartness. I saw myself sauntering about the sunlit streets, well dressed and acquainted with plenty of people with large houses in Berkeley, Grosvenor, or Portman Squares, free to attend fashionable functions and liberated from my previous provincialism. Fantasias of polite society swept through me in wave on wave of secret snobbishness; life in London when Hyde Park would be bright with flowers assumed the enchanting aspect of a chapter in an elegantly written novel about people with large incomes and aristocratic connections. Sighing for such splendours, I knew that I was only flattening my nose against the plate-glass window of an expensive florist's shop. Orchids were altogether beyond my income. I never doubted the authenticity of those enjoyments. My immature mind, as was natural, conjectured something magical in such allurements of prosperity. It was the spectacle of vivid life, and I was young to it.

As for the Packlestone people and their London season—well, it is just possible that they weren't quite as brilliant as I imagined. Ascot, Lords, a few dances and theatres, dull dinner-parties, one or two visits to the Opera—that was about all. Since I have grown older I have heard the hollow echoes in that social apparatus; but at that time I was only aware that it was an appropriate sequel to the smoothly moving scene in which I was involved. It was a contrast, also, to the rigorous routine of life at the Kennels. All this contributed to a feeling of finality in my proceedings.

The hunting season ended with an ironic glory at the point-to-points, where the inestimable Cockbird managed to win the Heavy Weight Race after Denis had set him an example in the Light Weights. Everyone agreed that it was a great day for the Kennels, and a couple of weeks afterwards I was back at Butley.

I had been away from Aunt Evelyn for nearly seven months. I found it none too easy to tell her all about my eventful absence from the quiet background which awaited my return. Everything was just the same as ever at Butley; and as such it was inevitable that I found it monotonous. Sadly I sold my brilliant chestnut for thirty-six guineas at Tattersalls. He was bought by a Belgian officer. I couldn't bring myself to part with any of the others; neither could I discuss my sporting future with Dixon, although he was undoubtedly aware of my difficulties. After an unpalatable interview with Mr. Pennett I succeeded in extracting an extra hundred pounds; and so I settled down to an uneventful summer, restless and inwardly dissatisfied, unable to make up my mind what to do next winter, and healthier than I'd ever been in my life, which (though I wasn't aware of it at the time) was saying a good deal from the physiological point of view.

I have said I found everything at Butley unchanged. This was not so, for faithful Miriam had retired from domestic service and her manner of doing so had been consistent with her character. During the winter Aunt Evelyn had persuaded her to go to the seaside for a fortnight's holiday, as her health had become noticeably bad. While at the seaside she unobtrusively died of heart failure. To the last, therefore, she managed to avoid being a trouble to anyone. This was a severe blow to Aunt Evelyn. She had been so much a part of the place that I had taken for granted everything she did. Now that she was gone I began to regret the occasions when I had shown her too little consideration.

Stephen Colwood, who was now a well-contented Artillery subaltern, had stayed for a week with us at the Kennels, and had departed saying that the Packlestone country was a fox-hunter's Paradise and had spoilt him for anything else.

And so my life lumbered on into July, very much with the

same sedate manner of progress which characterized Homeward's carrier's van. I went to see the Hunt horses sold at Tattersalls, at the end of May, and there I encountered many of the friendly Packlestone faces. After that I avoided London: the mystery and magnificence of Mayfair remained remote from my callow comprehension of terrestrial affairs.

PART NINE: IN THE ARMY

I

Sitting in the sunshine one morning early in September, I ruminated on my five weeks' service as a trooper in the Yeomanry. Healthier than I'd ever been before, I sat on the slope of a meadow a few miles from Canterbury, polishing a cavalry saddle and wondering how it was that I'd never learned more about that sort of thing from Dixon. Below me, somewhere in the horse-lines, stood Cockbird, picketed to a peg in the ground by a rope which was already giving him a sore pastern. Had I been near enough to study his facial expression I should have seen what I already knew, that Cockbird definitely disliked being a trooper's charger. He was regretting Dixon and resenting mobilization. He didn't even belong to me now, for I had been obliged to sell him to the Government for a perfunctory fifty pounds, and I was lucky not to have lost sight of him altogether. Apart from the fact that for forty-five months he had been my most prized possession in the world, he was now my only tangible link with the peaceful past which had provided us both with a roof over our heads every night.

My present habitation was a bivouac, rigged up out of a rick-cloth and some posts, which I shared with eleven other troopers. Outside the bivouac I sat, with much equipment still uncleaned after our morning exercises. I had just received a letter, and it was lying on the grass beside me. It was from someone at the War Office whom I knew slightly; it offered me a commission, with rank of captain, in the Remount Service. I had also got yesterday's *Times*, which contained a piece of poetry by Thomas Hardy. "What of the faith and fire within us, men who march away ere the barn-cocks say night is growing grey?" I did not need Hardy's "Song of the Soldiers" to warn me that the Remounts was no place for me. Also the idea of my being any sort of officer in the Army seemed absurd. I had already been offered a commission in my own Yeomanry, but how could I have accepted it when everybody was saying that the Germans might land at Dover any day? I was safe in the Army, and that was all I cared about.

I had slipped into the Downfield troop by enlisting two days before the declaration of war. For me, so far, the War had been a mounted infantry picnic in perfect weather. The inaugural excitement had died down, and I was agreeably relieved of all sense of personal responsibility. Cockbird's welfare was my main anxiety; apart from that, being in the Army was very much like being back at school. My incompetence, compared with the relative efficiency of my associates, was causing me perturbed and flustered moments. Getting on parade in time with myself and Cockbird properly strapped and buckled was ticklish work. But several of the officers had known me out hunting with the Ringwell, and my presence in the ranks was regarded as a bit of a joke, although in my own mind my duties were no laughing matter and I had serious aspirations to heroism in the field. Also I had the advantage of being a better rider than a good many of the men in my squadron, which to some extent balanced my ignorance and inefficiency in other respects.

The basis of my life with the "jolly Yeo-boys" was bodily fatigue, complicated by the minor details of my daily difficulties. There was also the uncertainty and the feeling of emergency which we shared with the rest of the world in that rumour-ridden conjuncture. But my fellow troopers were kind and helpful, and there was something almost idyllic about those early weeks of the War. The flavour and significance of life were around me in the homely smells of the thriving farm where we were quartered; my own abounding health responded zestfully to the outdoor world, to the apple-scented orchards, and all those fertilities which the harassed farmer was gathering in while stupendous events were developing across the Channel. Never before had I known how much I had to lose. Never before had I looked at the living world with any degree of intensity. It seemed almost as if I had been waiting for this thing to happen, although my own part in it was so obscure and submissive.

I belonged to what was known as the "Service Squadron", which had been formed about three weeks after mobilization. The Yeomanry, as a Territorial unit, had not legitimately pledged themselves for foreign service. It was now incumbent upon them to volunteer. The squadron commanders had addressed their mustered men eloquently on the subject, and those who were willing to lay down their lives without delay were enrolled in the Service Squadron which for a few weeks prided itself on being a *corps d'élite* under specially selected officers. Very soon it became obvious that everyone would be obliged to go abroad whether they wanted to or not, and the too-prudent "Home-service" men were not allowed to forget their previous prudence.

As I sat on the ground with my half-cleaned saddle and the

War Office letter, I felt very much a man dedicated to death. And to one who had never heard the hiss of machine-gun bullets there was nothing imaginatively abhorrent in the notion. Reality was a long way off; I had still to learn how to roll my "cloak" neatly on the pommel of my saddle and various other elementary things. Nor had I yet learned how to clean my rifle; I hadn't even fired a shot with it. Most of the letters I had received since enlisting had been bills. But they no longer mattered. If the War goes on till next spring, I ruminated, I shall be quite rich. Being in the army was economical, at any rate!

The bugle blew for twelve o'clock "stables", and I went down to the horse-lines to take Cockbird to the watering trough. Everyone had been talking about the hundred thousand Russians who were supposed to have passed through England on their way to France. Away across the hot midday miles the bells of Canterbury Cathedral refused to recognize the existence of a war. It was just a dazzling early autumn day, and the gaitered farmer came riding in from his fields on a cob.

As I was leading Cockbird back from watering I passed Nigel Croplady, who was one of the troop leaders. He stopped to speak to me for a moment, and asked whether I had heard from Denis Milden lately; this caused me to feel slightly less *déclassé*. Calling the officers "sir" and saluting them still made me feel silly. But I got on so comfortably with the other troopers that I couldn't imagine myself living in the farmhouse with the officers. The men in my troop included two or three bank clerks, several farmers' and small tradesmen's sons, a professional steeplechase jockey, and the son of the local M.P. (who had joined at the outbreak of war). They were all quite young. Discipline was not rigorous, but their conduct was exemplary. I soon found out, however, that they were by no means as efficient as I had expected. The annual training had been little more than a three weeks' outing. "Solidarity on parade" was not an impressive element in the Service Squadron, and squadron drill was an unsymmetrical affair. Nevertheless, we talked impressively among ourselves as though being ordered abroad was only a matter of weeks or even days, and our officers regaled us with optimistic news from the Western Front. Many of us believed that the Russians would occupy Berlin (and, perhaps, capture the Kaiser) before Christmas. The newspapers informed us that German soldiers crucified Belgian babies. Stories of that kind were taken for granted; to have disbelieved them would have been unpatriotic.

When Aunt Evelyn came over to see me one hot Sunday afternoon I assured her that we should soon be going to the Front. Her private feelings about "men who march away" had to be sacrificed to my reputability as a cavalryman. She brought with her some unnecessarily thick shirts and the news from Butley, where I was, I surmised, regarded as something of a hero. Enlistment in the Army had not yet become an inevitability. Everyone thought it splendid of me to set such an example. I shared their opinion as we went along the horse-lines to look at Cockbird. Aunt Evelyn was bearing up bravely about it all, but it was no good pretending that the War had brought any consolations for her, or for Dixon either.

Dixon had taken Cockbird to Downfield the day after mobilization, and had returned home just in time to interview some self-important persons who were motoring about the country requisitioning horses for the Army. Harkaway had been excused on grounds of old age, but the other two had been taken, at forty pounds apiece: the plump mowing-machine pony was not yet needed for a European war.

When we had finished making a fuss of Cockbird I took Aunt Evelyn up to inspect our bivouac; several of my companions were taking their Sabbath ease in the shade of the rick-cloth; they scrambled shyly to their feet and Aunt Evelyn was friendly and gracious to them; but she was a visible reminder to us of the homes we had left behind us.

As I lay awake after "lights-out", visual realizations came to me of the drawing-room at Butley, and Miriam's successor bringing in the oil-lamp; I had not liked it when I was seeing my aunt into the train at Canterbury—the slow train which took her home in the evening sunshine through that life-learned landscape, which, we all felt, was now threatened by barbaric invasion. I had never thought about her in that way while I was enjoying myself up at Packlestone, and my sympathetic feeling for her now was, perhaps, the beginning of my emancipation from the egotism of youth. I wished I hadn't told her that "we should probably be going out quite soon". She would be lying awake and worrying about it now. The ground was hard under my waterproof sheet, but I was very soon asleep.

*　　　*　　　*

The cloudless weather of that August and September need not be dwelt on; it is a hard fact in history; the spellbound serenity of its hot blue skies will be in the minds of men as long as they remember the catastrophic events which were under way in that autumn when I was raising the dust on the roads with the Yeomanry. But there was no tragic element in my own experience, though I may have seen sadness in the sunshine as the days advanced toward October and the news from France went from one extreme to the other with the retreat and advance of our expeditionary force.

I can remember the first time that I was "warned for guard" and how I polished up my boots and buttons for that event. And when, in the middle of the night, I had been roused up to take my turn as sentry, I did not doubt that it was essential that someone in a khaki uniform should stand somewhere on

the outskirts of the byres and barns of Batt's Farm. My King
and Country expected it of me. There was, I remember, a low
mist lying on the fields, and I was posted by a gate under a
walnut tree. In the autumn-smelling silence the village church
clanged one o'clock. Shortly afterwards I heard someone moving in my direction across the field which I was facing. The
significance of those approaching feet was intensified by my
sentrified nerves. Holding my rifle defensively (and a loaded
rifle, too) I remarked in an unemphatic voice: "Halt, who
goes there?" There was no reply. Out of the mist and the
weeds through which it was wading emerged the Kentish
cow which I had challenged.

*   *   *

By the third week in September the nights were becoming
chilly, and we weren't sorry when we were moved into the
Workhouse, which was quite near the farm where we had
been camping. Sleeping in the Workhouse seemed luxurious;
but it put an end to the summer holiday atmosphere of the
previous weeks, and there were moments when I felt less light-
hearted than I would have admitted to myself at the time.
Soon afterwards young Nunburne (the M.P.'s son) was
whisked away to Sandhurst, his father having decided that he
would be more suitably situated as a subaltern in the Guards.
His departure made a difference but it did not convince me
that I ought to become an officer myself, though Cockbird,
also, had in a manner of speaking, accepted a commission.

For the daily spectacle of Cockbird's discomforts (the most
important of which was the enormous weight of equipment
which he had to carry) had induced me to transfer him to the
squadron commander, who was glad to get hold of such a
good-looking and perfect-mannered charger. Having got a
tolerably comfortable horse in exchange, I now had the satisfaction of seeing Cockbird moving easily about with a light-

249

weight on his back and a properly trained groom to look after him. I felt proud of him as I watched his elegant and pampered appearance.

"Of course you'll be able to buy him back at the end of the War," said the squadron commander; but I knew that I had lost him; it was a step nearer to bleak realization of what I was in for. Anyhow, I thought, Dixon would hate to see old Cockbird being knocked about in the ranks. As for Cockbird, he didn't seem to know me since his promotion.

It must have been about this time that I began to be definitely bored with Yeomanry life. It was now becoming a recognized fact, even in the ranks, that we were unlikely to be sent to the Front in our present semi-efficient condition. It was said too, that "Kitchener had got a down on our Brigade". I remember riding home from a Brigade Field Day one afternoon at the end of September. My horse had gone lame and I had been given permission to withdraw from the unconvincing operations. During three or four leisurely miles back to the Workhouse I was aware of the intense relief of being alone and, for those few miles, free. For the first time since I'd joined the Army with such ardours I felt homesick. I was riding back to a Workhouse and the winter lay ahead of me. There was no hope of sitting by the fire with a book after a good day's hunting.

I thought of that last cricket match, on August Bank Holiday, when I was at Hoadley Rectory playing for the Rector's eleven against the village, and how old Colonel Hesmon had patted me on the back because I'd enlisted on the Saturday before. Outwardly the match had been normally conducted, but there was something in the sunshine which none of us had ever known before that calamitous Monday. Parson Colwood had three sons in the service, and his face showed it. I thought of how I'd said good-bye to Stephen the next day. He had gone to his Artillery; and I had gone to stay at the hotel in

Downfield, where I waited till the Wednesday morning and then put on my ill-fitting khaki and went bashfully down to the Drill Hall to join the Downfield troop. I had felt a hero when I was lying awake on the floor of the Town Hall on the first night of the war.

But the uncertainty and excitement had dwindled. And here I was, riding past the park wall of Lord Kitchener's country house and wondering how long this sort of thing was going to last. Kitchener had told the country that it would be three years. "Three years or the duration" was what I had enlisted for. My heart sank to my boots (which were too wide for my stirrups) as I thought of those three years of imprisonment and dreary discomfort. The mellow happy looking afternoon and the comfortable Kentish landscape made it worse. It wouldn't have been so bad if I'd been doing something definite. But there was nothing to write home about in this sort of existence. Raking up horse-dung before breakfast had ceased to be a new experience. And the jokes and jollity of my companions had likewise lost freshness. They were very good chaps, but young Nunburne had been the only one I could really talk to about things which used to happen before the War began. But there was burly Bob Jenner, son of a big farmer in the Ringwell Hunt; he was in my section, and had failed to get a commission on account of his having lost the sight of one eye. What I should have done without him to talk to I couldn't imagine. I had known him out hunting, so there were a good many simple memories which we could share. . . .

Escape came unexpectedly. It came about a week later. My horse was still lame and I had been going out on the chargers of various men who had special jobs in the squadron, such as the quartermaster-sergeant. One fortunate morning the farrier-sergeant asked me to take his horse out; he said the horse needed sharpening up. We went out for some fieldwork, and, as usual, I was detailed to act as ground scout. My notion of acting as ground scout was to go several hundred yards ahead of the troop and look for jumpable fences. But the ground was still hard and the hedges were blind with summer vegetation, and when I put the farrier-sergeant's horse at a lush-looking obstacle I failed to observe that there was a strand of wire in it. He took it at the roots and turned a somersault. My wide boots were firmly wedged in the stirrups and the clumsy beast rolled all over me. Two young men, acting as the "advance guard" of the troop, were close behind me. One of them dismounted and scrambled hurriedly through the hedge, while the other shouted to him to "shoot the horse", who was now recumbent with one of my legs under him. My well-meaning rescuer actually succeeded in extracting my rifle from its "bucket", but before he had time to make my position more perilous by loading it, Bob Jenner arrived, brought him to his senses with some strong language, and extricated me, half-stunned and very much crushed. The same day I was taken to a doctor's house in Canterbury. It would be hypocrisy to say that I was fundamentally distressed about my badly broken arm. I couldn't have got a respite from the Workhouse in any other way. But if I had been able to look into the future I should have learned one very sad fact. I had seen the last of my faithful friend Cockbird.

II

Staring at my face in a mirror two months after the accident, I compared my pallid appearance with the picture of health I used to see in a small scrap of glass when I was shaving with cold water in the Army. All my sunburnt health and hardihood had vanished with my old pair of breeches (which the nurse who looked after me had thrown away, saying that they made the room smell like a stable) but I had still got my skimpy tunic to remind me that I had signed away my freedom. Outside the doctor's house where I was lodged, another stormy December afternoon was closing in with torrents of rain. Would it ever stop raining, I wondered. And would my right arm ever be rid of this infernal splint? Anyhow, my December face matched the weather in exactly the same way as it had done in August and September.

The Yeomanry were now in a camp of huts close to the town. Every Saturday Bob Jenner or one of the others came to see me; while they were with me my ardour revived, but when I was alone again I found it more and more difficult to imagine myself sharing the discomforts which they described so lightheartedly. But I had only exchanged one prison for another, and after reading about the War in the newspapers for nine weeks, the "faith and fire" within me seemed almost extinguished. My arm had refused to join up, and I had spent more than an hour under an anaesthetic while the doctor screwed a silver plate on to the bone. The fracture wobbled every time I took a deep breath, and my arm was very much inflamed. When I was out for a walk with my arm in a sling I felt a fraud, because the people I passed naturally assumed that I had been to the Front. When my squadron commander came to see me I couldn't help feeling that he suspected me of not getting well on purpose. I still found it impossible to imagine myself as an officer. It was only half an hour's walk to the Yeomanry camp, but I could never get myself to go up there.

The weather had been as depressing as the war news. Like everybody else I eagerly assimilated the optimistic reports in the papers about Russian victories in East Prussia, and so on. "The Russian steam-roller"; how remote that phrase seems now! ... Often I prayed that the War would be over before my arm got well. A few weeks later the doctor said the bone had united and I had another operation for the removal of the plate. In the middle of January I was allowed to return home, with my arm still in a splint.

Since my accident I had received a series of letters from Stephen, who was with an ammunition column on the Western Front and apparently in no immediate danger. He said there wasn't an honest jumpable fence in Flanders; his forced optimism about next year's opening meet failed to convince me that he expected the "great contest", as he called it, to be over by then. Denis had disappeared into a cavalry regiment and was still in England. For him the world had been completely disintegrated by the War, but he seemed to be making the best of a bad job.

It was five and a half months since I had been home. I had left Butley without telling anyone that I had made up my mind to enlist. On that ominous July 31st I said long and secret good-byes to everything and everyone. Late in a sultry afternoon I said good-bye to the drawing-room. The sunblinds (with their cords which tapped and creaked so queerly when there was any wind to shake them) were drawn down the tall windows; I was alone in the twilight room, with the glowering red of sunset peering through the chinks and casting the shadows of leaves on a fiery patch of light which rested on the wall by the photograph of "Love and Death". So I looked my last and rode away to the War on my bicycle. Somehow I knew that it was inevitable, and my one idea was to be first in the field. In fact, I made quite an impressive inward emotional experience out of it. It did not occur to me that everyone else would be rushing off to enlist next week. My gesture was, so to speak, an individual one, and I gloried in it.

And now, although Aunt Evelyn fussed over me as if I were a real wounded soldier, I was distinctly conscious of an anti-climax. I had looked forward to seeing Dixon again in spite of the sad state of affairs in the stable. But before I had been in the house five minutes Aunt Evelyn had given me some news which took me by surprise. Dixon had gone away to join the Army Veterinary Corps. This had happened two days ago. He was forty-three, but he hadn't a grey hair, and he had stated his age as thirty-five. The news had a bracing effect on me. It wasn't the first time that Tom Dixon had given me a quiet hint as to what was expected of me.

The worst of the winter was over and my arm was mending. Aunt Evelyn talked almost gaily about my going back to the Yeomanry in the spring. She had twigged that it was a comparatively safe location, and I knew from her tone of voice that she was afraid I might do something worse. If she had been more subtle and sagacious she would have urged me to exchange into the Infantry. As it was she only succeeded in stiffening my resolve to make no mistake about it this time. I had made one false start, and as I'd got to go to the Front, the sooner I went the better. The instinct of self-preservation, however, made it none too easy, when I was sitting by the fire of an evening, or out for a walk on a mild February afternoon; already there were primroses in the woods, and where should I be in twelve months' time, I wondered. Pushing them up, perhaps! . . .

But I had struggled through the secret desperations of that winter, and I like to remember myself walking over one afternoon to consult Captain Huxtable about a commission in an infantry regiment. Captain Huxtable, who had always shown an almost avuncular concern for my career, had joined the Army in 1860. He was a brisk, freckled, God-fearing, cheerful little man, and although he was now over seventy, he didn't seem to have altered in appearance since I was a child. He was a wonderful man for his age. Chairman of the local bench, churchwarden, fond of a day's shooting with Squire Maundle, comfortably occupied with a moderate sized farm overlooking the Weald, he was a pattern of neighbourly qualities, and there was no one with whom Aunt Evelyn more enjoyed a good gossip. Time-honoured jokes passed between them, and his manner toward her was jovial, spruce, and gallant. He was a neat skater, and his compact homespun figure seemed to find its most appropriate setting when the ponds froze and he was cutting his neat curves on the hard, ringing surface; his apple-cheeked countenance, too, had a sort of blithe good humour which seemed in keeping with fine frosty weather. He was a man who knew a good Stilton cheese and preferred it over-ripe. His shrewd and watchful eyes had stocked his mind with accurate knowledge of the country-side. He was, as he said himself, "addicted to observing the habits of a rook" and he was also a keen gardener.

Captain Huxtable was therefore an epitome of all that was pleasant and homely in the countrified life for which I was proposing to risk my own. And so, though neither of us was aware of it, there was a grimly jocular element in the fact that it was to him that I turned for assistance. It may be inferred that he had no wish that I should be killed, and that he would have been glad if he could have gone to the Front himself, things being as they were; but he would have regarded it as a greater tragedy if he had seen me shirking my responsibility. To him, as to me, the War was inevitable and justifiable. Courage remained a virtue. And that exploitation of courage, if I may be allowed to say a thing so obvious, was the essential tragedy of the War, which, as everyone now agrees, was a crime against humanity.

Luckily for my peace of mind, I had no such intuitions when I walked across the fields to Butley that afternoon, with four o'clock striking in mellow tones from the grey church tower, the village children straggling home from school, and the agricultural serenity of the Weald widespread in the delicate hazy sunshine. In the tall trees near Captain Huxtable's house the rooks were holding some sort of conference, and it was with a light heart that I turned in at his gate. It happened that as I rang the front-door bell an airship droned its way over the house. Every afternoon that airship passed over our parish, on its way, so it was said, to France. The Captain came out now to watch it from his doorstep, and when it had disappeared he led me into his sanctum and showed me a careful pencil drawing of it, which he had made the first time its lustrous body appeared above his garden. Under the stiff little sketch he had written, "airship over our house", and the date. It was his way of "putting on record" a significant event. Sixteen months afterwards he probably jotted down some such memorandum as this: "Between 11 and 12 this morning, while we were getting in the last load of hay, I distinctly heard the guns in France. A very faint thudding noise but quite continuous as long as it was audible." But he wasn't able to make a neat pencil drawing of the intensive preliminary bombardment on the Somme.

III

As a result of my conversation with Captain Huxtable he wrote a letter about me to the Adjutant at the Training Depot of the Royal Flintshire Fusiliers, which was his old regiment. As far as he was concerned the Flintshire Fusiliers were, as he said, ancient history; but the Adjutant happened to be the nephew of an old brother officer of his, and he jovially remarked that he would perjure himself for once in a way by giving me a good character. For him his old "corps" ranked next below religion, and to be thus almost actively in touch with the regiment gave him deep satisfaction.

His room contained many objects associated with his army life; he had seen garrison service in India; there were mementoes of that; and his little water-colour foreign sketches which I had often seen before. His sword, of course, was hanging on the wall. Everything connected with Captain Huxtable's regimental career had suddenly become significant and stimulating. The Flintshire Fusiliers, which I had so often heard him speak about (and had taken so little interest in) had become something to be lived up to. I would be a credit to him, I resolved, as I went home across the dark fields.

The local doctor had said I might take the splint off my arm next day and that was a step in the right direction. I said nothing to Aunt Evelyn about my conspiracy with her old friend until a week later, when I received a favourable letter from the Adjutant. I was to make a formal application for a Special Reserve commission. The Special Reserve was a new name for the old Militia; a temporary commission in the New Army would have been much the same, but Captain Huxtable wanted me to do the thing properly. Greatly as he admired their spirit, he couldn't help looking down a bit on those Kitchener's Army battalions.

When I broke the news to Aunt Evelyn she said that of course I was doing the right thing. "But I do hate you doing it, my dear!" she added. Should I have to go all the way to Flintshire, she asked. I said I supposed I should, for the depot was there.

And although I agreed with her that it would have been nice if I'd been somewhere nearer, I had a private conviction that I wanted to make my fresh start among people who knew nothing about me. Dixon had said (when he brought Cockbird to Downfield the day after mobilization) that if I had to be in the ranks I ought to have done it somewhere where I wasn't so well known. I found afterwards that there was a great deal of truth in his remark. The Yeomanry would have been more comfortable for me if none of the officers had known me before I joined. I now felt strongly in favour of getting right away from my old associations. Captain Hux-table had given me all I needed in the way of a send-off. Aunt Evelyn was helping at the Voluntary Aid Detachment Hospital, which, as she said, took her mind off things.

Stephen, when I wrote and told him about it, replied that since I was so keen on getting killed I might as well do it properly dressed, and gave me the name of his military tailor, which was a rather unfortunate one—Craven & Sons. He had been expecting to get a week's leave, but it had been "stopped owing to the big strafe" which was imminent (the Battle of Neuve Chapelle happened soon afterwards).

Ordering my uniform from Craven & Sons was quite en-joyable—almost like getting hunting clothes. Situated in a by-way off Bond Street, the firm of Craven & Sons had been established a century ago in the cathedral city of Wintonbury: To the best of my knowledge the firm was exclusively mili-tary, though there may have been a demure ecclesiastical con-nection at the "and at Wintonbury" shop. I was warmly wel-comed by a florid gentleman with a free and easy manner; he might almost have been a major if he had not been so osten-sibly a tailor. He spoke affectionately of the Flintshire Fusiliers ("The Twenty-Fifth" he called them); he had "been up at the depot only the other day", and he mentioned a few of the first and second battalion officers by name; one might almost have imagined that he had played polo with them, so dashing was his demeanour as he twirled his blond moustache. This repre-sentative of Craven & Sons was like the royal family; he never forgot a name. He must have known the Army List from cover to cover, for he had called on nearly every officers' mess in the country during the periodical pilgrimages on which the prosperity of his firm depended. Newly gazetted subalterns found themselves unable to resist his persuasive suggestions, though he may have met his match in an occasional cur-mudgeonly colonel. Mr. Stoving (for that was his name) chatted his way courageously through the War; "business as usual" was his watchword. Undaunted by the ever more bloated bulk of the Army List, he bobbed like a cork on the lethal inundation of temporary commissions, and when I last saw him, a few months before the Armistice, he was still outwardly unconscious of the casualty lists which had lost (and gained) him such a legion of customers.

As soon as he had put me at my ease I became as wax in his hands. He knew my needs so much better than I did that when I paid a second visit to try on my tunics, there seemed no reason why he shouldn't put me through a little squad drill. But he only made one reference to the cataclysm of military training which was in progress, and that was when I was choosing khaki shirts. "*You can't have them too dark*," he insisted, when my eye wandered toward a paler pattern. "We have to keep those in stock—they're for the East of course—but it's quite unpermissible the way some of these New Army officers dress: really, the Provost-Marshal ought to put a stop to all these straw-coloured shirts and ties they're coming out in." He lifted his eyes in horror. . . .

A few weeks later (a second lieutenant in appearance only) I arrived at the training depot of the "Twenty-Fifth". The whole concern had recently migrated from the small peacetime barracks in Flintshire to a new camp of huts on the outskirts of Liverpool. On a fine afternoon at the end of April I got out of the local electric railway at Clitherland Station. Another evidently new officer also climbed out of the train, and we shared a cab up to the camp, with our brand new valises rolling about on the roof. My companion was far from orthodox in what he was wearing, and from his accent I judged him to be a Yorkshireman. His good-humoured face was surmounted by a cap, which was as soft as mine was stiff. His shirt and tie were more yellow than khaki. And his breeches were of a bright buff tint. His tunic was of the correct military colour, but it sat uneasily on his podgy figure. His name, he told me, was Mansfield, and he made no secret of the fact that he had chucked up a job worth £800 a year. "And a nice hope I've got of ever getting it back again!" he added.

When our luggage was unloaded we went to report ourselves at the orderly room. Everything was quiet and deserted, for the troops were drilling on a big field a few hundred yards up the road which went past the camp. We entered the orderly room. The Adjutant was sitting at a table strewn with documents. We saluted clumsily, but he did not look up for a minute or two. When he deigned to do so his eyes alighted on Mansfield. During a prolonged scrutiny he adjusted an eyeglass. Finally he leant back in his chair and exclaimed, with unreproducible hauteur, "*Christ! who's your tailor?*" This (with a reminder that his hair wanted cutting) was the regimental recognition which Mansfield received from his grateful country for having given up a good job in the woollen industry. My own reception was in accordance with the cut of my clothes and my credentials from Captain Huxtable.

IV

It is ten years since I uttered an infantry word of command: and I am only one of a multitude of men in whose minds parade ground phraseology has become as obsolete and derelict as a rusty kettle in a ditch. So much so that it seems quite illuminating to mention the fact. "At the halt on the left form platoon" now sounds to me positively peculiar, and to read *Infantry Training 1914* for a few minutes might be an almost stimulating experience. Though banished to the backs of our minds, those automatic utterances can still be recalled; but who can restore Clitherland Camp and its counterparts all over the country? Most of them were constructed on waste land; and to waste land they have relapsed. I cannot imagine any ex-soldier revisiting Clitherland in pensive pilgrimage. Apart from its deadening associations, it was in an unattractive neighbourhood. The district was industrial. Half a mile away were the chimneys of Bryant's Match Factory. Considerably closer was a hissing and throbbing inferno, which incessantly concocted the form of high explosive known as T.N.T.; when the wind was in the east the Camp got the benefit of the fumes, which caused everyone to cough. Adjoining the Camp, on the other side, was a large Roman Catholic cemetery. Frequent funeral processions cheered up the troops. The surrounding country, with its stunted dwelling-houses, dingy trees, disconsolate canal, and flat root-fields, was correspondingly unlikeable.

Unrolling my valise in a comfortless hut on that first afternoon, I was completely cut off from anything I had done before. Not a soul in the Camp had ever set eyes on me until today. And I was totally ignorant of all that I had to learn before I was fit to go to the Front. Fixing up my folding bed, in which I managed to pinch my finger, I listened to what this new world had to tell me. A bugle call was blown—rather out of tune—but what event it signalized I couldn't say. An officer's servant was whistling cheerfully, probably to a pair of brown shoes. A door banged and his army boots thumped hastily along the passage. Then a sedate tread passed along on the boards, evidently some senior officer. Silence filled a gap, and then I heard a dusty rhythm of marching feet; the troops were returning from the drill-field up the road. Finally, from the open space behind the officers' quarters, a manly young voice shouted: "At the halt on the left form close column of platoons." Clitherland Camp had got through another afternoon parade. I was in a soldier manufactory, although I did not see it in that way at the time.

The cell-like room was already occupied by one other

officer. He transpired as an unobtrusive ex-civil-engineer—a married man, and expecting to go to France with the next draft of officers. He was friendly but uncommunicative; in the evenings, after mess, he used to sit on his bed playing patience with a pack of small cards. It must not be assumed that I found life in the Camp at all grim and unpleasant. Everything was as aggressively cheerful and alert as the ginger-haired sergeant-major who taught the new officers how to form fours and slope arms, and so on, until they could drill a company of recruits with rigid assurance. In May, 1915, the recruits were men who had voluntarily joined up, the average age of the second lieutenants was twenty-one, and "war-weariness" had not yet been heard of. I was twenty-eight myself, but I was five years younger in looks, and in a few days I was one of this outwardly light-hearted assortment, whose only purpose was to "get sent out" as soon as possible.

The significant aspects of Clitherland as it was then can now be seen clearly, and they are, I think, worth reviving. It was a community (if anything could be called a community under such convulsive conditions) which contained contrasted elements. There were the ostensibly permanent senior officers of the pre-war Special Reserve Battalion (several of whom had South African War ribbons to make them more impressive); and there were the young men whose salutes they received and for whose future efficiency at the Front they were, supposedly, responsible. For these younger men there was the contrast between the Camp at Clitherland (in the bright summer weather of that year) and the places they were booked for (such as the Battle of Loos and the Dardanelles). It was, roughly speaking, the difference between the presence of life (with battalion cricket matches and good dinners at the *hotel de luxe* in Liverpool) and the prospect of death. (Next winter in the trenches, anyhow.) A minor (social) contrast was provided by the increasingly numerous batches of Service Battalion officers, whose arrival to some extent clashed with the more carefully selected Special Reserve commissions (like my own) and the public-school boys who came from the Royal Military College. I mention this "feeling" because the "temporary gentlemen" (disgusting phrase), whose manners and accents were liable to criticism by the Adjutant, usually turned out to be first-rate officers when they got to the trenches. In justice to the Adjutant it must be remembered that he was there to try and make them conform to the Regular "officer and gentleman" pattern which he exemplified. And so, while improvised officers came and went, Clitherland Camp was a sort of raft on which they waited for the moment of embarcation which landed them as reinforcements to the still more precarious communities on the other side of the Channel.

Those who were fortunate enough to return, a year or two later, would find, among a crowd of fresh faces, the same easy-going Militia majors enjoying their port placidly at the top of the table. For, to put it plainly, they weren't mobile men, although they had been mobilized for the Great War. They were the products of peace, and war had wrenched them away from their favourite nooks and niches. The Commanding Officer was a worthy (but somewhat fussy) Breconshire landowner. He now found himself in charge of 3,000 men and about 100 officers, and was inundated with documents from the War Office. His second-in-command was a tall Irishman, who was fond of snipe-shooting. Nature had endowed him with an impressive military appearance; but he was in reality the mildest of men. This kind and courteous gentleman found himself obliged to exist in a hut on the outskirts of Liverpool for an indefinite period.

There were several more majors; three of them had been to the Front, but had remained there only a few weeks; the difference between a club window and a dug-out had been too much for them. Anyhow, here they were, and there was the War, and to this day I don't see how things could have been differently arranged. They appeared to be unimaginative men and the Colonel probably took it as all in the day's work when he toddled out after mess on some night when a draft was "proceeding to the Front". Out on the Square he would find, perhaps, 150 men drawn up; discipline would be none too strict, since most of them had been fortifying themselves in the canteen. He would make his stuttering little farewell speech about being a credit to the regiment; going out to the Big Push which will end the War; and so on. And then the local clergyman would exhort them to trust in their Saviour, to an accompaniment of asides and witticisms in Welsh.

"And now God go with you," he would conclude, adding, "I will go with you as far as the station. . . ."

And they would march away in the dark, singing to the beat of drums. It wasn't impressive, but what else could the Colonel and the clergyman have said or done? . . .

Young officers were trained by efficient N.C.O.s; the senior officers were responsible for company accounts, kit inspections, and other camp routine. And the spirit of the regiment, presumably, presided over us all. I have reason to believe that Clitherland was one of the most competently managed camps in the country; high authorities looked upon it as exemplary.

Needless to say, I felt awestruck by my surroundings as I edged my way shyly into mess on my first evening. The cheerful crowd of junior officers sat at two long tables which culminated in the one across the top, which was occupied by the impressive permanencies of whom I have been writing. Old soldiers with South African, China and even Ashanti medal ribbons bustled in and out with plates.

Outside in the evening light, among the subalterns who waited for the Olympians to emerge from the ante-room, I had spoken to no one. Next to me now was a young man who talked too much and seemed anxious to air his social eligibility. From the first I felt that there was something amiss with him. And he was, indeed, one of the most complete failures I ever came across in the War. G. Vivian-Simpson had joined the battalion two or three months before, and for a time he was regarded as smart and promising. A bit of a bounder, perhaps, but thoroughly keen and likely to become competent. He was known among the young officers as "Pardon-me", which was his characteristic utterance. Little by little, poor "Pardon-me" was found out by everyone. His social pretensions were unmasked. (He had been an obscure bank clerk in Liverpool.) His hyphenated name became an object of ridicule. His whole spurious edifice fell to bits. He got into trouble with the Adjutant for cutting parades and failing to pass in musketry. In fact, he was found to be altogether unreliable and a complete cad. For two and a half years he remained ignominiously at the Camp. Fresh officers arrived, were fully trained, and passed away to the trenches. In the meantime guards had to be provided for the docks along the Mersey, and "Pardon-me" was usually in command of one of these perfunctory little expeditions. He must have spent some dreary days at the docks, but it was rumoured that he consoled himself with amorous adventures. Then, when he least expected it, he was actually sent to the Front. Luck was against him; he was introduced to the Ypres salient at its worst. His end was described to me as follows. "Poor old 'Pardon-me'! He was in charge of some Lewis gunners in an advance post. He crawled back to Company headquarters to get his breakfast. You remember what a greedy devil he was! Well, about an hour after he'd gone back to his shell-hole, he decided to chance his arm for another lot of eggs and bacon. A sniper got him while he was on his way, and so he never got his second breakfast!"

It was a sad story, but I make no apology for dragging it from its decent oblivion. All squalid, abject, and inglorious elements in war should be remembered. The intimate mental history of any man who went to the War would make un-heroic reading. I have half a mind to write my own.

In the meantime there is nothing more to be said about my first night in mess, and the next morning I began to acquire the alphabet of infantry training. Mansfield picked it up twice as quickly as I did. For he was a competent man, in spite of his New Army style of dress. And his "word of command" had fire and ferocity; whereas mine was much as might have been expected (in spite of my having acquired a passable "view holloa" during my fox-hunting life). Learning how to be a second-lieutenant was a relief to my mind. It made the War seem further away. I hadn't time to think about it, and by the end of each day I was too healthily tired to worry about any-thing.

Life in the officers' mess was outwardly light-hearted. Only when news came from our two battalions in France were we vividly reminded of the future. Then for a brief while the War came quite close; mitigated by our inexperience of what it was like, it laid a wiry finger on the heart. There was the battle of Festubert in the middle of May. That made us think a bit. The first battalion had been in it and had lost many officers. Those who were due for the next draft were slightly more cheerful than was natural. The next thing I knew about them was that they had gone—half a dozen of them. I went on afternoon parade, and when I returned to the hut my fel-low occupant had vanished with all his tackle. But my turn was months away yet. . . .

The following day was a Sunday, and I was detailed to take a party to church. They were Baptists and there were seven of them. I marched them to the Baptist Chapel in Bootle, won-dering what on earth to do when I got them to the door. Ought I say "Up the aisle; quick march?" As far as I can re-member we reverted to civilian methods and shuffled into the

Chapel in our own time. At the end of the service the bearded minister came and conversed with me very cordially and I concealed the fact that it was my first experience of his religion. Sunday morning in the Baptist Chapel made the trenches seem very remote. What possible connection was there?

Next day some new officers arrived, and one of them took the place of the silent civil-engineer in my room. We had the use of the local cricket ground; I came in that evening feeling peaceful after batting and bowling at the nets for an hour. It seemed something to be grateful for—that the War hadn't killed cricket yet, and already it was a relief to be in flannels and out of uniform. Coming cheerfully into the hut I saw my new companion for the first time. He had unpacked and arranged his belongings, and was sitting on his camp-bed polishing a perfectly new pipe. He looked up at me. Twilight was falling and there was only one small window, but even in the half-light his face surprised me by its candour and freshness. He had the obvious good looks which go with fair hair and firm features, but it was the radiant integrity of his expression which astonished me. While I was getting ready for dinner we exchanged a few remarks. His tone of voice was simple and reassuring, like his appearance. How does he manage to look like that? I thought; and for the moment I felt all my age, though the world had taught me little enough, as I knew then, and know even better now. His was the bright countenance of truth; ignorant and undoubting; incapable of concealment but strong in reticence and modesty. In fact, he was as good as gold, and everyone knew it as soon as they knew him.

Such was Dick Tiltwood, who had left school six months before and had since passed through Sandhurst. He was the son of a parson with a good family living. Generations of upright country gentlemen had made Dick Tiltwood what he was, and he had arrived at manhood in the nick of time to serve his country in what he naturally assumed to be a just and glorious war. Everyone told him so; and when he came to Clitherland Camp he was a shining epitome of his unembittered generation which gladly gave itself to the German shells and machine-guns—more gladly, perhaps, than the generation which knew how much (or how little, some would say) it had to lose. Dick made all the difference to my life at Clitherland. Apart from his cheerful companionship, which was like perpetual fine weather, his Sandhurst training enabled him to help me in mine. Patiently he heard me while I went through my repetitions of the mechanism of the rifle. And in company drill, which I was slow in learning, he was equally helpful. In return for this I talked to him about fox-hunting, which never failed to interest him. He had hunted very little, but he regarded it as immensely important, and much of the material of these memoirs became familiar to him through our conversations in the hut: I used to read him Stephen's letters from the Front, which were long and full of amusing references to the sport that for him symbolized everything enjoyable which the War had interrupted and put and end to. His references to the War were facetious. "An eight-inch landed and duly expanded this morning twenty yards from our mess, which was half-filled with earth. However, the fourth footman soon cleared it and my sausage wasn't even cracked, so I had quite a good breakfast." But he admitted that he was looking forward to "the outbreak of peace", and in one letter went so far as to say that he was "just about as bucked as I should be if I was booked for a week with the Pytchley and it froze the whole time". Dick got to know Stephen quite well, although he had never seen him, except in a little photograph I had with me. So we defied the boredom of life in the Camp, and while the summer went past us our only fear was that we might be separated when our turn came to go abroad. He gave me a sense of security, for his smooth head was no more perplexed with problems than a robin redbreast's; he wound up his watch, brushed his hair, and said his prayers morning and evening.

September arrived, and we were both expecting to get a week's leave. (It was known as "last leave".) One morning Dick came into the hut with a telegram which he handed me. It happened that I was orderly officer that day. Being orderly officer meant a day of dull perfunctory duties, such as turning out the guard, inspecting the prisoners in the guard-room, the cookhouses, the canteen, and everything else in the Camp. When I opened my telegram the orderly sergeant was waiting outside for me; we were due for a tour of the men's huts while they were having their mid-day meal. The telegram was signed Colwood; it informed me that Stephen had been killed in action. But the orderly sergeant was waiting, and away we went, walking briskly over the grit and gravel. At each hut he opened the door and shouted "Shun!" The clatter and chatter ceased and all I had to ask was "Any complaints?" There were no complaints, and off we went to the next hut. It was queer to be doing it, with that dazed feeling and the telegram in my pocket. . . . I showed Dick the telegram when I returned. I had seen Stephen when he was on leave in the spring, and he had written to me only a week ago. Reading the Roll of Honour in the daily paper wasn't the same thing as this. Looking at Dick's blank face I became aware that he would never see Stephen now, and the meaning of the telegram became clear to me.

PART TEN: AT THE FRONT

I

Dick and I were on our way to the First Battalion. The real War, that big bullying bogey, had stood up and beckoned to us at last; and now the Base Camp was behind us with its overcrowded discomforts that were unmitigated by *esprit de corps*. Still more remote, the sudden shock of being uprooted from the Camp at Clitherland, and the strained twenty-four hours in London before departure. For the first time in our lives we had crossed the Channel. We had crossed it in bright moonlight on a calm sea—Dick and I sitting together on a tarpaulin cover in the bow of the boat, which was happily named *Victoria*. Long after midnight we had left Folkestone; had changed our course in an emergency avoidance of Boulogne (caused by the sinking of a hospital ship, we heard afterwards), had stared at Calais harbour, and seen sleepy French faces in the blear beginnings of November daylight. There had been the hiatus of uncertainty at Etaples (four sunless days of north wind among pine-trees) while we were waiting to be "posted" to our battalion. And now, in a soiled fawn-coloured first-class compartment, we clanked and rumbled along and everything in the world was behind us. . . .

Victoria Station: Aunt Evelyn's last, desperately forced smile; and Dick's father, Canon Tiltwood, proud and burly,

271

pacing the platform beside his slender son and wearing cheeriness like a light unclerical overcoat, which couldn't conceal the gravity of a heart heavy as lead. What did they say to one another, he and Aunt Evelyn, when the train had snorted away and left an empty space in front of them? . . .

To have finished with farewells; that in itself was a burden discarded. And now there was nothing more to worry about. Everything was behind us, and the First Battalion was in front of us.

At nine o'clock we were none of us looking over bright, for we had paraded with kit at two in the morning, though the train, in its war time way, hadn't started till three hours later. There we sat, Dick and I and Mansfield (at last released from peace-time Army conventions) and Joe Barless (a gimlet moustached ex-sergeant-major who was submitting philosophically to his elevation into officerdom and spat on the floor at frequent regular intervals). On our roundabout journey we stopped at St. Pol and overheard a few distant bangs—like the slamming of a heavy door they sounded. Barless had been out before; had been hit at the first battle of Ypres; had left a wife and family behind him; knocked his pipe out and expectorated, with a grim little jerk of his bullet head, when he heard the guns. We others looked at him for guidance now, and he was giving us all we needed, in his taciturn, matter-of-fact way, until he got us safely reported with the First Battalion.

It felt funny to be in France for the first time. The sober-coloured country all the way from Etaples had looked lifeless and unattractive, I thought. But one couldn't expect much on a starved grey November morning. A hopeless hunting country, it looked. . . . The opening meet would have been last week if there hadn't been this war. . . . Dick was munching chocolate and reading the *Strand Magazine*, with its cosy reminder of London traffic on the cover. I hadn't lost sight of *him* yet, thank goodness. The Adjutant at Clitherland had

272

sworn to do his best to get us both sent to the First Battalion. But it was probably an accident that he had succeeded. It was a lucky beginning, anyhow. What a railway-tasting mouth I'd got! A cup of coffee would be nice, though French coffee tasted rather nasty, I thought. . . . We got to Béthune by half-past ten.

*   *   *

We got to Béthune by half-past ten: I am well aware that the statement is, in itself, an arid though an accurate one. And at this crisis in my career I should surely be ready with something spectacular and exciting. Nevertheless, I must admit that I have no such episode to exhibit. The events in my experience must take their natural course. I distinctly remember reporting at battalion headquarters in Béthune. In a large dusky orderly room in—was it a wine-merchant's warehouse?—the Colonel shook hands with me. I observed that he was wearing dark brown field-boots, small in the leg, and insinuating by every supple contour that they came from Craxwell. And since the world is a proverbially small place, there was, I hope, nothing incredible in the fact that the Colonel was a distant relative of Colonel Hesmon, and had heard all about how I won the Colonel's Cup. It will be remembered that Colonel Hesmon's conversational repertoire was a limited one, so it wasn't to be wondered at that my new Commanding Officer could tell me the name of my horse, or that I was already well acquainted with *his* name, which was Winchell. For the old Colonel had frequently referred to the exploits of his dashing young relative.

I mention this mainly because my first few minutes with my unit in France transported me straight back to England and the Ringwell Hunt. Unfortunately, the migration was entirely mental; my physical feet took me straight along a *pavé* road for about three miles, to Le Hamel, where my company was in billets. Anyhow, it was to my advantage that I was already known to Colonel Winchell as a hunting man. For I always found that it was a distinct asset, when in close contact with officers of the Regular Army, to be able to converse convincingly about hunting. It gave one an almost unfair advantage in some ways.

Mansfield (who had been received with reservations of cordiality), Dick (*persona grata* on account of his having been at Sandhurst, and also because no one could possibly help liking him at sight) and I (no comment required) were all posted to "C" company which was short of officers. The battalion had lately been much below full strength, and was now being filled up with drafts. We had arrived at a good time, for our Division was about to be withdrawn to a back area for a long rest. And the Givenchy trenches on the La Bassée Canal had taken their toll in casualties. For the time being, the Western Front received us into comparative comfort and domesticity. We found Captain Barton, the company commander, by a stove (which was smoking badly) in a small tiled room on the ground floor of a small house on the road from Béthune to Festubert. The smoke made my eyes water, but otherwise things were quite cheerful. We all slept on the floor, the hardness and coldness of which may be imagined. But then, as always, my sleeping-bag (or "flea-bag" as we called it) was a good friend to me, and we were in clover compared with the men (no one who was in the War need be reminded of that unavoidable circumstance).

Barton (like all the battalion officers except the C.O., the second-in-command, and the quartermaster, and four or five subalterns from Sandhurst) was a civilian. He was big, burly, good-natured, and easy-going; had been at Harrow and, until the War, had lived a comfortably married life on an adequate unearned income. He was, in fact, a man of snug and domesticated habits and his mere presence (wearing pince-nez) in a front-line trench made one feel that it *ought*, at any rate, to be cosy. Such an inherently amicable man as Barton was a continual reminder of the incongruity of war with everyday humanity. In the meantime he was making gallant efforts to behave professionally, and keep his end up as a commander. But that stove had no business to be making the room uninhabitable with its suffocating fumes. It really wasn't fair on a chap like old Barton, who had always been accustomed to a bright fire and a really good glass of port. . . .

So my company received me: and for an infantry subaltern the huge unhappy mechanism of the Western Front always narrowed down to the company he was in. My platoon accepted me apathetically. It was a diminished and exhausted little platoon, and its mind was occupied with anticipations of "Divisional Rest".

To revert to my earlier fact, "got to Béthune by half-past ten", it may well be asked how I can state the time of arrival so confidently. My authority is the diary which I began to keep when I left England. Yes; I kept a diary, and intend to quote from it (though the material which it contains is meagre). But need this be amplified? . . .

"*Thursday*. Went on working-party, 3 to 10.30 p.m. Marched to Festubert, a ruined village, shelled to bits. About 4.30, in darkness and rain, started up half a mile of light-railway lines through marsh, with sixty men. Then they carried hurdles up the communication trenches, about three-quarters of a mile, which took two hours. Flares went up frequently; a few shells, high overhead, and exploding far behind us. The trenches are very wet. Finally emerged at a place behind the first-and second-line trenches, where new trenches (with 'high-command breastworks') are being dug.

"*Saturday*. Working-party again. Started 9.45 p.m. in bright moonlight and iron frost. Dug 12—2. Men got soup in ruined house in Festubert, with the moon shining through matchwood skeleton rafters. Up behind the trenches, the frost-bound morasses and ditches and old earthworks in moonlight, with dusky figures filing across the open, hobbling to avoid slipping. Home 4.15.

"*Sunday*. Same as Saturday. Dug 12—2. Very cold.

"*Monday*. Went with working-party at 3 p.m. Wet day. Awful mud. Tried to dig, till 7.30, and came home soaked. Back 9.45. Beastly night for the men, whose billets are wretched."

I can see myself coming in, that last night, with Julian Durley, a shy, stolid-faced platoon commander who had been a clerk in Somerset House. He took the men's discomforts very much to heart. Simple and unassertive, he liked sound literature, and had a sort of metropolitan turn of humour. His jokes, when things were going badly, reminded me of a facetious bus conductor on a wet winter day. Durley was an inspiration toward selfless patience. He was an ideal platoon officer, and an example which I tried to imitate from that night onward. I need hardly say that he had never hunted. He could swim like a fish, but no social status was attached to that.

II

When I had been with the battalion a week we moved away from the La Bassée sector at nine o'clock on a fine bright morning. In spite of my quite mild experiences there, I felt that I'd seen more than enough of that part of the country. Barton and Durley and young Ormand (who was now second-in-command of the company) were always talking about the Givenchy trenches and how their dugout had been "plastered with trench-mortars and whizzbangs". Now that they were out of it they seemed to take an almost morbid delight in remembering their escapes. No one knew where we were moving to, but the Quartermaster had told Barton that we might be going south. "New Army" battalions were beginning to arrive in France, and the British line was being extended.

On our second day's march (we had done ten kilometres to a comfortable billet the first day) we passed an infantry brigade of Kitchener's Army. It was raining; the flat dreary landscape was half-hidden by mist, and the road was liquid mud. We had fallen out for a halt when they passed us. Four after four they came, some of them wearing the steel basin-helmets which were new to the English armies then. The helmets gave them a Chinese look. To tell the truth, their faces looked sullen, wretched, and brutal as they sweated with their packs under glistening waterproof capes. Worried civilian officers on horses, young-looking subalterns in new rainproof trench-coats; and behind the trudging column the heavy transport horses plodding through the sludge, straining at their loads, and the stolid drivers munching, smoking, grinning, yelling coarse gibes at one another. It was the War all right, and they were going in the direction of it.

Late that afternoon I walked out a little way from our billets. In the brooding stillness I watched the willows and poplars, and the gleaming dykes which reflected the faint flush of a watery sunset. A heron sailed slowly away across the misty flats of ploughed land. Twilight deepened, and a flicker of star-shells wavered in the sky beyond Béthune. The sky seemed to sag heavily over Flanders; it was an oppressive, soul-clogging country, I thought, as I went back to our company mess in the squalid village street, to find Dick polishing his pipe against his nose, Ormand and Mansfield playing "nap", and Durley soberly reading *The Cloister and the Hearth* in an Everyman edition. Already we were quite a happy family. "Old Man Barton", as we called him, had gone out to invite the Quartermaster to dinner with us. Until that evening I had only seen the Q.M. from a distance, but I was already aware that he was the bed-rock of the battalion (as befitted one on whom we relied for our rations). I saw him clearly for what he was, on that first evening (though not so clearly as I can see him now).

Joe Dottrell had been quartermaster-sergeant before the War: he was now Acting Quartermaster, with the rank of captain, since the real Q.M. had faded away into a "cushy job" at Army Headquarters. (He had, in fact, found that haven before the battalion went into action at the first battle of Ypres, whence it had emerged with eighty-five men and one officer—Joe Dottrell.) Whatever might happen, Joe was always there, and he never failed to get the rations up; no bombardment could have prevented him doing that. And what those "dixies" of hot tea signified no one knows who wasn't there to wait for them. He was a small, spare man—a typical "old soldier". He had won his D.C.M. in South Africa, and had a row of ribbons to match his face, which was weather-beaten and whiskyfied to purple tints which became blue when the wind was cold.

Joe Dottrell now entered, his cap hiding his bald brow, and his British-warm coat concealing his medal ribbons, and old man Barton beaming beside him.

"I've brought Dottrell in to jolly you all up," he said with his nervous giggle. "Have a drink, Joe," he continued, holding up a squat bottle of "Old Vatted Highland".

"Well, my lucky lads!" exclaimed Joe, in his Lancashire voice.

Accepting the proffered glass he wished us all "the best", and his presence gave us just that sense of security which we were in need of. But something went wrong in the kitchen, and the dinner was a disgrace. Barton "strafed" the servants until they were falling over one another, but Dottrell said the toasted cheese wasn't too bad, and "There's worse things in the world than half-warmed Maconochie", he remarked. (Maconochie, it will be remembered, was a tinned compound of meat and vegetables; but perhaps it has survived the War. If so, it has my sympathy.)

*　　*　　*

Next day we took it easy. The day after that we travelled to our destination. I have been looking at the map. The distance, by a straight line, was fifty miles. Sixty-five, perhaps, by road; an easy three hours' drive for the Divisional General in his car. Not so easy for the rank and file, whose experiences of migration were summarized well and truly by a private soldier, in a simple sentence which once met my eye while I was censoring the correspondence of my platoon. "Our company have been for a bath to-day and had a clean shirt given us and socks. We had to march five miles each way, so we had a good walk for it, didn't we? My feet are minus all the top skin. *Everywhere we go seems such a long way.*" In those last words one infantry private speaks for them all.

Our big move to the back area began at six a.m. We had to be up by then, for our kits had to be packed and ready by half-past seven. As soon as we had eaten our bacon and eggs in the stuffy billet by the light of a candle, the officers' servants began to pack up the tin plates and dishes, and I remember how I went out alone into the first grey of the morning and up the village street with the cocks crowing. I walked slowly up to some higher ground with a view of woods and steeples and colliery chimneys; rooks were cawing in some tall trees against the faint colours of a watery daybreak, and the *curé* came out of his gate in a garden wall and said good-morning to me as he passed. It was Sunday morning, and by eight o'clock there was a sound of church bells from far and near. Then a troop of mules and horses clattered along the road at their morning exercise, some of them led by turbaned Indians.

I sat on a milestone and watched the sun come out, and a thrush sang a little way off—the first I'd heard in France. But solitude was scanty and precious in the Army, and at half-past ten I was on parade.

We marched two miles into Lillers and entrained. The train started at noon. Ten hours later we detrained at a station three miles from Amiens. We had averaged four miles an hour, and it was now after ten; a dark, still night, with a little rain at times. Men, transport horses, officers' chargers, limbers, and field-kitchens (known as "the cookers") were unloaded. All this took two hours. We had some tea. . . . If I could taste that tea out of the dixies now I should write it all very much as it was. Living spontaneity would be revived by that tea, the taste of which cannot be recovered by any effort of memory.

Fifteen minutes after midnight we moved off. It was rumoured that we had only a few miles to go. On we went to the steady beat of the drums, halting for ten minutes at the end of each fifty. After the second halt the road seemed to become more hilly. About once in an hour we passed through a dark sleeping village. There was a lamp hung on a limber in the rear of the column. Twice I saw our shadows thrown on a white wall in a village. The first time it was a few colossal heads with lurching shoulders and slung rifles; and a second time, on a dead white wall, it was a line of legs; legs only; huge legs striding away from us as if jeering at our efforts to keep going. Movement became mechanical, and I found myself falling asleep as I walked. The men had the weight of their packs and equipment to keep them awake!

A little after six, just before it began to get light, we halted for the sixth time in a small town with a fine church. I sat on the steps at the church door with Dick beside me. Barton came and told us that we had another five kilometres to go "up a high hill". How we managed it I can't say, but an hour afterwards we entered a straggling village on the wooded uplands. As we hobbled in we were met by the Quartermaster, who had got there a few hours ahead of us with the Interpreter (a spindle-shanked Frenchman with a gentle soul and a large military moustache—exiled, poor man, from his jewellery shop at Pau).

As we were the first troops who had ever been billeted in the village, old Joe and Monsieur Perrineau had been having quite a lively time with the rustic inhabitants, who had been knocked up out of their beds and were feeling far from amiable as regards the Flintshire Fusiliers. Having seen the men into their ramshackle barns we sorted ourselves out into our own billets. Dick and I shared a small room in an empty cottage. My diary informs me that I slept from eleven till five. We had marched sixteen miles. It was no easy matter to move an infantry battalion fifty miles. Let those who tour the continent in their comfortable cars remember it and be thankful.

III

Dick and I and Mansfield were starting our active service with a peaceful interlude which we had no right to expect. We had "struck it lucky" as Mansfield remarked. Young Ormand made round eyes under his dark eyebrows as he gloated over the difference between Divisional Rest and those ruddy Givenchy trenches. He was a sturdy little public-school boy who made no secret of his desire to avoid appearing in the Roll of Honour. He wanted life, and he appeared capable of making good use of it, if allowed the opportunity. Dick remained silent; he usually kept his thoughts to himself, confirming other people's opinions with one of his brilliant smiles and the trustful look which he carried in his grey eyes. Julian Durley, too contented for speech, stretched his hands toward

281

the blazing wood fire which crackled cheerfully while the wind blustered comfortably around the cottage.

We were all five of us sitting round the fire in my billet, which had a good open grate, a few pieces of old furniture, and a clock which ticked sedately, as if there were no war on. The owner of the cottage was with the French army. There wasn't a man in the village under forty, and most of them looked gaffers of seventy. They complained that the Battalion was burning all their wood, but firewood was plentiful, since the village was only half a mile from a small forest, and there were trees all round it. This, and its rural remoteness, gave it an air of avoiding conscription. While we were sitting there, my servant Flook (who had been a railway signalman in Lancashire) blundered in at the door with a huge sack of firewood, which he dropped on the tiled floor with a gasp of relief and an exclamation in the war jargon which is so difficult to remember, which made us all laugh. He explained that the people had been playing up hell to the Interpreter, so he'd slipped round to an adjacent woodstack as soon as it was dark to get some more of the "stoof" before the trouble began. Having emptied the sack in a corner he went out for another cargo.

Memories of our eight weeks at Montagne are blurred, like the war jargon which was around me then. I remember it by the light of a couple of ration candles, stuck in bottles; for our evenings were almost homely, except on the few occasions when we went out for a couple of hours of night-work. And even that was quite good fun, especially when old man Barton dropped his pince-nez in the middle of a wood. Mansfield's lurid language was another source of amusement. By daylight we were "training for open warfare". Colonel Winchell was very much on his toes and intent on impressing the Brigadier with his keenness and efficiency. He persistently preached "open warfare" at us, prophesying a "big advance" in the spring.

So we did outpost schemes at the forest's edge, and open-order attacks across wheat-fields and up the stubbled slopes, while sandy hares galloped away, and an old shepherd, in a blue frieze cloak with a pointed hood, watched us from the nook where he was avoiding the wind.

Every evening, at sunset, the battalion fifes and drums marched down the village street with martial music to signify that another day was at an end and the Flintshire Fusiliers in occupation. Ploughmen with their grey teams drove a last furrow on the skyline; windmills spun their sails merrily; rooks came cawing home from the fields; pigeons circled above farmstead stacks with whistling sober-hued wings; and the old shepherd drove his sheep and goats into the village, tootling on a pipe. Sometimes a rampart of approaching rain would blot out the distance, but the foreground would be striped with vivid green, lit with a gleam of sun, and an arc of iridescence spanned the slate-coloured cloud. The War was fifty kilometres away, though we could hear the big guns booming beyond the horizon.

I was happy as I trudged along the lanes in the column, with my platoon chattering behind me and everything gilt with the sun's good humour. Happier still when I borrowed the little black mare no one could ride and cantered about the open country by myself, which I did two or three afternoons a week. The black mare was well bred, but had lost the use of one eye. She had a queer temper, and had earned an evil reputation by kicking various officers off or bolting back to the transport lines with them after going half a mile quite quietly. She was now used as a pack-pony for carrying ammunition, but by gentle treatment I gained her confidence and she soon became a sort of active-service echo of my old favourites. Dick rode out with me as often as he could persuade the Transport Officer to let him have a horse.

When riding alone I explored the country rather absent-mindedly, meditating on the horrors which I had yet to experience; I was unable to reconcile that skeleton certainty with the serenities of this winter landscape—clean-smelling, with larks in the sky, the rich brown gloom of distant woods, and the cloud shadows racing over the lit and dappled levels of that widespread land. And then I would pass a grey-roofed chateau, with its many windows and no face there to watch me pass. Only a bronze lion guarding the well in the middle of an overgrown lawn, and the whole place forlorn and deserted. Once, as I was crossing the main road from Abbeville to Beauvais, I watched the interminable column of a French army corps which was moving southward. For the first time I saw the famous French field-guns—the "75's".

But even then it wasn't easy to think of dying. . . . Still less so when Dick was with me, and we were having an imitation hunt. I used to pretend to be hunting a pack of hounds, with him as my whipper-in. Assuming a Denis Milden manner (Denis was at Rouen with the cavalry and likely to remain there, in spite of the C.O.'s assumptions about open warfare) I would go solemnly through a wood, cheering imaginary hounds. After an imaginary fox had been found, away we'd scuttle, looking in vain for a fence to jump, making imaginary casts after an imaginary check, and losing our fox when the horses had done enough galloping. An imaginary kill didn't appeal to me, somehow. Once, when I was emerging rapidly from a wood with loud shouts, I came round a corner and nearly knocked the Brigadier off his horse. He was out for a ride with his staff-captain; but no doubt he approved of my sporting make-believe, and I didn't dare to stop for apologies, since the Brigadier was a very great man indeed. Dick enjoyed these outings enormously and was much impressed by my hunting noises. The black mare seemed to enjoy it also.

Thus, in those delusive surroundings, I reverted fictitiously to the jaunts and jollities of peace time, fabricating for my young friend a light-hearted fragment of the sport which he had not lived long enough to share. It was queer, though, when we met some of the black-bearded Bengal Lancers who were quartered in one of the neighbouring villages. What were they doing among those wooded ridges, with the little roads winding away over the slopes toward a low yellow sunset and the nowhere of life reprieved to live out its allotted span?

*   *   *

Christmas came—a day of disciplined insobriety—and the First Battalion entered 1916 in a state of health and happiness. But it was a hand-to-mouth happiness, preyed upon by that remote noise of artillery; and as for health—well, we were all of us provisionally condemned to death in our own thoughts and if anyone had been taken seriously ill and sent back to "Blighty" he would have been looked upon as lucky. For anybody who allowed himself to think things over, the only way out of it was to try and feel secretly heroic, and to look back on the old life as pointless and trivial. I used to persuade myself that I had "found peace" in this new life. But it was a peace of mind which resulted from a physically healthy existence combined with a sense of irresponsibility. There could be no turning back now; one had to do as one was told. In an emotional mood I could glory in the idea of the supreme sacrifice.

But where was the glory for the obscure private who was always in trouble with the platoon sergeant and got "medicine and duty" when he went to the medical officer with rheumatism? He had enlisted "for the duration" and had a young wife at home. It was all very well for Colonel Winchell to be lecturing in the village schoolroom on the offensive spirit, and the spirit of the regiment, but everyone knew that he was booked for a brigade, and some said that he'd bought a brigadier's gold-peaked cap last time he was on leave.

When I instructed my platoon, one or two evenings a week, I confined myself to asking them easy questions out of the infantry training manual, saying that we had got to win the War (and were certain to) and reading the League Football news aloud. I hadn't begun to question the rights and wrongs of the War then; and if I had, nothing would have been gained by telling my platoon about it—apart from the grave breach of discipline involved in such heart-searchings.

Early in the New Year the first gas-masks were issued. Every morning we practised putting them on, transforming ourselves into grotesque goggle-faced creatures as we tucked the grey flannel under our tunics in flustered haste. Those masks were an omen. An old wood-cutter in high leather leggings watched us curiously, for we were doing our gas-drill on the fringe of the forest, with its dark cypresses among the leafless oaks and beeches, and a faint golden light over all.

One Sunday in January I got leave to go into Amiens. (A rambling train took an hour and a half to do the eighteen-mile journey.) Dick went with me. After a good lunch we inspected the Cathedral, which was a contrast to the life we had been leading. But it was crowded with sight-seeing British soldiers; the kilted "Jocks" walked up and down the nave as if they had conquered France, and I remember seeing a Japanese officer flit in with curious eyes. The long capes which many of the soldiers wore gave them a mediaeval aspect, insolent and overbearing. But the background was solemn and beautiful. White columns soared into lilies of light, and the stained-glass windows harmonized with the chanting voices and the satisfying sounds of the organ. I glanced at Dick and thought what a young Galahad he looked (a Galahad who had got his school colours for cricket).

Back in the company mess at Montagne we found the Quartermaster talking to Barton, who was looking none too bright, for old Joe seemed to think that we might be moving back to the Line any day now.

Young Ormand had got his favourite record going on his little gramophone. That mawkish popular song haunts me whenever I am remembering the War in these afterdays:

> *And when I told them how wonderful you were,*
> *They wouldn't believe me; they wouldn't believe me;*
> *Your hands, your eyes, your lips, your hair,*
> *Are in a class beyond compare. . . .*

and so on. His records were few, and all were of a similar kind. I would have liked to hear a Handel violin sonata sometimes; there was that one which Kreisler had played the first time I heard him. . . . And I'd have liked to hear Aunt Evelyn playing "The Harmonious Blacksmith", on that Sunday evening when we began to pull ourselves together for "the Line". . . . In her last letter she had said how long the winter seemed, in spite of being so busy at the local hospital. She was longing for the spring to come again. "Spring helps one so much in life." (In the spring, I thought, the "Big Push" will begin.) Her chief bit of news was that Dixon was in France. Although he had enlisted in the Army Veterinary Corps he was now attached to the Army Service Corps, and was a sergeant. "He seems quite happy, as he has charge of a lot of horses," she wrote. I wondered whether there was any chance of my seeing him, but it seemed unlikely. Anyhow, I would try to find out where he was, as soon as I knew where our division was going. Dottrell thought we were for the Somme trenches, which had lately been taken over from the French.

*   *   *

But before we left Montagne Colonel Winchell sent for me and told me to take over the job of Transport Officer. This was an anti-climax, for it meant that I shouldn't go into the trenches. The late Transport Officer had gone on leave, and now news had come that he had been transferred to a reserve battalion in England. Mansfield remarked that God seemed to watch over some people. He seemed to be watching over me too. Everyone in "C" company mess expressed magnanimous approval of my appointment, which was considered appropriate, on account of my reputation as a fox-hunting man. I entered on my new duties with "new-broom" energy. And the black mare was now mine to ride every day. For the time being I remained with "C" company mess, but when we got to the Line I should live with Dottrell and the Interpreter. It was a snug little job which would have suited Barton down to the ground.

There was one thing which worried me; I disliked the idea of Dick going into the front line while I stayed behind. I said so, and he told me not to be an old chump. So we had a last ride round the woods, and the next morning, which was raw and foggy, we turned our backs on the little village. The First Battalion never had such a peaceful eight weeks again for the remainder of the War.

We crossed the Somme at Picquigny: after that we were in country unknown to us. I rode along with the rattle and rumble of limber and wagon wheels, watching the patient dun-coloured column winding away in front; conscious of what they were marching to, I felt myself strongly identified with this queer community, which still contained a few survivors from the original Expeditionary Force battalion which had "helped to make history" at Ypres in October, 1914. Most of the old soldiers were on the strength of the Transport, which numbered about sixty.

On the roll of the Transport were drivers, officers' grooms, brakesmen, and the men with the nine pack animals which carried ammunition. Then there was the transport-sergeant (on whose efficiency my fate depended), his corporal, and a farrier-corporal; and those minor specialists, the shoeing-smith, saddler, carpenter, and cook. Our conveyances were the G.S. wagon (with an old driver who took ceaseless pride in his horses and the shining up of his steelwork), the mess wagon (carrying officers' kits, which were strictly limited in weight), the company cookers (which lurched cumbersomely along with the men's dinners stewing away all the time), the watercart, and a two-wheeled vehicle known as "the Maltese cart" (which carried a special cargo connected with the Quartermaster's stores and was drawn by an aged pony named Nobbie). There were also the limbers, carrying the machine-guns and ammunition.

The transport-sergeant was a Herefordshire man who could easily be visualized as a farmer driving to market in his gig. The C.O. had told me that the transport had been getting rather slack and needed smartening up; but I was already aware that Dottrell and the transport-sergeant could have managed quite easily without my enthusiastic support; they knew the whole business thoroughly, and all I could do was to keep an eye on the horses, which were a very moderate assortment, though they did their work well enough.

So far I have said next to nothing about the officers out-side my own company, and there is nothing to be said about them while they are on their way to the Line, except that their average age was about twenty-five, and that I had known the majority of them at Clitherland. It was a more or less untried battalion which marched across the Somme that misty morning. But somehow its original spirit survived, fortified by those company sergeant-majors and platoon sergeants whose duties were so exacting; how much depended on them only an ex-infantry officer can say for certain; ac-cording to my own experience, everything depended on them. But the Army was an interdependent concern, and when the Brigadier met us on the road Colonel Winchell's face assumed a different expression of anxiety from the one which it wore when he was riding importantly up and down the column with the Adjutant at his heels. (The Adjutant, by the way, became a Roman Catholic priest after the War, and it doesn't surprise me that he felt the need for a change of mental atmosphere.) The Brigadier, in his turn, became a more or less meek and conciliatory man when he encountered the Divisional General. And so on, up to Sir John French, who had lately been replaced by Sir Douglas Haig.

We went thirteen miles that day. I remember, soon after we started on the second day, passing the end of an avenue, at the far end of which there was an enticing glimpse of an ancient château. My heart went out to that château: it seemed to symbolize everything which we were leaving behind us. But it was a bright morning, and what had I got to complain about, riding cockily along on my one-eyed mare while Dick was trudging in front of his platoon? . . . .

On the third day, having marched thirty-three miles altotogether, we entered Morlancourt, a village in the strip of undulating landscape between the Somme and the Ancre rivers. This was our destination (until the next day, when the troops went up to the trenches, which were four or five miles away). It was an ominous day, but the sun shone and the air felt keen; as we marched down to Morlancourt a flock of pigeons circled above the roofs with the light shining through their wings. It was a village which had not suffered from shell-fire. Its turn came rather more than two years afterwards.

We were all kept busy that afternoon: Barton and the other company commanders were harassed by continuous "chits" from battalion H.Q. and, as young Ormand remarked when he came to leave his gramophone in my care, "everyone had fairly got the breeze up". The only person who showed no sign of irritability was the Quartermaster, who continued to chaff M. Perrineau, with whom he stumped about the village mollifying everyone and putting difficulties to rights.

Late in the evening I was sent off to a hamlet a mile away to find out (from the billeting officer of the New Army battalion we were relieving next day) certain details of routine connected with the transport of rations to the Line. This billeting officer recognized me before I remembered who he was. His name was Regel (which he now pronounced Regal). I had forgotten his existence since we were at school together. He now dictated his methodical information, and when I had finished scribbling notes about "water-trolley horses", "mule-stable just beyond first barricade", and so on, we talked for a while about old days.

"How's your cousin Willie?" I asked, for want of anything else to say. His chubby face looked embarrassed, and he replied (in a low voice, for there were two other officers in the room), "He's on the other side—in the artillery.". . .

I remembered then that Willie (a very nice boy) had always gone home to Hanover for the holidays. And now he might be sending a five-nine shell over at us for all we, or he, knew. It was eleven o'clock when I got back to Morlancourt. Dottrell was having a glass of rum and hot water before turning in. He had already found out all the details which I had scribbled in my notebook.

IV

Morlancourt was tucked away among the fold of long slopes and bare ridges of ploughland. Five roads entered the village and each road, in its friendly convergence with the others, had its little crop of houses. There was a church with a slated tower and a gilt vane, round which birds wheeled and clacked. In the hollow ground in the middle, where the five roads met, there was a congregation of farm buildings round an open space with a pond on one side of it. It seemed a comfortable village when one looked down on its red and grey roofs and its drab and ochre walls.

The long lines of the high ground hid the rest of the world: on the ridge one saw a few straggling trees, a team of greys ploughing or dredging, and some horsemen or a hooded farm-cart moving along the white edge of the skyline. The wind piped across the open, combing the thorn bushes which grew under high banks, and soughing in isolated plane trees and aspens. It was a spacious landscape of distant objects delicately defined under an immense sky. The light swept across it in a noble progress of wind and cloud, and evening brought it mystery and sadness. At night the whole region became a dusk of looming slopes with lights of village and bivouac picked out here and there, little sparks in the loneliness of time. And always the guns boomed a few miles away, and the droning aeroplanes looked down on the white seams of the reserve trench lines with their tangle of wires and posts.

Here, while the battalion began its "tours of trenches" (six days in and four days out), I had my meals comfortably with mild M. René Perrineau and Joe Dottrell. I slept in a canvas hut close to the transport lines, falling asleep to the roar and rattle of trench warfare four miles away, and waking to see, on sunny mornings, the shadows of birds flitting across my canvas roof, and to hear the whistling of starlings from the fruit trees and gables of the farm near by. After breakfast I would sit for a while reading a book by the fire in Dottrell's billet, while the soldier cook sang "I want to go to Michigan" at the top of his voice about three yards away. But however much he wanted to go to Michigan, he was lucky not to be in the trenches, and so was I; and I knew it as I toddled down to the transport lines to confer with Sergeant Hoskins about getting some carrots and greenstuff for the horses and indenting for some new nosebags and neckpieces for the limber harness. Some of the horses were looking hidebound, and I promised the sergeant that I'd buy a couple of hundredweight of linseed for them when I went on leave. Linseed was a cosy idea; it reminded me of peacetime conditions.

Our serious activities began after lunch. At half-past two I mounted the black mare, and old Joe soused himself into the saddle of his pony Susan (a veteran who had sustained a shrapnel wound on the near hip at the first battle of Ypres) and the transport moved off along the Bray road with the rations for the battalion. As the days lengthened the expedition started later, for we couldn't go beyond Bray until after dusk. It was a roundabout journey of seven miles, and if we started at three we were never home before ten. But home we came, to find Monsieur Perrineau solacing himself with Ormand's gramophone: "But when I told them how wonderful you were" or "Just a little love, a little kiss". (Perrineau was hoping to go on leave soon, and his wife was waiting for him at Pau.)

There were times when I felt that I ought to be somewhere else; I always went up to see my company, and when they were in the front line I was reluctant to leave them. One night (during the second time they were in) I arrived while our batteries were busily retaliating after a heavy afternoon bombardment by the Germans. I had some difficulty in getting up to the front line as the communication trenches were badly knocked about. But I found the five "C" company officers none the worse for having been "strafed" with trench-mortars, and my visit seemed to cheer them. I came home across the open country that night (which saved three miles) and it was a relief to leave it all behind me—the water-logged trenches, and men peering grimly at me from under their round helmets: riding home there was friendly gloom around me, while the rockets soared beyond the ridge and the machine-guns rattled out their mirthless laughter. I left the mare to find her way to the gap in the reserve trench line: she never hesitated though she had only been up that way once by daylight. I was seeing the War as a looker-on, it seemed.

*   *   *

I had written to Dixon, telling him all about my new job, and I now received a reply. We were, apparently, in the same army corps, so he couldn't be so very many miles away.

"I have been wondering, sir," he wrote, "whether it might possibly be fixed up for me to exchange into your battalion as transport-sergeant. You say your sergeant has been in France since the beginning, so he's done his bit all right! It would be quite like old times for me to be your transport-sergeant. That was a rotten business about Mr. Colwood being killed, sir. We shall all miss him very much when this War is over."

Dixon's letter sent me off into pleasant imaginings; to have him near me would make all the difference, I thought. Everything I had known before the War seemed to be withering away and falling to pieces: Denis seldom wrote to me, and he was trying to get a job on the Staff; but with Dixon to talk to I should still feel that the past was holding its own with the War; and I wanted the past to survive and to begin again; the idea was like daylight on the other side of this bad weather in which life and death had come so close to one another. I couldn't get used to the idea of Stephen being dead. And Denis had become so remote that I seldom remembered him, though I couldn't say why it was.

So, by the time I was showing Dottrell the letter, I had made up my mind that Dixon's exchange was as good as settled. Joe read the letter through twice. "Your old groom must be a good sport," he remarked, pouring himself out a couple of inches of O.V.H. and adding a similar amount of water. "But it would take a deal of wangling to work his exchange. And if you want my private opinion, young George, he'd far better stay where he is. We'll find ourselves in much less cushy places than this, and you say he's turned forty-five...." He handed me the letter. "And you might find yourself back with 'C' company again if we had some casualties. Things change pretty quick nowadays. And I don't mind betting there'll be a few changes when Kinjack rolls up to take command of the battalion!"

I nodded wisely. For everyone now knew that Winchell had got his brigade, and Major Kinjack was expected (from the Second Battalion) in a week or two. And Kinjack had a somewhat alarming reputation as a disciplinarian. He was, according to Dottrell, who had known him since he was a subaltern, "a bloody fine soldier but an absolute pig if you got the wrong side of him". Old man Barton was in a twitter about the new C.O., his only hope being, he said, that Kinjack would send him home as incompetent. Barton came in at this moment, for the battalion had returned from the trenches the day before.

"Why, Barton," exclaimed Dottrell, "you look as if you'd just come out of quod!"

Barton's hair had been cut by an ex-barber (servant to the medical officer) who had borrowed a pair of horse-clippers to supplement his scissors. Barton giggled and rubbed his cropped cranium. He said it made him feel more efficient, and began to chaff Dick (who had come in to ask if he might go for a ride with me that afternoon) about his beautifully brushed hair. "Kinjack'll soon have the horse-clippers on your track, young man!" he said. Dick smiled and said nothing.

We arranged to go for a ride, and he went off to inspect the company's dinners. When he had gone Barton remarked that he wished he could get Dick to take more care of himself up in the Line. "I sent him out on a short patrol two nights ago, but he stayed out there nearly an hour and a half and went right up to the Boche wire." Old Joe agreed that he was a rare good lad: no cold feet about him; the country couldn't afford to lose many more like that. . . .

And he got on to his favourite subject—"The Classes and the Masses". For Joe had been brought up in the darkest part of Manchester, and he prided himself on being an old-fashioned socialist. But his Socialism was complicated by his fair-minded cognizance of the good qualities of the best type of the officer class, with whom he had been in close contact ever since he enlisted. He clenched a knotted fist. "This war," he exclaimed in his husky voice, "is being carried on by the highest and the lowest in the land—the blue-blooded upper ten and the poor unfortunate people that some silly bastard called 'the Submerged Tenth'. All the others are making what they can out of it and shirking the dirty work. Selfish hogs! And the politicians are no better."

"That's right, Joe. That's the stuff to give 'em!" said Barton.

And they both drank damnation to the (enigmatic) part of the population which was leaving all the dirty work to the infantry. Their generalizations, perhaps, were not altogether fair. There was quite a lot of blue blood at G.H.Q. and Army Headquarters. And Mansfield and Durley, to name only two of our own officers, were undoubtedly members of "the middle class", whatever that may be.

*　　　*　　　*

My ride with Dick was a great success. Over the rolling uplands and through an occasional strip of woodland, with the sun shining and big clouds moving prosperously on a boisterous north-west wind, we rode to a village six or seven miles away, and had tea at an unbelievable shop where the cakes were as good as anything in Amiens. I wouldn't like to say how many we ate, but the evening star shone benevolently down on us from among a drift of rosy clouds while we were cantering home to Morlancourt. But about a fortnight later, when Dick was up in the trenches, I received a letter in reply to the one I had sent Dixon. Someone informed me that Sergeant Dixon had died of pneumonia. Major Kinjack arrived to take command a day or two afterwards.

V

Lieutenant-Colonel Kinjack (to give him his new rank) exceeded all our expectations. He was the personification of military efficiency. Personal charm was not his strong point and he made no pretension to it. He was aggressive and blatant, but he knew his job, and for that we respected him and were grateful. His predecessor had departed in his Brigadier's cap without saying good-bye to anyone. For that we were less grateful; but as Dottrell said: "He'd had Brigadier on the brain ever since he came back off leave, and now he'd never be satisfied till he'd got a Division and another decoration to go with it." Dottrell had just got his D.S.O., so he had no cause to feel jealous, even if he had been capable of that feeling, which he wasn't. His only complaint was that they didn't make his "acting rank" permanent. He aired that grievance several evenings a week, especially when he had got back late with the ration party, and his references to the "permanent" Quartermaster (at Army Headquarters) were far from flattering.

Colonel Kinjack stopped one night in Morlancourt, and on the following afternoon I guided him up to the Line, going by the short cut across the open country and the half-dug and feebly wired reserve trench which, we hoped, would never be utilized. The new C.O. had inspected the Transport in the morning without active disapproval, but he was less pleased when our appearance on the ridge (half a mile behind the front line) attracted a few shells, none of which exploded near us. This was considered quite a good joke in the battalion, and I was often reminded afterwards of how I'd got Kinjack welcomed with whizz-bangs.

"The Boches saw Kinjack coming all right. The Transport Officer made sure of that!" Barton would say, with a chuckle.

For in spite of my easy job, it was supposed that I could be a bit of a daredevil if I liked. Not that I wanted to be, that afternoon; Kinjack frightened the life out of me, and was so sceptical of my ability to find the way that I began to feel none too sure about it myself. . . . It is, however, just conceivable that at that time I didn't care what happened to the new Colonel or anybody else. . . .

That same day, at about midnight, I was awakened by Dottrell, who told me that I was to go on leave next morning. I drove to the station in the Maltese cart; the train started at 9.30, crawled to Havre, and by ten o'clock next day I was in London. I had been in France less than four months. As regards war experience I felt a bit of an impostor. I had noticed that officers back from their ten days' leave were usually somewhat silent about it. Then, after a few weeks, they began to look forward to their next leave again, and to talk about this future fact. But there wasn't much to be said about mine, for it was bitterly cold and a heavy fall of snow knocked my hopes of hunting on the head. So I remained quietly with Aunt Evelyn at Butley, telling myself that it was a great luxury to have a hot bath every day, and waiting for a thaw. If it thawed I should have two or three days with the Ringwell on Colonel Hesmon's horses. And I should stay at Hoadley Rectory. But no thaw came, and I returned to France without having been to the Rectory, which had been a painful idea in any case. The Rector evidently felt the same, for he wrote me a sad letter in which he said "as I think of all the suffering and death, the anxieties and bereavements of this terrible struggle, I feel that in our ignorance we can only rest on the words, 'What I do thou knowest not now but thou shalt know hereafter'. Obedience and self-sacrifice for right and truth in spite of suffering and death is Christianity. . . ." I received this letter on my last day at Butley. Sitting alone in the schoolroom late at night, I felt touched by the goodness and patience of my old friend, but I was unable to accept his words in the right spirit. He spoke too soon. I was too young to understand. And England wasn't what it used to be. I had been over to say good-bye to Captain Huxtable that afternoon; but the War was making an old man of him, though he did his best to be bright. And kind Aunt Evelyn talked bitterly about the Germans and called them "hell-hounds". I found myself defending them, although I couldn't claim acquaintance with a single one of them (except Willie Regel, and I shouldn't have known him by sight if I'd met him).

Looking round the room at the enlarged photographs of my hunters, I began to realize that my past was wearing a bit thin. The War seemed to have made up its mind to obliterate all those early adventures of mine. Point-to-point cups shone, but without conviction. And Dixon was dead. . . .

Perhaps, after all, it was better to be back with the battalion. The only way to forget about the War was to be on the other side of the Channel. But the fire burnt brightly and the kettle was hissing on the hob. It was nice to be wearing my old civilian clothes, and to make myself a cup of tea. Old Joe will be on his way home with the transport now, I thought, contrasting my comfort with him joggling along the Bray road in this awful weather. His bronchitis had been bad lately, too. Dick was a thought which I repressed. He would be getting his leave soon, anyhow. . . . The Rector said we were fighting for right and truth; but it was no use trying to think it all out now. There were those things to take back for the others—a bottle of old brandy for Dottrell and some smoked salmon for "C" company mess—I mustn't make any mistake about that when I get to town in the morning, I thought. . . .

And the next evening I was on the boat at Southampton; the weather had turned mild again; it was a quiet evening; I watched the red and green lights across the harbour, and listened to the creaking cries of the gulls, like the sound of windlasses and pulleys, as they swooped in circles or settled on the smooth dusk of the water. From the town came the note of a bugle, a remote call, like the last thought of home. And then we were churning across the dark sea, to find France still under snow.

*   *   *

There was a continuous rumble and grumble of bombardment while we were going up with the rations on the day after I got back from leave. As we came over the hill beyond Bray the darkness toward Albert was lit with the glare of explosions that blinked and bumped. Dottrell remarked that there seemed to be a bit of a mix-up, which was his way of saying that he didn't altogether like the look of things that evening.

When we arrived at the ration dump the quartermaster-sergeant told us that the battalion had been standing to for the past two hours. It was possible that the Boches might be coming across. "C" company was in the front line. The noise was subsiding, so I went up there, leaving Joe to pay his nightly call at battalion headquarters.

Stumbling and splashing up a communication trench known as Canterbury Avenue, with the parcel of smoked salmon stuffed into my haversack, I felt that smoked salmon wasn't much of an antidote for people who had been putting up with all that shell-fire. Still, it was something. . . . Round the next corner I had to flatten myself against the wall of that wet ditch, for someone was being carried down on a stretcher. An extra stretcher-bearer walking behind told me it was Corporal Price of "C" company. "A rifle-grenade got him . . . looks as if he's a goner. . . ." His face was only a blur of white in the gloom; then, with the drumming of their boots on the trench-boards, Corporal Price left the War behind him. I remembered him vaguely as a quiet little man in Durley's platoon. No use offering *him* smoked salmon, I thought, as I came to the top of Canterbury Avenue, and, as usual, lost my way in the maze of saps and small trenches behind the front line. Watling Street was the one I wanted. Finding one's way about the trenches in the dark was no easy job when one didn't live up there. I passed the dug-outs of the support company at Maple Redoubt. Candles and braziers glinted through the curtain-flaps and voices muttered gruffly from the little underground cabins (which would have been safer if they had been deeper down in the earth). Now and again there was the splitting crack of a rifle-shot from the other side, or a five-nine shell droned serenely across the upper air to burst with a hollow bang; voluminous reverberations rolled along the valley. The shallow blanching flare of a rocket gave me a glimpse of the mounds of bleached sandbags on the Redoubt. Its brief whiteness died downward, leaving a dark world; chilly gusts met me at corners, piping drearily through crannies of the parapet; very different was the voice of the wind that sang in the cedar tree in the garden at home. . . .

Pushing past the gas-blanket, I blundered down the stairs to the company headquarters' dug-out. There were twenty steps to that earthy smelling den, with its thick wooden props down the middle and its precarious yellow candlelight casting wobbling shadows. Barton was sitting on a box at the rough table, with a tin mug and a half-empty whisky bottle. His shoulders were hunched and the collar of his trench-coat was turned up to his ears. Dick was in deep shadow, lying on a bunk (made of wire-netting with empty sandbags on it). It was a morose cramped little scene, loathsome to live in as it is hateful to remember. The air was dank and musty; lumps of chalk fell from the "ceiling" at intervals. There was a bad smell of burnt grease, and the frizzle of something frying in the adjoining kennel that was called the kitchen was the only evidence of ordinary civilization—that and Barton's shining pince-nez, and the maps and notebooks which were on the table. . . .

Smoked salmon from Piccadilly Circus was something after all. It cheered Barton immensely. He unpacked it; he sniffed it; and no doubt it brought the lights of London into his mind.

"Gosh, if only this war would stop!" he exclaimed. "I'd be off to Scott's oyster-bar like a streak of light and you'd never get me away from it again!"

He held the smoked salmon under Dick's nose and told him what a lucky young devil he was to be going on leave in two or three days' time. Dick wasn't as bright as usual; he'd got a rotten headache, he said. Barton told him he'd better let Ormand go out with the wiring-party instead of him. But he said no, he'd be all right by then, and Ormand had been out last night. Barton told me they'd had a lively time with the C.O. lately: "He gave orders for the whole of the front line to be re-wired; we've been at it every night, but he came up this morning with his big periscope, strafing like hell about the gaps along by the mine-craters. He says the wire isn't strong enough to stop a wheelbarrow—why a wheelbarrow God knows!" He laughed, rather hysterically; his nerves were on edge, and no wonder. . . . For, as he said, what with the muck everything was in since the snow melted, and being chivvied by Kinjack, and then being "crumped" all the afternoon, life hadn't been worth living lately. The odd thing was that good old Barton seemed equally concerned because the snowy weather had prevented me from having any hunting while on leave. And Dick agreed that it had been very rough on me.

Mansfield and Ormand came in at that moment; these two were very good friends, and they always seemed to be cheering one another up. They had left Durley on duty in the front trench. They wanted to hear all about the "shows" I had been to in London, but I couldn't tell them anything (though I wished I could) for I hadn't been to a theatre, and it was no use talking about the Symphony Concert at Queen's Hall, which now made me feel rather a prig.

Dick was still lying in his dark corner when I said good-night and groped my way up the steps, leaving them to make the most of the smoked salmon. Going down Canterbury Avenue it was so pitch black that I couldn't see my own hand; once or twice a flare went up in the spectral region on the shoulder of the hill behind me; lit by that unearthly glare the darkness became desolation.

*   *   *

Coming up from the transport lines at twelve o'clock next morning I found Joe Dottrell standing outside the Quartermaster's stores. His face warned me to expect bad news. No news could have been worse. Dick had been killed. He had been hit in the throat by a rifle bullet while out with the wiring-party, and had died at the dressing-station a few hours afterwards. The battalion doctor had been a throat specialist before the War, but this had not been enough.

The sky was angry with a red smoky sunset when we rode up with the rations. Later on, when it was dark, we stood on the bare slope just above the ration dump while the Brigade chaplain went through his words; a flag covered all that we

were there for; only the white stripes on the flag made any impression on the dimness of the night. Once the chaplain's words were obliterated by a prolonged burst of machine-gun fire; when he had finished, a trench-mortar "canister" fell a few hundred yards away, spouting the earth up with a crash...
A sack was lowered into a hole in the ground. The sack was Dick. I knew Death then.

*   *   *

A few days later, when the battalion was back at Morlancourt, and Kinjack was having a look round the Transport lines, he remarked that he wasn't sure that I wasn't rather wasted as Transport Officer. "I'd much rather be with 'C' Company, sir." Some sort of anger surged up inside me as I said it. . . . He agreed. No doubt he had intended me to return to my platoon.

VI

Easter was late in April that year; my first three tours of trenches occupied me during the last thirty days of Lent. This essential season in the Church calendar was not, as far as I remember, remarked upon by anyone in my company, although the name of Christ was often on our lips, and Mansfield (when a canister made a mess of the trench not many yards away from him) was even heard to refer to our Saviour as "murry old Jesus!" These innocuous blasphemings of the holy name were a peculiar feature of the War, in which the principles of Christianity were either obliterated or falsified for the convenience of all who were engaged in it. Up in the trenches every man bore his own burden; the Sabbath was not made for man; and if a man laid down his life for his friends it was no part of his military duties. To kill an enemy

304

was an effective action; to bring in one of our own wounded was praiseworthy, but unrelated to our war-aims. The Brigade chaplain did not exhort us to love our enemies. He was content to lead off with the hymn "How sweet the name of Jesus sounds"!

I mention this war-time dilemma of the Churches because my own mind was in rather a muddle at that time. I went up to the trenches with the intention of trying to kill someone. It was my idea of getting a bit of my own back. I did not say anything about it to anyone; but it was this feeling which took me out patrolling the mine-craters whenever an opportunity offered itself. It was a phase in my war experience— no more irrational than the rest of the proceedings, I suppose; it was an outburst of blind bravado which now seems paltry when I compare it with the behaviour of an officer like Julian Durley, who did everything that was asked of him as a matter of course.

Lent, as I said before, was not observed by us. Barton got somewhere near observing it one evening. We had just returned to our dug-out after the twilight ritual of "standing-to". The rations had come up, and with them the mail. After reading a letter from his wife he looked at me and said: "O Kangar, how I wish I were a cathedral organist!" (I was known as "the Kangaroo" in "C" company.) His remark, which had no connection with any religious feeling, led us on to pleasant reminiscences of cathedral closes. Nothing would be nicer, we thought, than to be sauntering back, after Evensong, to one of those snug old houses, with a book of anthems under our arms—preferably on a mild evening toward the end of October. (In his civilian days Barton had attended race meetings regularly; his musical experience had been confined to musical comedy.)

The mail that evening had brought me a parcel from Aunt Evelyn, which contained two pots of specially good jam.

Ration jam was usually in tins, and of tins it tasted. Barton gazed affectionately at the coloured label, which represented a cherry-growing landscape. The label was a talisman which carried his mind safely to the home counties of England. He spoke of railway travelling "Do you remember the five-thirty from Paddington? What a dear old train it was!" Helping himself to a spoonful of cherry jam he mentally passed through Maidenhead in a Pullman carriage. . . . The mail had also brought me the balance sheet of the Ringwell Hunt. These Hunt accounts made me feel homesick. And it appeared that the late Mr. S. Colwood had subscribed ten pounds. He must have sent it early in September, just before he was killed. No doubt he wrote the chèque in a day dream about hunting. . . .

In the meantime we were down in that frowsty smelling dug-out, listening to the cautious nibbling of rats behind the wooden walls; and above ground there was the muffled boom of something bursting. And two more officers had been killed. Not in our company though. The Germans had put up another mine that afternoon without doing us any damage. Their trenches were only a hundred and fifty yards from ours; in some places less than fifty. It was a sector of the line which specialized in mines; more than half of our 750-yard frontage was pitted with mine-craters, some of them fifty feet deep. . . .

"They were digging in front of Bois Français Trench again last night," I remarked.

Barton had just received a message from battalion headquarters saying that the company front was to be thoroughly patrolled.

"I'll take O'Brien out with me to-night," I added.

Barton's ruddy face had resumed the worried expression which it wore when messages came from Kinjack or the Adjutant.

"All right, Kangar; but do be careful. It puts the fear of

God into me when you're out there and I'm waiting for you to come in."

It put the fear of God into me too, but it was the only escape into freedom which I could contrive, up in those trenches opposite Fricourt and Mametz. And I was angry with the War.

*   *   *

Memory eliminates the realities of bodily discomfort which made the texture of trench-life what it was. Mental activity was clogged and hindered by gross physical actualities. It was these details of discomfort which constituted the humanity of an infantryman's existence. Being in the trenches meant among other things having a "trench-mouth".

I can see myself sitting in the sun in a nook among the sandbags and chalky debris behind the support line. There is a strong smell of chloride of lime. I am scraping the caked mud off my wire-torn puttees with a rusty entrenching tool. Last night I was out patrolling with Private O'Brien, who used to be a dock labourer at Cardiff. We threw a few Mills' bombs at a German working-party who were putting up some wire and had no wish to do us any harm. Probably I am feeling pleased with myself about this. Now and again a leisurely five-nine shell passes overhead in the blue air where the larks are singing. The sound of the shell is like water trickling into a can. The curve of its trajectory sounds peaceful until the culminating crash. A little weasel runs past my outstretched feet, glancing at me with tiny bright eyes, apparently unafraid. One of our shrapnel shells, whizzing over to the enemy lines, bursts with a hollow crash. Against the clear morning sky a cloud of dark smoke expands and drifts away. Slowly its dingy wrestling vapours take the form of a hooded giant with clumsy expostulating arms. Then, with a gradual gesture of acquiescence, it lolls sideways, falling over into the attitude of a swimmer on his side. And so it dissolves into nothingness. Perhaps the shell has killed someone. Whether it has or whether it hasn't, I continue to scrape my puttees, and the weasel goes about his business. The sun strokes the glinting wings of an aeroplane, foraging away westward. Somewhere on the slope behind me a partridge makes its unmilitary noise—down there where Dick was buried a few weeks ago. Dick's father was a very good man with a gun, so Dick used to say. . . .

*　　*　　*

Down in the reserve line I was sitting in the gloom of the steel hut (like being inside a boiler) reading a novel by candlelight while Barton and Mansfield snored on their beds and my servant Flook sang "Dixieland" in some adjoining cubbyhole. Being in reserve was a sluggish business; in the front line we were much less morose. Outside there was a remote rumble going on, like heavy furniture being moved about in a room overhead. But the little wooden weather-vane on the roof kept on spinning and rattling as though nothing were amiss with the world. Then the patter of rain began, and I shivered and turned chilly and thought of home and safety. It was time to be going up with that working-party. We should be out from eight till midnight, piling sandbags on the parapet of the front-line trench, which had suffered from the wet weather.

It was a pitch dark night. As we were going up across the open to the support line, the bombardment, about two miles away in the low country on our left, reached a climax. The sky winked and flickered like a thunderstorm gone crazy. It was a battle seen in miniature against a screen of blackness. Rocket-lights, red and white, curved upward; in the rapid glare of bursting explosives the floating smoke showed rufous and tormented; it was like the last hour of Gomorrah; one couldn't imagine anything left alive there. But it was only a small local attack—probably a raid by fifty men, which would be reported in two lines of the G.H.Q. communiqué. It would soon be our turn to do a raid. The Brigadier had made it quite clear that he "wanted a prisoner". One would be enough. He wanted to make certain what troops were in front of us.

*   *   *

For identification purposes a dead body would be better than nothing, Kinjack said. O'Brien and I went out one moonlight night into a part of no-man's-land where there were no mine-craters. We had been instructed to bring in a dead body which (so our Observation Officer said) was lying out there. The Germans had been across the night before, cutting our wire, and the Lewis-gun officer was certain that he had inflicted severe casualties on them. Anyhow, a pair of boots could be seen sticking up out of a shell-hole. But when we arrived at the boots we found them attached to the body of a French soldier who had been there several months. I didn't like this much; but O'Brien whispered to me: "T'Colonel shall have t'boot," and the boot, with half a leg on it, was sent down to Kinjack, as a proof of our efficiency.

Prisoners were seldom seen at that time. I never saw one myself until the Somme battle began in the summer. The landscape was in front of us; similar in character to the one behind us, but mysterious with its unknown quality of being "behind the Boche line". We could see the skeleton villages of Fricourt and Mametz, and the ruinous cemetery (which the men called "the rest camp"). But the enemy was invisible. On still nights our sleepy sentries heard him cough from the far side of the craters. He patrolled, and we patrolled. Often when I was crawling about on my belly, I imagined a clod of earth to be a hostile head and shoulders watching me from a shell-hole. But patrols had a sensible habit of avoiding per-

309

sonal contact with one another. Men in the Tunnelling Company who emerged, blinking and dusty white, from the mine-shafts, had heard the enemy digging deep underground. They may even have heard the muffled mutter of German voices. But, apart from the projectiles he sent us, the enemy was, as far as we were concerned, an unknown quantity. The Staff were the people who knew all about him. . . .

*　　　*　　　*

Spring arrived late that year. Or was it that spring kept away from the front line as long as possible? Up there it seemed as though the winter would last for ever. On wet days the trees a mile away were like ash-grey smoke rising from the naked ridges, and it felt very much as if we were at the end of the world. And so we were; for that enemy world (which by daylight we saw through loopholes or from a hidden observation post) had no relation to the landscape of life. It had meant the end of the world for the man whose helmet was still lying about the trench with a jagged hole through it. Steel hats (which our Division had begun to wear in February) couldn't keep out a rifle bullet. . . .

By five o'clock on a frosty white morning it would be daylight. Trees and broken roofs emerged here and there from the folds of mist that drifted in a dense blur; above them were the white shoals and chasms of the sky flushed with the faint pink of dawn. Standing-to at dawn was a desolate affair. The men stamped their feet and rats scurried along the crannied parapets. But we'd had our tot of rum, and we were to be relieved that afternoon. . . . Dandelions had begun to flower along the edges of the communication trenches. This was a sign of spring, I thought, as we filed down Canterbury Avenue, with the men making jokes about the estaminet in Morlancourt. Estaminet! What a memory-evoking word! . . . It was little enough that they had to go back to.

As for me, I had more or less made up my mind to die; the idea made things easier. In the circumstances there didn't seem to be anything else to be done. I only mention the fact because it seems, now, so strange that I should have felt like that when I had so much of my life to lose. Strange, too, was the thought of summer. It meant less mud, perhaps, but more dust; and the "big push" was always waiting for us.

Safe in Morlancourt, I slept like a log. Sleep was a wonderful thing when one came back from the Line; but to wake was to remember. Talking to Joe Dottrell did me good. A new transport officer had arrived—a Remount man from England. It was said that he had been combed out of a cushy job. I was glad I'd given up the transport. Glad, too, to be able to ride out on the black mare.

After the ugly weather in the trenches a fine afternoon in the wood above Méaulte was something to be thankful for. The undergrowth had been cut down, and there were bluebells and cowslips and anemones, and here and there a wildcherry tree in blossom. Teams of horses, harrowing the uplands, moved like a procession, their crests blown by the wind. But the rural spirit of the neighbourhood had been chased away by supply sheds and R.E. stores and the sound of artillery on the horizon. Albert (where Jules Verne used to live), with its two or three chimney-stacks and the damaged tower of the basilica, showed above a line of tall trees along the riverside; a peaceful medley of roofs as I watched it, but in reality a ruined and deserted town. And in the foreground Bécourt church tower peeped above a shoulder of hill like a broken tooth.

Anyhow the black mare had got the better of the new transport officer. That was something, I thought, as I jogged home again.

*　　　*　　　*

My faithful servant Flook always contrived to keep me supplied with oranges when we were up in the trenches. An orange, and taking my sodden boots off whenever I got the chance (though it was against the rules), were my two favourite recreations in the front line. Flook called me (with an orange) at two in the morning; I had to relieve Ormand, who had been on duty since midnight. The orange woke me up. But it was a wet night, and I'd been out with the wiring-party from ten till twelve. Lugging coils of concertina wire along a narrow trench swilling with mud and water wasn't much fun. Stumbling with it over shell-holes and trip-wires was worse. However, we had got quite a lot out. . . .

Once I'd shaken off my stupor it wasn't so bad to be out in the night air. The rain had stopped and Ormand had nothing to report. For the next two hours I should loiter up and down with my knobkerrie in my hand; now and again I had a whack at a rat running along the parados. From one "bay" to another I went, stopping for a word in an undertone with the sentries; patient in their waterproof sheets they stood on the firestep, peering above the parapet until bleak daylight began to show itself. The trench was falling in badly in places after the rain. . . .

Then there was the bombing-post up a sap which went thirty or forty yards out into no-man's-land. Everything had been very quiet, the bombers muttered. . . .

Back in the main trench, I stood on the firestep to watch the sky whitening. Sad and stricken the country emerged. I could see the ruined village below the hill and the leafless trees that waited like sentries up by Contalmaison. Down in the craters the dead water took a dull gleam from the sky. I stared at the tangles of wire and the leaning posts, and there seemed no sort of comfort left in life. My steel hat was heavy on my head while I thought how I'd been on leave last month. I remembered how I'd leant my elbows on Aunt Evelyn's front gate. (It was my last evening.) That twilight, with its thawing snow, made a comfortable picture now. John Homeward had come past with his van, plodding beside his weary horse. He had managed to make his journey, in spite of the state of the roads. . . . He had pulled up for a few minutes, and we'd talked about Dixon, who had been such an old friend of his. "Ay; Tom was a good chap; I've never known a better. . . ." He had said good-bye and good-night and set his horse going again. As he turned the corner the past had seemed to go with him. . . .

And here I was, with my knobkerrie in my hand, staring across at the enemy I'd never seen. Somewhere out of sight beyond the splintered tree-tops of Hidden Wood a bird had begun to sing. Without knowing why, I remembered that it was Easter Sunday. Standing in that dismal ditch, I could find no consolation in the thought that Christ was risen. I sploshed back to the dug-out to call the others up for "stand-to".